CITY AND COUNTRYSIDE IN LATE MEDIEVAL

AND RENAISSANCE ITALY

CITY AND COUNTRYSIDE
IN LATE MEDIEVAL AND
RENAISSANCE ITALY

ESSAYS PRESENTED TO PHILIP JONES

EDITED BY

TREVOR DEAN AND
CHRIS WICKHAM

THE HAMBLEDON PRESS
LONDON   AND   RONCEVERTE

Published by The Hambledon Press, 1990

102 Gloucester Avenue, London NW1 8HX (U.K.)

309 Greenbrier Avenue, Ronceverte WV 24970 (U.S.A.)

ISBN 1 85285 035 3

British Library Cataloguing in Publication Data

City and countryside in late Medieval and Renaissance Italy:
   essays presented to Philip Jones.
   1. Italy, 1300-1494
   I. Dean, Trevor   II. Wickham, Chris   III. Jones, Philip
   945.05

Library of Congress Cataloging-in-Publication Data

City and countryside in late medieval and Renaissance Italy:
   essays presented to Philip Jones/edited by Trevor Dean
   and Chris Wickham.
   Includes bibliographical references.
   1. Italy – Civilization – 1268-1559.
   2. Italy – Civilization – 476-1268.
   3. Cities and towns – Italy – History.
   4. Italy – Rural conditions.
   5. City-states – Italy – History.
   I. Jones, P.J. (Philip James)   II. Dean, Trevor
   III. Wickham, Chris, 1950-
DG443. C58 1990
945 – dc20   90-5346 CIP

Printed on acid free-paper and bound in
Great Britain by Billings Ltd, Worcester.

Contents

Illustrations

Foreword

This book has a double purpose: to honour Philip Jones, one of the leading historians of medieval Italy in any country, and to present a body of original work on late medieval Italian society to an English-speaking audience. Some aspects of Italy in this period have been studied as much as any fields of research have been studied anywhere: one sometimes has the impression that fifteenth-century Florence is known person by person and stone by stone. Cities generally have been better explored than the countryside. Florence in particular needs little introduction to an English readership. It is very much a stamping-ground for British and American scholars, although there is quite as much work on the city also in French, German and, of course, Italian. Italy has always been very diverse and even neighbouring cities have had quite different histories.

This book seeks to balance the predominant weight of Italian history-writing in Britain and America by giving attention to Siena rather than Florence (essays by Waley, Pinto, Paton) and to other cities, such as Naples (Abulafia), Camerino (Law), Lucca (Wickham) and Ferrara (Dean), that are less frequently discussed in English. When we find ourselves in the Florentine lands (de la Roncière), we examine the countryside rather than the city. The countryside can also be found, set against city politics, in several other essays (Chittolini, Stephens, Wickham). We hope by this means to convey a more representative view of Italian society, through its diversity, to anyone who reads the book as a whole.

The book has two main themes that run interlaced through the essays: the structures of society and their cultural representations. As regards the first, the structures of local and rural power are discussed by Wickham and de la Roncière; the force of rural geography by Larner; the city's dominance over the countryside by Chittolini; urban politics and socio-economic relationships by Waley, Pinto, Abulafia, Law and Dean. The complexity of patronage networks comes out in most of these essays, both in the city and in the country, as does the consequent need to pattern, justify and explain them. Chittolini, Abulafia and Law in particular confront this issue with discussions of ideological interpretation and ritual mediation of these relationships, that link straight into the theme of culture. Stephens and Paton pick this up in their analyses of religious sensibility and preaching and it is taken on by Cardini and Denley in their discussions of teaching and intellectual life in the cities. These themes do not, of course, cover the whole array of current writing on late medieval and Renaissance Italy, but we believe that the essays will serve, through their interconnection and the density of their interpretations, as an introduction to this writing, as well as making an original contribution to the understanding of the period.

We have been helped and encouraged by many people during the genesis of this book. We would especially like to thank Carla Jones for her essential help and advice in its preparation. We are also very grateful to Brasenose College, Oxford and to several of the contributors for their generous financial assistance.

Some of Philip Jones' closest associates in Italian studies who, for various reasons, have not been able to contribute to this volume wish to have their names associated with it, in order to send Philip their best wishes: Marvin Becker, Humfrey Butters, Giovanni Cherubini, Emilio Cristiani, Riccardo Francovich, Richard Goldthwaite, Mike Knapton, Franco Venturi and Stuart Woolf. We are indebted to them for their encouragement of the project.

Essays by Franco Cardini and Charles de la Roncière were translated by Chris Wickham; those by Giorgio Chittolini and Giuliano Pinto by Trevor Dean.

Trevor Dean
Chris Wickham

March 1990

Philip Jones: An Appreciation

Karl Leyser

Philip Jones belongs to a school of medievalists for whom the stark realities of being have always come before the pathos of their idealisation. This may seem strange in one who is so much at home in the intellectual and artistic life of fourteenth- and fifteenth-century Italy but he quite rightly does not allow us to forget that humanists, like many others, had to make their way in the worlds of court – and city – intrigue and were anxious about their own careers. Philip takes a certain delight in uncomfortable paradox. Whereas most historians, working on Renaissance Italy and its society, are instinctive townsmen and bourgeois, he reminds us throughout that there was a countryside and a rural nobility and that they mattered. He once told me, half in earnest and half joking, that he feared he might be accused of un-Florentine activities for his resolute concern with the harder, underlying exploitative routines outside the city walls – and within them. Yet it is very characteristic of him that behind even his sternest and most demanding analysis of economic developments, minutely traced through the evidence, there is a deep sense of humanity and compassion. I recall one of his most penetrating articles, 'From Manor to Mezzadria', where he not only exposes the economic, but also the personal tyranny to which the *mezzadri* were subjected by their landlords.

As a historian Philip was first formed by Reginald Lennard at Wadham, and Reggie Lennard kindled in him his abiding interest in agrarian history and the belief in its fundamental, underlying importance also for cultural understanding, matters usually ignored by the addicts of *Geistesgeschichte*. Lennard was not only the master of complex agrarian structures and those who were their beneficiaries and victims, he also illustrated these themes from sources far away from the traditional economic historian's arsenal, like the account and the survey. Reggie would quote from Thomas Hardy's *Woodlanders* or the *Mayor of Casterbridge* to illustrate a point about, say, marriage customs. This instinct for range and breadth also breathes in Philip's work. At the same time it is held together by a deeply disillusioned view of the nature of most regimes and the false imagery of their conflicts. Where the modern admirers of the late medieval Florentine polity, and the historians who lament its drift towards despotism, take fifteenth-century eulogists of republicanism at their word, Philip shows that there were in fact not so many differences between these professed opposites. Both were oligarchies, out for the same ends.

This strain may have stemmed from his experience as a graduate at Magdalen College. He had been elected to a Senior Demyship there in 1946 and soon joined a circle of K.B. McFarlane's pupils. They formed a group of which John Cooper, who became a life-long friend, was the centre. What were its characteristics? They shared a certain distrust of authority and a critical abrasiveness in their discussions of current orthodoxies in historical interpretations. More positively theirs was a passionate quest not only for the mainsprings but also for the less obvious legal and proprietorial arrangements which, they believed, must be grasped to explain how power was wielded in a given society. For Philip that came to mean, among other things, a ceaseless, avid and never sated search for reading, a mastery of the secondary literature quite out of the ordinary. His example here is daunting to his fellow scholars. Visit Bodley any day and he can be found there. His flair for *grands thèmes* and controversies leads to their critical exploration, and they are then harnessed to his subject matter. His own analysis rests on very large and deep intellectual foundations indeed, and as a historian Philip is not one to fire from the hip.

To programme a *Festschrift* for him is no easy task given the richness, range and variety of his own achievement. True, Italy stands at the heart of it, but it is not often that a single scholar masters so many facets and themes of its uniquely rich and almost over-endowed civilisation, side-by-side with the enduring realities of its social fabric. He does not shun the *vue d'ensemble*, as his *Storia economica*, for Einaudi, testifies. In Italy his name inspires awe, and his is altogether a stunning body of work. Not surprisingly he has attracted a large number of graduate pupils, some of whom have already enriched the English repertoire of medieval Italian historical studies. Philip is no easy master to please and satisfy, as not only his graduates but also his Brasenose undergraduates and the many others from elsewhere whom he taught the Italian Renaissance Special Subject must know. He can be formidable, and the scholarly criteria he commands and wants to inculcate are rigorous, not to say intimidating. But they, the pupils, will also have discovered that these qualities are blended with patience, tolerance and humour. He takes enormous care with them all, the able and the stragglers. Underneath an at times peppery surface there are in Philip large funds of sympathy, warmth and helping kindness. In Italy he is, if anything, renowned for his joviality and there he enjoys dining out. As a teacher and mentor he stands for the best in more than one tradition and his attachment to Leeds, to B.N.C. and the Oxford Faculty, each of whom he served for many years, is stirring. He is also a wise, staunch and unshakable friend.

Philip Jones

Bibliography of Philip Jones

Compiled by Trevor Dean
Books and Articles

'The Vicariate of the Malatesta of Rimini', *English Historical Review*, lxvii (1952)

'A Tuscan Monastic Lordship in the Later Middle Ages: Camaldoli', *Journal of Ecclesiastical History*, v (1954)

'An Italian Estate, 900-1200', *Economic History Review*, s. 2, vii (1954-55)

'Le finanze della badia cistercense di Settimo nel XIV secolo', *Rivista di storia della chiesa in Italia*, x (1956)

'Florentine Families and Florentine Diaries in the Fourteenth Century', *Papers of the British School at Rome*, xxiv (1956) (Studies in Italian Medieval History presented to E.M. Jamison)

'The End of Malatesta Rule in Rimini', in *Italian Renaissance Studies*, ed. E.F. Jacob (London, 1960)

Translation of G. Luzzatto, *An Economic History of Italy from the Fall of the Roman Empire to the Beginning of the 16th Century* (London, 1961)

'Per la storia agraria italiana nel medioevo: lineamenti e problemi', *Rivista storica italiana*, lxxvi (1964)

'Communes and Despots: The City State in Late-Medieval Italy', *Transactions of the Royal Historical Society*, s. 5, xv (1965)

'L'Italia agraria nell'alto medioevo: problemi di cronologia e di continuità', *Settimane di studio*, xiii (1965)

'Medieval Agrarian Society in its Prime: Italy', in *Cambridge Economic History of Europe*, i (2nd ed., Cambridge, 1966)

'From Manor to Mezzadria: a Tuscan Case-Study in the Medieval Origins of Modern Agrarian Society', in *Florentine Studies*, ed. N. Rubinstein (London, 1968)

The Malatesta of Rimini and the Papal State: A Political History (Cambridge, 1974)

'La storia economica. Dalla caduta dell'Impero romano al secolo XIV', in *Storia d'Italia Einaudi*, II. i. (Turin, 1974)

'Economia e società nell'Italia medievale: la leggenda della borghesia', in *Storia d'Italia Einaudi, Annali*, i. *Dal feudalesimo al capitalismo* (Turin, 1978)

Economia e società nell'Italia medievale (Turin, 1980)

'Travel Notes of an Apprentice Florentine Statesman, Giovanni di Tommaso Ridolfi', in *Florence and Italy: Renaissance Studies in Honour of Nicolai Rubinstein*, ed. P. Denley and C. Elam (London, 1988)

Reviews

Review of C.E. Boyd, *Tithes and Parishes in Medieval Italy* in *History*, xl (1955), 154-5

Notice of *Chronicon Salernitanum*, ed. U. Westerbergh in *Medium Aevum* xxvii (1958), 27-28

Notice of W.M. Bowsky, *Henry VII in Italy* in *Eng. Hist. Rev.*, lxxvi (1961), 703

Review of R.L. Reynolds, *Europe Emerges. Transition toward an Industrial World-wide Society 600-1750* in *Ec. Hist. Rev.* s.2, xiv (1961-2) 605-7

Review of D. Waley, *The Papal State in the Thirteenth Century* in *History*, xlvii (1962), 184-86

Review of K. Beloch, *Bevölkerungsgeschichte Italiens* in *Eng. Hist. Rev.*, lxxvii (1962), 723-27

Review of J. Heers, *Gênes au XVᵉ siècle* in *Eng. Hist. Rev.*, lxxviii (1963), 126-31

Review of G.A. Brucker, *Florentine Politics and Society, 1348-1378* in *History*, xlviii (1963), 56-59

Review of E. Cristiani, *Nobiltà e popolo nel comune di Pisa* in *Ec. Hist. Rev.*, s.2, xvi (1963-4), 402-4

Review of R.S. Lopez, *Naissance de l'Europe*, ibid. pp. 375-76

Review of L. Ruggini, *Economia e società nell'Italia 'annonaria'*, ibid. pp. 399-402

Review of J.C. Davis, *The Decline of the Venetian Nobility as a Ruling Class* in *Italian Studies*, xix (1964), 119-21

Review of *Cambridge Economic History of Europe*, iii in *Ec. Hist. Rev.*, xvii (1965), 570-78

Review of L. Martines, *The Social World of the Florentine Humanists, 1390-1460* in *History*, l (1965), 77-78

Review of R. De Roover, *The Rise and Decline of the Medici Bank, 1397-1494* in *History*, l (1965), 74-76

Review of M.H. Keen, *The Laws of War in the late Middle Ages*; N. Denholm-Young, *History and Heraldry*; M. Wade Labarge, *A Baronial Household of the Thirteenth Century*; and L. Gautier, *Chivalry*, in *The New Statesman* lxx (1965), 192

Notice of N. Rodolico, *Saggi di storia medievale e moderna* in *Eng. Hist. Rev.*, lxxxi (1966), 379

Review of J. Day, *Les Douaires de Gênes, 1376-1377* in *Eng. Hist. Rev.*, lxxxi (1966), 814-15

Review of J.K. Hyde, *Padua in the Age of Dante*; J. Larner, *Lords of Romagna*; and E.R. Chamberlin, *The Count of Virtue* in *The New Statesman*, lxxi (1966), 815

Review of V. d'Alessandro, *Politica e società nella Sicilia aragonese* in *Eng. Hist. Rev.*, lxxxii (1967), 601-2

Review of *Manuale di mercatura di Saminiato de' Ricci*, ed. A. Borlandi in *Eng. Hist. Rev.*, lxxxii (1967), 602-3

Notice of V. d'Alessandro, *Le pergamene degli Umiliati di Cremona* in *Eng. Hist. Rev.*, lxxxii (1967), 825-26

Review of N. Rubinstein, *The Government of Florence under the Medici (1434 to 1494)* in *History*, lii (1967), 318-20

Review of H. Baron, *The Crisis of the Early Italian Renaissance* in *History*, liii (1968), 410-13

Review of *Venice and History. The Collected Papers of Frederic C. Lane* in *History*, liv (1969), 262-64

Review of E.L. Cox, *The Green Count of Savoy. Amadeus VI and Transalpine Savoy in the Fourteenth Century* in *History*, lv (1970), 243-44

Notice of R. De Roover, *S. Bernardino of Siena and Sant'Antonino of Florence: The Two Great Economic Thinkers of the Middle Ages* in *Eng. Hist. Rev.*, lxxxv (1970), 160-61

Review of M. Becker, *Florence in Transition*, i in *Eng. Hist. Rev.*, lxxxv (1970), 563-67

Review of R.A. Goldthwaite, *Private Wealth in Renaissance Florence* in *Italian Studies*, xxv (1970)

Review of C. Klapisch-Zuber, *Les maîtres du marbre: Carrare 1300-1600*, in *Times Lit. Supp.* 1970, p. 1138.

Review of R-H. Bautier, *The Economic Development of Medieval Europe* in *Times Lit. Supp.* 1972, p. 165

Review of C.M. de la Roncière, *Un changeur florentin du Trecento: Lippo di Fede del Sega* in *Eng. Hist. Rev.*, xc (1975), 604-6

Review of J. Heers, *Parties and Political Life in the Medieval West* in *History*, lxiv (1979), 446-48

Review of D.J. Osheim, *An Italian Lordship: the Bishopric of Lucca in the Late Middle Ages* in *Speculum*, liv (1979), 410-12

Review of S. Epstein, *Wills and Wealth in Medieval Genoa 1150-1250* in *History*, lxxi (1986), 496-97

Notice of M. Ascheri, *Siena nel Rinascimento* in *Eng. Hist. Rev.*, ciii (1988), 481

Review of R. Bizzocchi, *Chiesa e potere nella Toscana del Quattrocento* in *Nuova rivista storica*, lxxii (1988), 478-79

List of Contributors

David Abulafia	Gonville and Caius College, Cambridge
Franco Cardini	Università degli Studi, Florence
Giorgio Chittolini	Università degli Studi, Milan
Trevor Dean	Roehampton Institute, London
Charles de la Roncière	Université de Provence
Peter Denley	Queen Mary and Westfield College, University of London
John Larner	University of Glasgow
John Law	University College of Swansea
Karl Leyser	Oxford
Bernadette Paton	Oxford
Giuliano Pinto	Università degli Studi, Florence
John Stephens	University of Edinburgh
Daniel Waley	Lewes
Chris Wickham	University of Birmingham

1

Rural Communes and the City of Lucca at the Beginning of the Thirteenth Century

Chris Wickham

What was going on in the Tuscan countryside around 1200? One cannot easily generalise. The hinterland of every city was different; even individual villages could be very dissimilar in their basic characteristics. Philip Jones, in his 1968 article 'From Manor to Mezzadria', identified one framework of analysis in one of those complex paradoxes that are so typical of his writing. The manor, ill-documented since Carolingian times, had not disappeared in most of the region but rather was hidden by leases of whole estates to aristocrats; when we regain a documentation that tells us how estates were really organised, from the late twelfth century onwards, manorial relationships reappear again. Nonetheless, it is precisely this documentation that tells us that around 1200 such relationships were going into a precipitous decline; what was left of the manor was little more than terminology. 'Servile' groups (*manentes*) by now coexisted uneasily with free tenants on low money rents, and, increasingly, on more 'modern' rents in kind, some of which could be called commercial rents, directed towards the great markets in the cities. More local differentiations can be identified: Philip Jones himself showed that the manor began to dissolve rather earlier in the territory of Lucca, in fact. But the patterns of the late twelfth and early thirteenth centuries remain those that he described, and any more specific socio-economic analyses are still to be understood through his synthesis.[1]

A second framework is that of the rural commune. Communes appeared in cities in Italy, as is well known, in the years around 1100. But in rural settlements, too, we begin to find formalised collective activities for the first time in the twelfth century, in the wake of the cities; consuls, often elected annually, came to lead villages, backed by village councils

---

[1] P.J. Jones, 'From Manor to Mezzadria', in *Florentine studies*, ed. N. Rubinstein (London, 1968), pp. 206-18; for Lucca, idem, 'An Italian Estate, 900-1200', *Economic History Review*, ser. 2, vii (1954). I am grateful to Julia Barrow, Leslie Brubaker and Trevor Dean for criticising a draft of this text.

and sometimes by relatively formal documents detailing their rights and duties. These developments represented a new collective identity for villages and their inhabitants. They have often been represented as the peasant counterattack against the signorial or tenurial powers of lords; and, indeed, where such counterattacks took place, rural communes were in their forefront.[2] This was not the only cause of their appearance, however, for communes can be found in both peaceful and tense villages, and in centres of signorial power and signorial weakness alike, at least once they became generalised in a given region (a process that was complete in the territory of Lucca, in all likelihood, by 1200). Indeed, one of the precise features of rural communes is the variability of their local roles according to the importance of different local political or economic issues, ranging across opposition to lords, the control of roads, the administration of common lands, the administration of justice, the organisation of churches, or the collection of city taxes. This very variation makes the rural commune interesting: for it allows us to assess how important each of these issues actually was in each locality.

In this essay I shall use these two frameworks of analysis as starting points for the interpretation of the society of one particular village, Tassignano, in the rich plain of Lucca, lying about 6 km. east of the city walls. We know quite a lot about Tassignano, as it happens, thanks to the richness of Lucchese archives: sixty-five land charters survive from the village just from the fifty years 1175-1225. Tassignano is no more typical than anywhere else is, but at least its economic environment can be understood before we start; and its very specificities will, I hope, give us further insights into the problems of local societies in the Lucca plain in general around 1200, as well as into the social and political links that were already tying its inhabitants to the nearby city.

One document is more illuminating than any other for the development of its local society, a court-case of 1206 involving its rural commune. In April 1206 Fiorentino, one of the consuls of the commune of Tassignano, laid a plea against Albertino and Bandino di Soffreduccio, as patrons of the local church of S. Stefano, before the *consules foretanorum* of Lucca, judges of the newly constituted court for the *contado*.[3] The dialogue form of the plea, which represents the case as an argument between the parties – a standard feature of Lucchese court documents of the period – allows the claims set out by each side to be understood; we can indeed at least in part work out what was really going on as well. Fiorentino's principal aim was

---

[2] See, classically, R. Caggese, *Classi e comuni rurali nel medio evo italiano* (Florence, 1907-8); G. Salvemini, 'Un comune rurale nel secolo XIII', now in idem, *La dignità cavalleresca nel comune di Firenze e altri scritti* (Milan, 1972), pp. 274-97; the most recent general survey is A. Castagnetti, *Le comunità rurali dalla soggezione signorile alla giurisdizione del comune cittadino* (Verona, 1983).

[3] A[rchivio di] S[tato di] L[ucca, Diplomatico], Archivio de'Notari 14 Nov. 1206.

to contest the power of the church patrons over the commune of Tassignano, especially in the matter of elections. He claimed for the commune the right to elect its own consuls, who would then be able to elect *guardiani* (roughly, local watchmen), with the agreement of a local board of *consiliarii*: saving only the rights of the city, to whom the commune was directly subject for civic taxation. He stated that he and his associates were consuls of Tassignano 'inasmuch as it is the parish or neighbourhood (*vicinia*) of S. Stefano'; that there had been consuls in the *vicinia* for a hundred years; and that the *vicinia* had been subject to a *consulatus* for forty. These claims were opposed by Albertino, who said that his father (with other men) had organised the election of these consuls for forty years or, later on in the case, fifty; that they had sworn the consular oath in his presence; and that at the beginning of this dispute (probably in 1205) it was he who had called in the city consuls – in other words that the local commune was only attached to the city through the intermediacy of the church patrons. (Fiorentino contested this last point, saying that the city's intervention had been neutral as to the rights of the parties; later Albertino and Bandino conceded the issue.) Albertino claimed further that in former times all the *rustici* of Tassignano had been *manentes seu servi* (subject tenants) of the patrons and the church, except one single household of incomers, and that now three quarters were. Fiorentino said the figure had never been more than half, and for the last forty years it had been only a sixth. Later he extended this, to claim that only five or ten families out of the eighty-three in the *vicinia* were now *manentes*; the latter were included in the commune, though.

The argument then shifted to who the consuls were and what they did. Bandino said that he himself had been one of the consuls one year, and that they had had the Island Ditch dug, had put up a toll-booth on the road, and had paid for a feast with the profits. Fiorentino said that there were two sets of consuls, one or two for the patrons and three or four for the *populus*, and that Bandino had been consul for the patrons only (which the latter conceded); both sets had had the ditch dug. Albertino said that the consuls swore according to the text of the communal *breve* (which Fiorentino agreed), and that the *breve* contained an oath to the church and the patrons (which Fiorentino denied, except for the oath of the patron's consul); the *breve* was in fact a new one, after the old one was formally destroyed in a previous dispute. Fiorentino agreed that this last point was true, but said that the *breve* the consuls swore to was actually quite often changed, if the consuls and *consiliarii* agreed to do so and that the commune, not the patrons, had control of its content. (Albertino, predictably enough, denied this.) Fiorentino further stated that on the occasion that a certain Aldebrandino had been appointed consul by the patrons, a decade previously, the *vicini* had rejected him, and he had only served as patronal consul; once, as well, the patrons had appointed the guardians, but these too were boycotted by the *vicini*.

So ran the main lines of the dispute, as clear as I can make them (they are not all quite so clear in the text). The city judges made the sort of 'compromise' that cities often made when faced with disputes of this kind, conceding most of the case to the patrons: the latter were to have the right to choose the consuls, and only if they did not turn up were the consuls to have the power to choose their successors; guardians, however, could be chosen by the commune. Evidently the city did not feel disturbed by the power that the patrons of S. Stefano might exert over the commune of Tassignano, presumably because the village was no political threat; the city could routinely include it in its jurisdiction (justice was certainly not one of the rights at issue in 1206), and the patrons were largely city-based, as we shall see. We certainly need not conclude from the judgement, anyway, that the patrons were actually in the right – or even, for that matter, in the wrong. But some of the points at issue can be decided on from the texts for Tassignano that we have. There was certainly never a time in which all its inhabitants were *manentes* of the church and its patrons, for we have plenty of documents from independent landowners who were certainly local, while other inhabitants were tenants of other city owners; in this case the position of the commune is supported. Conversely, it is likely that taxes were paid through the village church, not directly by the commune, for S. Stefano was liable in 1187 to pay a massive *datium* and *fodrum* of £9 to King Henry VI, which was too large a sum to be just for the church's own estates – the implication is that it was a communal tax that the church had to pay. (It had trouble paying, in fact, and had to borrow money from a member of one of the families of the church patrons; it did not manage to pay the money back, either.)[4] This would support the claim of the church patrons that they were in some respects legal mediators for the commune. Other unsupported arguments the parties made were perhaps not even meant to be credible; it was not uncommon in the period to include claims for tactical purposes, to be conceded when compromise became possible. These arguments tell us at least what each side regarded as important for its case, nonetheless; and some points were, more or less explicitly, agreed to or assumed by both sides, and can be regarded as fairly firm.

Let us look at some of these latter points; for these, since they show how both sides regarded Tassignano, will enable us to see more clearly in what ways Tassignano was typical of the Lucchesia. One assumption shared by both sides was that the commune of the village was defined as that of the preexisting *vicinia* of the church: in Tassignano, there is no doubt that the parish constituted the field of action of the developing commune. On the other hand, the church and its patrons were not always conceptually

---

[4] *R[egesto del] C[apitolo di] L[ucca]*, ed. P. Guidi and O. Parenti (Rome, 1910-39), nn. 1560, 1618.

separated either; the same *manentes*, for example, were indifferently of one or the other. It is thus not surprising that the men of Tassignano never denied that the patrons of the church had some local authority *as* patrons, which extended to definitely secular activities like participating in the digging of ditches. Elsewhere, however, it is much less evident that similar local potentates claimed such authority. The patrons of S. Stefano were in fact more visible even in church documents than were patrons in other places. For example, in the neighbouring village of S. Margherita, barely a kilometre away, the commune is first documented in 1148, when the *consules communiter vicinorum ecclesie* consented to a sale of church land: this is in fact a very characteristic early reference to a Lucchese commune, once again showing how closely linked it was to the parish. In the same year, the church of S. Stefano also sold land with lay consent, but the format is quite different: *cum consensu patronum et vicinum*, with the patrons very much to the forefront and the villagers not yet structured by communal officials.[5] We cannot go into the problematic issue of communal origins here, but it is likely that rural communes first existed as informal bodies with *ad hoc* representatives, and only later began to institutionalise the office of consuls and the like, with, eventually, a *breve* to give the remit of their office; the Tassignano documents would certainly fit this pattern.[6] But the specific role of S. Stefano's patrons from the start of the documentation for community activity is unusually extensive, and can be linked to another topic in the 1206 case, the issue of *manentes*.

Fiorentino and the patrons argued about how many *manentes* there were in Tassignano, but at least agreed that there had once been a good few in the village, constituting even on Fiorentino's figures half of the population in 1150 or thereabouts. Also implicit in the argument is the assumption that the number mattered: the more *manentes* there were, the more likely it was that the patrons had the right to nominate the local consuls. Exactly how to define *manentes* is not an easy task. They appear in the twelfth- and thirteenth-century Lucchesia as free men, capable of making contracts, but subject in some way to the justice of their lords, and above all tied to the land.[7] They were probably not really 'serfs', in the sense that this is generally understood, that is to say updated versions of the unfree tenants

---

[5] *RCL* 1044; *Reale archivio di stato di Lucca. Regesti*, ed. G. degli Azzi Vitelleschi (Lucca, 1903-11), ii. 583.

[6] Tassignano's destroyed *breve* may have resembled that for Moriano dating from *c.* 1170, A[rchivio] A[rcivescovile di] L[ucca], + +A98, a very informal text, quite unlike a later communal statute; or the slightly more formal AAL, AB50, anno 1223, for Sesto Moriano, or D. Corsi, 'Il "breve" dei consoli e del podestà del comune di S. Maria a Monte', *Atti dell'Accademia Lucchese di scienze, lettere ed arti*, n.s. x (1959). I will discuss the issue of communal origins, and its relationship to the parish, at greater length elsewhere.

[7] A few symptomatic examples: *RCL* 993, 1472, 1727, 1729; ASL, S. Maria Forisportam, 27 Aug. 1188.

of the Carolingian period; there is, at any rate, very little sign of such a category in the intervening centuries. But they were certainly among the most subject people in the contemporary landscape, explicitly excluded from the rural commune in Marlia (5 km. north of Tassignano) in 1193, for example, as also from any rights to urban privileges in Lucca in 1224. In these instances, as at Tassignano, the key element is the judicial one, for the subjection of peasants to a lord's justice implied a degree of social control over such peasants that could be extended very easily to the denial of their right to participate in collective activity, or, as in Tassignano, to the direct control of any collective activity they did engage in. It seems likely that the specifically demeaning characteristics of *manentia* did indeed develop with the expansion of signorial justice in the late eleventh century and early twelfth, although not everyone subject to local signorial rights was a *manens*.[8]

The Lucca plain did not have many territorial *signorie* in it; with one or two exceptions, such as the episcopal lordship of Moriano north of the city, the territory inside a six-mile radius of Lucca's walls was directly subject to urban jurisdiction. Inside the twelfth- and thirteenth-century Sei Miglia, signorial rights (generally restricted to low justice) tended to be associated above all with the scattered properties of some particularly privileged ecclesiastical and lay lords.[9] The patrons of S. Stefano di Tassignano, with at least half the village their very subject tenants, were in this respect rather more privileged than most: property was normally highly fragmented in this period, with dozens of absentee owners in each village, not to speak of local peasant proprietors, and few other documented villages out of the hundred-odd in the Sei Miglia had as large a proportion of property associated with a single owner as did Tassignano. It does at least look as if the local patrons had relaxed their control over many of their *manentes* in the late twelfth century, for there were certainly fewer of the latter in 1206 than there had been; the patrons may simply have thought to control the village by indirect means, through the church and the consulate. They certainly could not, however, have moved in the other direction and crystallised their local control into a territorial *signoria* over the village, as lords elsewhere generally tried to do, for the city was too close and too jealous of its authority. It is indeed a truly striking testimony to the local hegemony of urban jurisdiction that Albertino and

---

[8] AAL, AE90, a.1193 for Marlia; for Lucca in 1224, see P. Vaccari, *L'affrancazione dei servi della gleba nell'Emilia e nella Toscana* (Bologna, 1926), pp. 83-86. For *manentes* in general, apart from Vaccari, the classic account, see E. Conti, *La formazione della struttura agraria moderna nel contado fiorentino*, i (Rome, 1965), pp. 182-92, 216-17, and F. Panero, *Terre in concessione e mobilità contadina* (Bologna, 1984), pp. 207-76.

[9] D.J. Osheim, *An Italian Lordship* (Berkeley, 1977); C.J. Wickham, 'Economia e società rurale nel territorio lucchese durante la seconda metà del secolo XI', in *S. Anselmo vescovo di Lucca*, ed. A. Spicciani and C. Violante, in press.

Bandino's attempts to maintain control over a village they dominated tenurially was couched so largely in the terminology of patronage, the giving of feasts and the swearing of oaths, rather than according to the sharper lines of legal power and privilege. The local landed power of the patrons was nonetheless greater than that of most landlords in the Lucca plain, including several who had rather more global wealth and power than Albertino and his colleagues. This in itself is one explanation for the tension of 1206 in the first place. Few other villages in the Sei Miglia had a local landowning family with as much power as the patrons had in Tassignano; few other villages show as much tension between classes. The communes in other villages crystallised with much less difficulty and with much more local autonomy than that at Tassignano. The Tassignanesi did not have to fight a consolidated and domineering *signoria*, like the peasants in some of the well-known and more dramatic Italian peasant conflicts of the twelfth and early thirteenth century, on Monte Amiata or in the Veneto; but they had to struggle more than other Lucchese villages for a measure of independence. They duly did so, with disputed elections, boycotts and destruction of documents, running on for over a decade.[10]

Tassignano's real atypicality, then, lies in the fact that the 1206 case occurred at all: the church patrons may not have had the local hegemony considered normal by lords in much of Italy and elsewhere in Europe, but they had more control over the village than was common around Lucca, and the village thus reacted against them, as a collectivity. In other respects, however, Tassignano was more like other places in the Lucca plain. Its focus on its church was, for example, wholly typical of the area. The Lucca plain has always been an area of highly dispersed settlement, divided into very small units, with little to distinguish one village from the next, and with at times even a certain amount of confusion between them. Thickly settled, it is also not an area with extensive common lands, especially in places like Tassignano which are in alluvial plain, well away from the woods and pastures of the surrounding hills: it is noteworthy how little of the 1206 dispute hung on collective economic activity, which could come to act as a focus for village identity elsewhere. Nor could territorial *signorie*, the usual framework for rural communal identity, act as such a focus here; for, as we have seen, these were virtually absent as well. Under these circumstances, the parishes of the plain, themselves a relatively recent development – indeed not completely formed before the early twelfth century – were the most visible territorial structures for early rural communes to crystallise around; many communes are first documented, like that at S. Margherita, simply as approving church transactions, or, more combatively, as trying to control the appointment of the local priest.

[10] For the Veneto, see Castagnetti, *ubi supra*; for the Amiata, Salvemini, *ubi supra*, and O. Redon, 'Seigneurs et communautés rurales dans le contado de Sienne au XIIIe siècle', *Mélanges de l'Ecole française de Rome*, xci (1979), 149-95, 619-57.

It is also wholly unsurprising that the richest owners in Tassignano should be defined as the patrons of the church, for the latter acted, rather more than elsewhere in Italy, as the pole of reference for all local power.[11]

Tassignano was also like other villages in the network of links between it and the city. Institutionally, as I have argued, Lucca was the direct ruler of the village, undisputed as such by either side in 1206. (Fiorentino, indeed, made a blatant play towards the judges, stating at one point 'maxima utilitas est habere consules civitatis et populi Lucani in Tassignano et in aliis villis'; Albertino refused to reply, on the grounds of its irrelevance to the case.) In social terms, however, the city was a focus for its surrounding villages as well, and this requires further attention. Who were the patrons, for a start? Essentially, they were city notables. They consisted of a group of linked families, a *consorteria*, of which Albertino and Bandino themselves were perhaps the least important and most local; at any rate, they and their father Soffreduccio di Ugolino are not very widely attested in Lucchese land documents, and are called *de Tassiniano* in city texts. But Bandino was a *treuguanus* in 1212, a prominent city judge; whether or not he lived in the city, he had status there. His kin and *consortes* in control of S. Stefano consisted of more important people still, including Antelminello di Antelmino, a *consul maior* in 1173, and a member of a substantial landowning family, with their own towerhouse in Lucca, and a reputation for throwing their weight around inside the city walls: they would become, as the Antelminelli, one of the major Lucchese families of the next century or so.[12] They were doubtless major urban figures *because* of their rural power, including that at Tassignano; not only was the city's territorial authority not menaced by local hegemonies such as this one, but the wielders of city authority depended for their urban status precisely on such hegemonies. (Fiorentino and the rural commune ought to have known they were going to lose in 1206, unless they hoped for strictly factional support from the Antelminelli's enemies; factional enmity was certainly high in this period, and there had even been a brief civil war focussed on the city in 1203.)[13]

[11] On settlement see C.J. Wickham, 'Frontiere di villaggio in Toscana nel XII secolo', in *Castrum iv*, ed. J.M. Poisson, in press. For parishes see L. Nanni, *La parrocchia studiata nei documenti lucchesi dei secoli VIII-XIII* (Rome, 1948), pp. 107-90. Some examples of communes and the church: *RCL* 1262-63 (Fibbialla), 1481 (Ciciana); ASL, Arch. de'Notari 30 June 1157 (S. Concordio); S. Ponziano 31 Jan. 1207 (Marlia).

[12] Bandino as *treuguanus*: ASL, S. Ponziano 3 Apr. 1212; AAL, +145, anno 1213 (mod. dating 1212). Antelminello as *consul maior*: AAL, +M80, anno 1173; as a city potentate, e.g. *RCL* 1652, a.1192. I am grateful for many references for these men and others to the kindness of Arnold Esch.

[13] For a *summa* of analysis on the rural element in city politics, see P.J. Jones, 'Economia e società nell'Italia medievale: la leggenda della borghesia', in *Storia d'Italia. Annali*, i (Turin, 1978), pp. 220-30; for 1203, the most circumstantial chronicle is *Le croniche di Giovanni Sercambi*, ed. S. Bongi (Rome, 1892) i, 12-14.

The villagers in Tassignano were, not surprisingly, less closely linked to the city than the patrons were; but they, too, show some substantial urban involvement which was not exclusively linked to the patronal *consorteria*, and partially ran counter to it. If around half the villagers were directly dependent on the patrons, the other half were not. Up to the middle of the twelfth century, most of these were local peasant or quasi-peasant owners or their tenants. In the later twelfth century, particularly from the 1170s, we begin to find city churches accumulating land in the village (it was, as usual, these churches which preserved the documents we have), and also the nearby rural monastery of Pozzeveri, dependent on the rural aristocratic family of the Porcaresi. We could well see these developments as the Tassignanesi looking for patrons, perhaps rivals of the Antelminelli, both in the city and outside it, to offset the power of the families who controlled the church. Tassignano owners also sold out to laymen who were certainly predominantly citizens; by the early decades of the thirteenth century there was a lot of lay property-owning by city-dwellers in the village, and by now markedly fewer local owners turn up in the documents. Fiorentino was such an owner; in 1195 he got a tenant-house from his future son-in-law as part of their marriage negotiations, which probably indicates that Fiorentino was also rich enough to have tenants.[14] By 1206, however, there may not have been so many like him: those not subject to the church patrons had sold out to largely urban lords.

These patterns can be found with minor variations in many villages around Lucca in the same period: the years around 1200 seem to have seen a considerable expansion of city landowning, and this was everywhere at the expense of the formerly independent peasantry, at least where it involved the acquisition of land rather than the immigration of its owners. This was largely, of course, the result of the economic supremacy of the city and its markets. Tassignano had been fully integrated into the market structure already by 1100, specialising in grain, as leases make clear; its inhabitants thus automatically looked to city buyers when they were short of money – as well as to city patrons when they needed social and political backing. Citizens, when they gained control over local land, brought the requirements of the markets still further into village society, for they were certainly taking rents in produce to sell in the city, and may have bought land at least in part according to purely marginalist economic calculations.[15] These developments were by no means necessarily to the advantage of the Tassignanesi, for city creditors were coercive and threatening; but they must have contrasted markedly with the much more

[14] AAL, *H96. There are too many Tassignano land transactions with external owners to list here; very many are registered and indexed in *RCL*.

[15] For such calculations and references to leases, see A. Esch, *Lucca im XII. Jahrhundert*, 1974 Habilitationsschrift for the Univ. of Göttingen, in course of publication. I am very grateful to the author for letting me see it.

static social and economic obligations of the *manentes* of the church patrons. We do not know what sorts of rents the latter paid – probably grain rents for the city markets just like their neighbours, given the city orientation of their landlords; but the social presuppositions of their subjection went back to an earlier age, creating the disjunctions in types of obligation that Philip Jones described in 1968. The social condition of the *manentes* gave political coherence and tension to the developing commune; their freer neighbours, like Fiorentino, gave it leaders and an independent sphere of action; neighbouring villages (all of which were more autonomous), and above all, these close economic links to the city provided an awareness of alternative and sometimes less totalising systems of subjection. This was a recipe for trouble, and trouble duly followed.

On economic grounds, even if not political ones, the city may have seemed like a potential ally for the commune of Tassignano against its patrons; while one must not naively assume that open, commercially-orientated exploitation is always preferable to seigneurial subjection, it is at least worth stressing that the 1206 document gives no hint of any hostility to the city on anyone's part.[16] The city did, however, also tend to undermine the social coherence and autonomy of rural communes. In 1206 it did so directly and consciously by backing Albertino and Bandino; it tended to do so elsewhere rather more slowly and gradually, by the simple means of attracting potential communal leaders towards its walls. Fiorentino was prepared to lead the commune of Tassignano against S. Stefano's patrons, for whatever reason; but he would have been unlikely to do so had he moved to Lucca. Many middling landowners like Fiorentino did precisely that. In Paganico, for example, a village 2 km. further from the city than Tassignano, our best-documented owner around 1200 is a certain Cortafugga di Panfollia, who appears as a witness, a land-measurer, an arbitrator, and a landowner, in over fifty documents between 1182 and 1215. He is found associated with Paganico's consuls, and is just the sort of person who became a consul in other Lucchese villages, but he is never said to be a consul himself in all these texts. He did buy a house in the city though, and spent some of his time there; by the time of his grandsons, in the mid thirteenth century, the family, while maintaining its land in Paganico, is described in the sources as an entirely urban one. The economic, or perhaps the political, framework of the city was evidently more enticing than the possibilities offered locally by

[16] Cities elsewhere could also actively aid lords who were trying, against the resistance of rural communes, to establish the commercial rents in kind that would supply markets: e.g. G. Dameron, 'Episcopal lordship in the diocese of Florence and the origins of San Casciano Val di Pesa, 1230-1247', *Journal of Medieval History*, xii (1986), a valuable comparison with my Tassignano material. In the Lucchesia, such rents were already normal a century earlier, as Jones, 'Manor', and Esch, *ubi supra*, have shown.

Paganico's weak consulate.[17]

Rural communes are often presented as the entirely collective creation of their inhabitants, reacting against the domination of their lords, or crystallising the more inchoate local structures of previous centuries into new institutions.[18] These processes undoubtedly occurred, in the Lucchesia as elsewhere. I would also emphasise the importance of a third element: rural communes were the vehicle used by local élites to establish dominance over their neighbours. To men like Fiorentino or Cortafugga, prosperous country-dwellers with a certain local status, the rural world of 1200 provided certain clearly-defined possibilities. They could try to dominate their villages from above, with the help of the most important local landowners (churches, or aristocratic families like the Porcaresi or the Antelminelli), as local notables at the base of the 'feudal' hierarchy in the eleventh and twelfth centuries had often done.[19] Alternatively they could gain local hegemony by working through their neighbours, rich and poor alike, to help set up or stabilise a rural commune; this would bring less direct power, perhaps, but in practice as much local influence, and influence that was less liable to challenge. (Such a choice, made by Fiorentino, led him to quite a considerable challenge, of course; but being a leader of the Tassignanesi may well have been preferable to being a client of the Antelminelli.) A third choice was the world of the city, no less than two hours' walk from Paganico and Tassignano, and locus of a far wider range of chances for advancement than village life, though a place where one would lose, at least at first, the satisfaction of local importance. We do not know if these three possibilities were mutually exclusive; people could certainly own houses and spend time in both city and country, for example. But in the end the conflict of interest was there, and, of the three, the city would win. The result is very clear in terms of the expansion of city ownership, as Plesner showed for Florence; but the effect on local social links themselves was certainly no less. The coherence of twelfth-century rural communes in the Lucchesia was largely created by a tight-knit network of local middling owners and prosperous peasants, who had a certain independent local base; we can see such networks often enough in mid twelfth-century charters. At the start of the thirteenth century, such

[17] Cortafugga: e.g. AAL, +I31, anno 1182; ++D47, anno 1185; *RCL* 1571-72, 1597, 1768, 1800, 1803, 1819, 1830; Archivio capitolare di Lucca, Q123, annis 1214-15 (for his house in Lucca and his death); Q112, anno 1224; Q103, anno 1224; AAL ++V70, anno 1257; *A77, annis 1265-70, for his heirs. Paganico's own consuls are not at all well documented: only AAL, ++H34, anno 1190, predates 1225. These patterns in Lucca anticipate by half a century the very similar Florentine processes described by J. Plesner, *L'emigrazione dalla campagna alla città libera di Firenze nel XIII secolo* (Florence, 1979), though many of Plesner's examples were rather farther away from the city than is Tassignano.

[18] See n. 2, with S. Reynolds, *Kingdoms and Communities in Western Europe 900-1300* (Oxford, 1984), pp. 122-38.

[19] Cf. C.J. Wickham, *The Mountains and the City* (Oxford, 1988), pp. 256-68, 324-40.

groups vanish from our documentation; many villages just became collections of tenants of a disparate array of landlords. The commune that every village had by 1200 could be given cohesion by a grouping of tenants of a single lord, as at Tassignano; even there their *leader* was a local middling owner. Where, as at Paganico, there was no such community of subjection (any number of external owners owned in Paganico), and major local owners were leaving, the commune lost identity: the city sucked its life out. Communes continued to exist, and became in the thirteenth century very firmly institutionalised; but they lost status, becoming simply the local administrative arm of the city, at most frustrating city policy (particularly its taxation and its justice) as much as they could.[20]

These generalisations are necessarily, of course, based on more than just the 1206 Tassignano case; they give context to it. Tassignano's local atypicality may be not only the unusually high degree of tension (by the standards of the Lucchesia) between a landlord and his tenants but also the preparedness of local independent owners, for their own good reasons of course, to stay and fight; less united groups, focussed on dependent tenants, found cohesion harder. The 1206 Tassignano case also allows us to understand an important feature of rural communes as a group: that they were essentially organising devices, whose meaning changed according to the needs of each village. Some communes were directed against lords; others towards the exploitation of common land; others still towards the running of the local church or, later, the undermining of city control in the countryside. We may be able to make some predictions as to how each commune might behave when we have analysed the landowning structure of each village: how many local owners there were and how rich they were; how much land was owned by how many external owners; how closely the village was tenurially or commercially linked to the city and how fast this changed; how much common land there was and who controlled it; and so on. We must also then look at what communes actually do in the documents at our disposal, so that we can understand how these patterns were transformed into social action. The issue of what communes were *for* and how their purpose changed is among the most useful means of comprehending the social questions that mattered most to the inhabitants of each village. Only by such a means shall we come to understand what was going on in the countryside in general in 1200, or in any other period.

---

[20] For later communes and the city, see D. Osheim, 'Countrymen and the Law in Late Medieval Lucca', *Speculum* lxiv (1989); A.I. Pini, *Città, comuni e corporazioni nel medioevo italiano* (Bologna, 1986), pp. 88-91, 102-5.

2

Intellectuals and Culture in Twelfth- and Thirteenth-Century Italy

Franco Cardini

In the Italian communes of the twelfth to fourteenth centuries there developed, slowly but surely, not only a new type of culture, but also a new type of cultural figure: the intellectual. Something similar certainly happened beyond the Alps, most obviously in Paris, in the world of the university; nonetheless, it was above all in the Italian communes that the social, civic and economic conditions existed which could ensure that, in a relatively short space of time, the trained and cultured layman – jurist, notary or doctor – would become indispensable to the development of the community in which he lived. In the cities culture soon became widely needed and consumed, and therefore the presence of those who could produce culture became ever more valued and essential.[1]

How far did the Italian intellectual really have an organic role for the governing classes of the period, if at all? A simple reply cannot be given, as this essay aims to look at Italian society as a whole over two centuries of history, at a wide and hardly homogeneous geographical area and at a period of important and rapid changes. It is certain, all the same, that if we look at certain jurists and notaries, and even at certain writers, poets or chroniclers who in one way or another were close to the holders of power, we find ourselves dealing with men who often influenced that power, as well as of course being themselves conditioned by it, and acting as a support to it, whether deliberately or not: that is to say, we find ourselves dealing with people capable of controlling their own political relationships.

The relationship between intellectuals and power will be the subject of this essay. In one sense the intellectual of the communal period was only rarely himself a real political figure for, as Max Weber commented, having political influence is very different from having power, if we

---

[1] This is a survey article, with only a minimum of notes; it is nonetheless appropriate to state here how much it owes to Philip Jones's work, in particular his 'Economia e società nell'Italia medievale: la leggenda della borghesia', *Storia d'Italia. Annali* i (Turin, 1978), pp. 185-372.

understand the latter word as meaning the ability to impose sanctions. At first sight we will almost always be having to deal with men who were not the direct holders of power, for this was initially still in the hands of great ecclesiastics and the lay aristocracy, and later extended to entrepreneurs, bankers and merchants: intellectuals were restricted to the role of *prominenti*, 'the mouths of the law', 'opinion-makers'. This was of course not a small role; following Salvemini, one can see that it was not by chance that in late thirteenth-century Florence the judges and notaries, that is to say the 'lay intellectuals' *par excellence*, always ended up, no matter what their socio-economic location, on the side of the magnates. We can see our intellectuals as mediators between rulers and subjects, as long as we keep in mind the relatively dynamic and fluid characteristics of the power of the period. This will bring our analysis very close to the Gramscian notion of the intellectual as having an organic relationship to a given social system. If we use a different definition of power, that of participation in decision-making,[2] the objective power of intellectuals in the communal period is immediately apparent, even if also very heterogenous, from the simple fact that their presence in the society and the political struggles of the period was far from secondary or purely decorative.

This new figure in the complex world of the Italian peninsula was the product of several different developments. In northern and central Italy, there were on the one hand some of the great feudal courts (Monferrato, the Malaspina, the da Romano, the Alberti, the Guidi, the Aldobrandeschi, Montefeltro and so on), with their intellectual patronage; on the other hand, many of the cities of the North (and in Tuscany, Lucca, Siena and Arezzo) had their own cultural traditions, generally based on the bishop and the cathedral school. In the South there was the Norman, and then Staufer, court of Palermo, faced with which some of the still flourishing cultural centres of more distant parts of the kingdom (most obviously the cities of Puglia) gradually weakened: this was, from the late thirteenth century, matched – but never fully supplanted – by the new Angevin court at Naples. In the Palermo of the Norman kings and of Frederick II, there developed, by the first half of the century, an elaborate courtly culture, which was focussed under Roger II on a group of Arab functionaries and scholars (Edrisi being the best known).

To say that this culture was 'courtly' is not a statement made purely for the sake of form. The key point is rather that, following the traditions of 'sacral kingship' and of Oriental centralising bureaucracy, known in the Mediterranean above all thanks to the models of the courts of Byzantium and of the Arab princes, the residence of the sovereign was the heavenly centre of the country: the locus of power and glory, but also of delightful

[2] A. Kaplan and H. Lasswell, *Power and Society* (London, 1950), p. 75.

and voluptuous living. The celebration of the palaces and gardens of Palermo by the Arab poets of the Norman chancery always had a precise political meaning, which is made clear by the emphasis they placed on the omnipotence of the ruler, living as he did surrounded by beauty and wealth.[3] When understood in this way, the court of Palermo takes on the character of a 'place of joy' that is very similar to the role of the feudal court in troubadour poetry. There developed a courtly *koine* that in the thirteenth century, thanks to the cultural model of Frederick II's circle, began to expand throughout the peninsula. If, then, we wish to recognise, as we should, that one of the basic traits of the cultural development of Italy was its polycentrism, we must realise that an important historical component of that development was the southern court culture. This does not mean that the South did not have its own notable civic traditions: but the latter had incomparably more importance in the North and Centre. It is principally these that we will henceforth discuss.

The Italian cities of the twelfth century had a civic identity that is obvious to anyone who looks at them. The communal movement was already established, and was going through its 'consular phase', as it is called, with the city aristocracies in power (though the details of this phase were very different from city to city). Urban centres were expanding: this reflected a demographic growth that can be recognised in the whole of Europe, but in Italy it was reinforced by a considerable amount of immigration from the countryside as well, and resulted in the building of new and extended walls around many cities precisely in the twelfth century. It was in this atmosphere that there developed the first clear signs of a patriotic civic culture: this was focussed on the cults of patron saints and their relics, on the local pride that resulted in the construction of solider and longer walls and greater cathedrals, and on the civic memory that was developing in a Latin literature of chronicle and panegyric.

One sign of this is that in the twelfth century the legends of some of the great city saints took on their definitive form, and with this their cults: S. Ranieri at Pisa; S. Petronio at Bologna; S. Miniato at Florence; S. Massimo at Reggio Emilia. The patron saints of the city communes were often bishops, and the sense of identity of the citizens tended to focus itself on these diocesan cults – though this does not take away from the fact that there was frequent friction and discord between the bishop and the local ruling classes (whose principal families tended to have members who were canons of the cathedral). Bishop, cathedral chapter, and commune were in this period three forces making up the political framework of the city which were allied together, or were mutually opposed, in different ways in

---

[3] See examples in F. Gabrieli and U. Scerrato, *Gli Arabi in Italia* (Milan, 1979).

each city; the result of these tensions marked the history (and the intellectual history) of each urban centre. In the maritime cities, especially Genoa and Pisa, one can add a new element of city identity: participation in the Crusades – particularly the First Crusade – and in the anti-Saracen campaigns immediately before and after it. Thus, in Genoa, the chronicle of Caffaro proudly identified the birth of the Genoese Mediterranean empire with the liberation of the cities of the East from the Arabs and with the enormous booty which represented that liberation so gloriously: above all, the relics of St. John and the so-called 'Sacred Chain' of Caesarea, which is still in the treasury of the cathedral. In Pisa, the *Carmen in victoria Pisanorum* exalts the Pisan victory over the North African port of al-Mahdiyah in 1087, as a holy enterprise. A few decades later another poem was dedicated to another anti-Muslim campaign, this time in the Balearic islands. The poets praised their home towns by comparing them to the two great cities at the centre of Christian imagery, Rome and Jerusalem; from now on many cities became the 'new Rome' or the 'second Rome' (as in the poem that Mosè del Brolo dedicated to his own city of Bergamo in 1112-13), or the 'new Jerusalem'. The tradition of a link with ancient Rome was particularly generalised, and is even seen in some of the cities of the south, such as Salerno, which was influenced by the monastery of Montecassino, a great centre of classical studies and of the transcription of Latin texts.[4] One of Montecassino's monks became bishop Alfano of Salerno, learned in medicine (as we would expect, given that his city was then the capital of medical studies in the West), but also a literary scholar, capable of weaving together praises of Salerno as equal in splendour to Rome with praises of Gregory VII as a Roman hero, defender against the German 'barbarians' of the dignity and liberty of a great and refined church, itself worthy heir of ancient Rome.[5] At Rome itself a text like the famous *Mirabilia Urbis Romae*, set down in the first half of the twelfth century by Benedetto, canon of S. Pietro, shows, with its heap of legends about each classical monument, a tenacious urban cult of the past, soaked in respect and nostalgia, in which one can sometimes see through the legendary surface to a sort of primitive lay pride in the ancient city.[6]

In the Italian cities of the twelfth century, and already by the second half of the eleventh, there thus emerged an environment rich in new developments (even if not in itself entirely new, for in these centres urban life had never entirely disappeared, even in the darkest centuries, and there had been no real break with the Roman imperial past). This was the

---

[4] See for this G. Pasquali, *Storia della tradizione e critica del testo*, 2nd edn. (Florence, 1971), p. 176.

[5] For Alfano see P. Delogu, *Mito di una città meridionale* (Naples, 1977).

[6] *Codice topografico della città di Roma* iii, eds. R. Valentini and G. Zucchetti (Rome, 1946), pp. 1-65.

environment of the man of 'lay' culture. The adjective needs closer definition. Not all such men were lay in the legal sense. Alfano of Salerno and Benedetto of Rome were clerics, and indeed men of episcopal or canonical rank, but they had a lay perspective. They were not, that is to say, men of an exclusively religious or clerical culture, but experts in science and the secular arts (ranging from Latin poetry to medicine), ready to express and involve their knowledge in themes that were no longer narrowly religious. Sometimes, too, the man of culture of the early communal period, who always saw his role as being that of serving civic interest, was legally a layman – not a small fact, in a period in which culture was so dominated by clerics that the word *clericus* meant both 'member of the clergy' and 'scholar', while *laicus* described the uncultured, *idiotae* or *illiterati*. (Not by chance did the University of Paris develop out of the episcopal school; and ecclesiastics still kept almost unchallenged, even if not total, control of all levels of teaching there.) City life brought, however, growing importance to the intellectual professions, which could certainly be practised, at least initially, by clerics, but which nonetheless were all destined to end up in the hands of laymen. One thinks of those of doctor, notary, judge, and legist. A look at the last of these categories is perhaps the best way of letting us enter the reality of lay communal culture.

It was in Italy that, in the first half of the twelfth century, the autonomous dignity of civil law was rediscovered, as was the sacredness of that dignity, insofar as it derived immediately and directly from the sacredness of imperial power itself. The legend that associates the rebirth of legal studies with a *translatio* very similar to the 'holy thefts' of relics that had preceded and accompanied the crusades is in itself very significant. At the sack of Amalfi in 1135, the Pisans were supposed to have removed a precious codex of the *Corpus iuris civilis* of Justinian, which they treated as a relic, showing it surrounded by candles to the bareheaded. It is irrelevant here how true this account is; but its meaning, that of the city's takeover of secular legal culture, is clear. From the early years of the century, in monastic and cathedral schools, it had been taught that law was subordinate to ethics (and thus to theology) inasmuch as it dealt with norms of behaviour, and to logic (and thus to the seven 'liberal arts') inasmuch as it was based on the textual interpretation of legislation. Nevertheless, the never-broken link with Rome had also allowed the survival of legal schools in the imperial (and thus lay) tradition, in centres such as Rome, Ravenna and Pavia. A legal school developed in Bologna too, perhaps, as has been proposed, protected in the eleventh century by the Countess Matilda, who made use of Bolognese judges in her courts; alternatively, perhaps it was already so prestigious as to attract her attention and protection. It is clear that the legal experts of Bologna were laymen: the *legis doctor* Pepone, whom we see in 1076 at a legal tribunal of Matilda's Marturi in Tuscany, was *advocatus* (that is to say legal representative in the secular courts) of the monastery of San Salvatore di Monte Amiata. Similarly, the great legist Irnerio was advocate of San Benedetto di Polirone; and we know that canon law did not permit clerics to exercise that office.

It is beyond doubt that the major role in the foundation of the great tradition of legal studies at Bologna belongs to Irnerio, *lucerna iuris* (lamp of the law), as the glossator Odofredo called him in the mid thirteenth century. Irnerio, the *magister in artibus* of the first three decades of the twelfth century, was responsible, as Francesco Calasso so clearly showed, for the separation of law from both ethics and logic.[7] With him the concept of the autonomy of law was founded and, with this, the problem of the relationship between law and the whole social and interior life of mankind began to be seen in new terms. Furthermore, although Irnerio recognised the importance of the concept of *aequitas* (by which law is only created when the emperor, who is *lex animata in terris*, confers life on it through his power and will), he also came to attribute an entirely special role to the interpreters of legal texts, that is to say to the jurists, as mediators: this role thus had a number of objectively political meanings. The powerful work of Irnerio and his followers was, in the course of the century, accompanied by the redaction of systematic legal treaties, the *summae*; for example those of Rogerio, Piacentino, and above all Giovanni Bassiano in the late twelfth century, and the two by Azzone in the early thirteenth. It should be noted that at the same time the bases of canon law were also being laid down.

Closely connected to law were the study of rhetoric and the studies connected to the profession of notary, which was close to the centre of the complex activities of the communal ruling classes. The tension between them is linked to the problem of the writing down of communal statutes.

Rhetoric in the medieval West was a development from the models of Cicero and Quintilian, and had resulted in a discipline of better writing that was to rise to a level of considerable importance in a communal world dominated by politics and diplomacy. The first treatise of this discipline, the *ars dictandi*, was written at Montecassino, where Alberico wrote his *Breviarium dictaminis* in the 1090s. But it was at Bologna that the *ars dictandi* found its real place, at the same time as the development of civil and canon law. Kantorowicz and Haskins have shown how a real training in the *ars dictandi* existed at Bologna, which resulted in the production of important treatises: the *Praecepta dictaminis* of Alberto Samaritani; the *Rationes dictandi prosaice* of Ugo; the anonymous *Rationes dictandi*; the *Introductiones prosaici dictaminis* of Bernardo da Bologna; the *Ars dictandi* of Guido da Bologna.

In the early thirteenth century, the most interesting master of rhetoric then teaching at Bologna was certainly Boncompagno da Signa, several of

---

[7] F. Calasso, *Medio evo del diritto* i (Milan, 1954), pp. 503ff.

whose works survive, such as the *Rhetorica antiqua* and the *Rhetorica novissima*, as well as many lesser writings. Thanks to his garrulousness and his imaginativeness, the work of Boncompagno is a precious source of information about the culture and society of the city communes. He was, furthermore, the model and teacher for other writers. One should add to his name that of Bene da Firenze, who taught at Bologna as well, was author of a *Summa recte dictandi* and a *Summa dictaminis*, and whose ability attracted the attention of Frederick II himself. It was from the University of Bologna and from this group of experts in style and rhetoric that Pier della Vigna came, who in 1220 entered the service of the emperor and became imperial chancellor. A fourth member of the group was Guido Faba, author of the *Gemma purpurea*, certainly the best known rhetorical manual of the entire thirteenth century, and of a volume of *Parlamenta*, that is to say orations in the vulgar tongue, Italian: with him it is clear that the *ars dictandi*, and its equivalent for the spoken word, the *ars arengandi*, had become by now two genres indispensable for city political life. These new communal intellectuals – masters of law and rhetoric, notaries, doctors – were, in many ways, the creators of urban cultural self-consciousness.

Feudal society had, for a long time, been able to live independently of the world of the city, although in Italy (unlike the lands beyond the Alps, with the partial exception of the South of France) urban society was a constant and unavoidable presence. Even when in the eleventh century the Italian cities began to be more densely populated again, the basic socio-cultural framework of the feudal world remained the same inside them: urban aristocracies, while engaging in entrepreneurial activities that would later lead to the development of the 'bourgeois' world, remained linked to landed property and to signorial mental structures: artisans and labourers remained essentially peasants without land. The two basic counterposed categories of courtly culture, the culture of a feudal *curia*, were *curialitas*, 'courtesy', and *rusticitas*, the rusticity of those still linked to agricultural toil. This is the dichotomy that one finds, for example, in the romances.

The new urban intellectual, often from humble or at least modest origins, found the justifications of his culture and dignity, and his social motivation, in the city. He was not linked to the feudal world, except by often ambiguous relationships of clientele; and if he needed to work to live, his would not be manual labour. A new set of oppositions introduced themselves into society; as well as the old contrast between producers and consumers, there developed a series of opposed categories of producers at different levels. To *rusticitas* there was now counterposed not only *curialitas* (though this remained important, and was reinterpreted by the intellectuals according to their own needs and interests: one instance is thirteenth-century poetry) but *civilitas* or *urbanitas*. Now, 'rustic' meant not only everything not courtly, but also everything not urban; symptomatically, 'courtliness' and 'urbanity' tended to become more closely linked, with the idea of the court transferring itself from the castle, remote among its woods and mountains, to the more refined houses of the city aristocracy – a development that is very clear, for example, in Tuscan poetry.

On the other hand, the intensification of economic relationships, of commerce and of the dynamic process of the circulation of wealth were quite as important as causes for the rapid growth, in a society that remained very largely illiterate, of a specific type of intellectual worker capable of registering agreements and transactions, and of writing documents in legally valid forms. This was the notary, who held *publica fides* (the automatic assumption that every document written by him was legally valid), and who as a result was an ideal mediator between prestige and power. That the level of prestige and indeed culture characteristic of notaries rose considerably in the thirteenth century can be seen from the frequency with which they also appear as poets, chroniclers, 'writers' in the artistic sense of the word. Even the theoretical manuals of the notarial art developed in eloquence in this period: some early thirteenth-century texts, like the *Summa notariae* from Belluno or the *Formularium* from Florence, are simple and fairly elementary collections of formulae and models for practical purposes; but, from the 1220s onwards, we have completer manuals, enriched by their own specific theoretical orientation. It is not by chance that in Bologna itself, at the same time as the greatest exuberance of legal and rhetorical studies, there appeared the first great formulary that considered, in order, all the branches of notarial activity, Ranieri's *Summa artis notariae*. At the start of the 1230s, another jurist, Martino da Fano, wrote a similar *Formularium*.

The problems of how to fit this notarial practice correctly into the framework of Roman law long dominated the relationship between jurists, legal theorists and notaries; Roman law was felt as a great ethical and cultural inheritance, whereas the work of the notary, however well rewarded, seemed like a mechanical heaping up of trite formulae. Between 1242 and 1254 the great Bolognese jurist Salatiele deigned to enter the debate, offering to the notaries with great hauteur two successive editions of an *Ars notariae* in four books, of which only one, the last, was a collection of formulae, whereas the first three consisted of a very basic *summa* of Roman law. Salatiele's text made clear not so much the gaps in the knowledge or the basic superficiality in legal matters of the notarial profession (even though this was certainly what he intended), but rather the inability of some older law teachers to realise that times had changed since the start of the century. By the 1250s, legists could no longer look down on the *practici*, precisely because notarial 'practice' had become a refined and essential instrument for mediation between law and customs, on one side, and the needs of a society that was continuing to evolve, even in its most basic structures, on the other. Indeed, a few years after the appearance of the second edition of Salatiele's book, another Bolognese jurist, Rolandino de' Passeggeri, wrote his *Summa artis notariae*, which showed a quite different sensibility and a quite different understanding of this new environment, while setting out very clearly the need to fit notarial formulae to the progress of legal studies.

At the same time as these developments, there appeared an interesting, and in many ways curious, political-legal popularising literature, directly connected both to writings on law and rhetoric and to ethical and political tracts. There had always been manuals focussed on the education of princes, which were a classical tradition revived in the West from the Carolingian period onwards;[8] to these there were now added works that offered advice of all types to communal officials, and in particular to the *podestà*. Boncompagno da Signa, with his endless output, was the major source of this type of literature. Its most important model was, however, the *Oculus pastoralis*; this was wrongly attributed to Giovanni da Viterbo, but the latter did write another text in this tradition, the *Liber de regimine civitatum*. (The short poem *De regimine et sapientia potestatis* should also be remembered in this context.) This vast and complex podestarial literature was systematised by the *De regimine principum* of the Augustinian Egidio Romano, a pupil of Aquinas, who finished his profound meditation on the duties of sovereigns around 1279. It is significant that a few decades later the Franciscan Paolino Minorita, in his *De regimine rectoris*, written in Venetian, translated Egidio's discourse into city terms, making urban rulers equivalent to kings.

Such podestarial literature fitted very well into the power-balances of the communal elites. The generalised practice by which the various city communes were accustomed to select their *podestà* for his period of office (which lasted on average a few months) from outside the city, from a relatively restricted circle of allies, resulted in the development during the thirteenth century of a sort of 'circulating professional aristocracy': this consisted of members of aristocratic houses of urban or feudal origin (the *podestà* had to be a knight) who moved from city to city in the exercise of the podestarial office. These officials came from 'Lombardy' in the medieval sense of the word (that is to say, the whole of the North), Tuscany, and the Marche: the rural aristocracy of the latter in particular, who tended to have few economic resources, became specialists in the office. The exercise of this profession meant not only the growth of ever tighter and more effective social relationships between cities, but also the creation of a network of competencies, in effect a 'podestarial culture' made up of political, diplomatic, procedural and behavioural skills. It is this culture that was underpinned and enriched by the literature that we have just looked at.

[8] See M.L. Picascia, 'La guerra come costume, la pace come ideale', and M. Pereira, 'L'educazione familiare alla fine del medioevo', in *Per una storia del costume educativo (età classica e medio evo)* (Milan, 1983), respectively pp. 33-52 and 109-23.

The *podestà* on his entry into office swore fidelity to the city statutes. Like the other practical disciplines, that of the writing of statutes developed in the course of the thirteenth century out of an empirical mode, and became ever more closely related to the world of legal culture. It is certainly not by chance that in Bologna itself the network of local norms was consciously inserted into the framework of legal theory, and gave rise to a particularly careful set of statutes, between 1245 and 1267. Bologna remained for the rest of the century at the forefront of the updating of statutes, followed by Florence. In 1284 the judge Alberto di Gandino published his *De statutis*, in which the discipline of writing statutes, too, became closely delimited, defined and discussed.

In the second half of the thirteenth century, then, one finds oneself dealing with a legal and rhetorical culture with precise and mature features. The great intellectuals who accompanied the emergence of the *popolo* and the establishment of the *comune delle arti* in the cities of the thirteenth and fourteenth centuries were complex figures: notaries and masters of rhetoric, writers, teachers, poets, even philosophers, but also politicians with deep roots in the struggles between the factions. It was from this same environment that there developed a characteristic scientific teaching that produced notable results; these included Dante's *Convivio*, and a series of 'vulgarisations' of encyclopaedic and educative works. This elite of political intellectuals included Guittone d'Arezzo, Cino da Pistoia (a poet and jurist, pupil of Dino del Mugello and Lambertino de' Ramponi), Brunetto Latini and Guido Cavalcanti. Cino was very influential on the greatest legal thinker of the fourteenth century, Bartolo da Sassoferrato.

The relationship between city statutes and legal theory was never simple or free of polemic. This can be seen in the *quaestiones statutorum*, elaborate dialectical exercises that spread well outside the universities, and in which nearly all the jurists of the century after 1250 joined in: Francesco, son of the great Accursio, Alberto, son of Odofredo (this was, as one can see, the beginning of the 'dynasties' of jurists), Guido da Suzzara, Lambertino de' Ramponi, Dino del Mugello, Alberto di Gandino, Cino da Pistoia. *Libri magni* were written, vast repertories for consultation, rich repositories of juridical material. These were not pedantic disquisitions, as some recent historians have thought; the fact is that the communes had begun in a delicate and uncertain legal situation, and never entirely got out of it. Cities were conscious of not possessing full rights of self-government or legislation, linked as they were to the universalist pretensions of imperial law. When Boncompagno da Signa wrote his book on statutes, it is significant that he called it *Cedrus*, for statutes in his time grew up more or less everywhere, in exuberant disorder, just like trees; he stated what was then still true, that contemporary statutes were written and given executive force in defiance of imperial authority, and that they only reflected local custom, as well as the political will that gave to the commune the objective force to make itself felt. In the early thirteenth century, the memories of the dispute between Barbarossa and the cities were still alive. But it became clear that it would be necessary to put this forest of cedars in order, and to turn them into a garden. The theoretical consideration of statutory practice should be understood in the context of this vigorous effort of rationalisation.

Boncompagno was a formidable observer of the reality of the communes of his time, and knew how to identify acutely how much would never be able to function in them; his discussion of the office of *podestà* shows this clearly. At the start of the thirteenth century, this office was usually in the hands of minor feudatories, ignorant of government and law (with the exception, Boncompagno said, of his friend Ugolino Gosia, a university teacher and member of a lineage of teachers). A few decades later, the situation had changed significantly; not only had the podestarial literature developed, evidently responding to a real need, but it was also not uncommon to find as *podestà* lawyers who had graduated from Bologna and Padua. In 1239 Genoa chose as *podestà* the jurist Jacopo Balduini, a disciple of Azzone; he used his period of office to carry out a monumental revision of local statutes. In this way the development of communal institutions, together with the advancement of individual professional and political careers, significantly based on the possession of legal knowledge, came ever more closely to be connected to the university, an institution that had come to be present throughout Italy.

That the word 'university' has survived to mean the institution in which one completes a higher education is symptomatic of the importance that the medieval antecedents of this institution had already achieved in their own time. At that time the word *universitas* was by no means technically specific; in the category of *universitates*, that is to say the corporate organisations through which associative and productive life was structured, the *universitas studiorum* was only one of many, alongside the *universitates mercatorum, fabrorum*, and so on. On the other hand, the very fact that in the twelfth century there developed a corporation of lay scholars, teachers and students, is symptomatic both of the growth in importance of laymen not of feudal extraction, and of the expansion and affirmation at all levels of city life of the corporate movement. It should nonetheless be noted that the term *universitas studiorum* appears later than the period we are looking at.

Until the twelfth century the monopoly over higher education was held by the church, through its monastic and cathedral schools. (At lower levels, education was entirely private, and is difficult to reconstruct in its basic contours.) In that century, in most of Europe, schools began to appear that were no longer (or not always, or not tightly) linked to the ecclesiastical schools; lay masters could be found teaching in them. In Italy an early example was the great medical school at Salerno, which however remained on its own for a long time. If one says 'medieval university', one thinks first and foremost of Paris, and perhaps Oxford: universities which were born as corporations of masters, in which one studied above all the 'mother' of all the disciples, theology.

In Italy, the origin of the university was different: it found its prototype in Bologna, which was, if anything, a corporation of students – although originally it was a few great masters who founded the tradition there – and which was, in conformity with the needs and nature of the communal movement, a centre of legal studies. After the fundamental research of Giorgio Cencetti, the hypothesis that the University of Bologna had any sort of ecclesiastical origin has been abandoned. It was the notarial school that was its original nucleus, which brings us back to Irnerio, and to Pepone before him: as long as we understand the word 'school' more conceptually than institutionally. It is probable, all the same, that the original mechanism underlying the development of the institution was fairly simple, based as it must have been on the principal elements of corporative association. Probably a master made a *societas* with his pupils, agreeing with them the methods and costs of their teaching, and the masters for their part made an association among themselves. The fact that they were experts in Roman law did not put them entirely at their ease with the nascent communal movement, at least at first. Like their common teacher Irnerio, the great Bolognese jurists of the mid twelfth century felt that no law could be set above that of the empire, and that the authority of the German and Roman emperor was the sole source and guarantee of legitimacy, and therefore of civil peace. It is not chance that in 1158 the 'four doctors', all pupils of Irnerio – Bulgaro, Jacopo, Martino and Ugo – came to Roncaglia, where the young emperor Frederick I, expressing admiration for them, asked their advice about which were the *iura regalia* appertaining to the crown. It was certainly in part to compensate these masters for their favourable response that Frederick promulgated the constitution known from its first word as *Habita*, in which he conceded privileges to the masters and students of the Bologna schools that removed them from the jurisdiction of the city authorities and from the danger of penalties in the case of debt.[9] This constitution was not restricted to Bologna, and in this respect allowed a development that could expand well beyond that city.

Although the constitution *Habita* cannot in any way be considered a foundation charter for the University of Bologna, it is certain that from now on there began a complex evolution that led to the organisation of *nationes*, which organised students according to their provenance, and which were in turn grouped into two *universitates*, of the *cismontani* and the *ultramontani*. By the start of the thirteenth century, the schools of Bologna were run by the students, in an *universitas scholarium*, and lectures were no

---

[9] A. Marongiu, 'La costituzione "Habita" di Federico I', *Clio* i (1965), 3-24.

longer held in the private houses of the masters, but in the great churches of the city. Also, after long periods of tension, the commune had finally got its hands on the university, if only in the sense that it took on the burden of paying professional stipends; slowly, it also gained the right to control the organisation of courses. This development took place because it had become clear that the university was a source of prestige and gain for the city; hence the provisions of the city authorities against the flight of masters, and hence also the offers that other cities made to them, with the aim of trying to organise universities in their turn. In this way, Modena succeeded in taking from Bologna a famous master, Pillio, in 1182; other temporary experiments included that of Vicenza, begun in 1204, Arezzo in 1213-16, Vercelli in 1228, and Piacenza in 1248. More successful developments were the secession from Bologna that gave rise to the University of Padua in 1222, which was to have a great future; the foundation of Siena in 1246; and that of Perugia at the end of the century. Qualitatively different was the case of Naples, where in 1224 Frederick II founded a general *Studium* with the specific task of preparing officials to rule the kingdom of Sicily. This foundation has been seen as the first state university of Europe, and it was certainly not the result of the initiative of masters or students, but of the will of the sovereign. Many of the masters in Naples were southerners, but had studied in Bologna. This experiment was partly directed against the tendency, general in Europe in the period, to discourage 'university nomadism', the pilgrimage of students in search of knowledge, which had been typical of the previous century and had given to twelfth-century culture its characteristic international features. By the end of the 1220s, the basic structures of intellectual activity in the Italian peninsula were all established.

Thirteenth-century Italian culture was not only university culture, just as it was not only that of the church; there were other sources and needs as well. Frederick II, who was as we have seen aware of the possibilities of the new university system, also set himself up, in the wake of his Arab and Norman predecessors on the Sicilian throne, at the centre of a cultural world that had, if only briefly, a role that was certainly more developed and effective than that of many universities. This was centred on the *Magna Curia*, where the cultivated and generous sovereign freely welcomed scholars, supported research and debate, and did not himself disdain to become involved in scientific work and in subtle and open-minded discussions.[10] It is well-known that Frederick's scientific interests, as well as his love of hunting, spurred him to write the *De arte venandi cum avibus*. Equally well-known is his relationship with Michael Scot, the great astrologer and translator of Ptolemy, Avicenna and Aristotle; but one should not forget the mathematician Leonardo

---

[10] A. De Stefano, *La cultura alla corte di Federico II imperatore* (Palermo, 1938).

Fibonacci, who dedicated his *Liber quadratorum* to Frederick in 1224 and the *Liber Abaci* to Michael in 1228; or Adamo di Cremona, who wrote for Frederick the *Tractatus de regimine iter agentium vel peregrinantium*, a hygiene manual for crusaders. Zoology, astrology, mathematics and medicine were only some of the disciplines which were pursued at court, and which found Frederick to be an attentive and able interlocutor. Greek and Arab science converged in order to give to Frederician scientific culture that experimental style which, elsewhere in contemporary Western culture, was repressed in favour of abstract speculation.

Thirteenth-century Italy, was, nonetheless, a period of wide and careful scientific speculation. Astronomy, suspended between science and magic (as we would say, but the phrase does not mean much), was represented by the geometric studies of Bartolomeo da Parma, by the *Theorica planetarum* of Gherardo da Sabbioneta, and above all by the *Liber astronomicus* of Guido Bonatti. Mathematics certainly derived great advantage from, and was renewed by, this speculation, but was at the same time stimulated by new mercantile developments: the Genoese, Pisans, and Venetians, who habitually visited African, Egyptian, Palestinian, Syrian and Byzantine ports, or who actually lived there for part of the year, learned a large number of new accounting techniques that could often be translated into new elements of mathematical theory. It is sufficient in this context to name once more the Pisan Leonardo Fibonacci, whose *Liber Abaci* was one of the routes by which Indo-Arabic numbers came to the West. Mathematics was related to astronomy, and also to music; indeed, all three were among the disciplines of the *quadrivium*. Music, in fact, made important steps forward in the thirteenth century as well, in the field of performance and also that of theory: in the last half of the century Marchetto da Padova wrote the *Pomerium in arte musicae mensuratae* and the *Lucidarium in arte musica planae*, in which he set in motion the discourse that would culminate in the so-called *Ars nova*.

Medical studies had had their stronghold in the South, in the school of Salerno. This tradition continued in the Norman period, as one can see for example in the *De balneis puteolanis* of Pietro da Eboli, but in the thirteenth century it began to decline; instead, medicine began to increase in importance in Bologna and, especially, Padua. In Bologna there was Taddeo d'Alderotto, whose commentary on Hippocrates was inspired by the formal techniques of the glossators; in Padua, there was the great Pietro d'Abano, the extent of whose 'Averroism' is still disputed, but who was certainly the ancestor of a Paduan medical school characterised by a strong tendency to empiricism. His open-mindedness – which brought upon him suspicions of heresy – is reflected in his most important work, the *Conciliator differentiarum philosophorum et praecipue medicorum*, where the principle of the autonomy of medical science is underlined, along with the need to study it according to its own principles. Doctors remained the principal researchers into the secrets of the body and its health, but there were surgeons as well, authors of tracts on *Chirurgia*: Ugo and Teodorico Borgognone from Lucca; Guglielmo da Saliceto; Guido Lanfranchi; Rolando Capelluto from Parma; and the first great anatomist, Mondino de' Liuzzi. And there was the doctor Aldobrandino da Siena, who lived in France and wrote in French, whose *Livres pour la santé garder* are translations of maxims about hygiene and diet taken from the Ancients and the Arabs.

Anatomy and physiology thus left the world of traditional medieval encyclopaedism deriving from Solinus and Isidore of Seville, in order to regain knowledge taken on the one hand from the Classical world, and on the other from direct observation. A typical example, in another field, of this new way of posing problems is an agricultural treatise, the *Ruralium commodorum libri XII* of Pietro de' Crescenzi, who used Roman agricultural texts (Varro, Cato, Columella), but also took up, with a great freedom and wealth of data, a living popular tradition, and, beyond the symbolic botany of the herbalists, drew directly from experience. A translation of part of this work into Florentine in the fourteenth century had a long and wide circulation, a proof that the experimental message had been received; the treatise was used as a mine of practical advice and of real solutions to the various problems of the cultivation of fields. With Pietro de' Crescenzi we are at the beginning of an extensive and important late medieval and Renaissance tradition, that will include names like Paganino Bonafede, Michelangelo Tartaglia and Corniolo della Cornia, who in his turn stands at the start of a whole technical-literary genre, both learned and popular, that can still be found in modern agricultural almanacs.[11]

Learning had matured enough by the end of the thirteenth century for a new encylopaedism which went beyond the traditional encyclopaedias of Isidore and of Vincent of Beauvais, and which took on the results of the reworking of medieval culture that had emerged both from Scholastic thought and from the many-sided cultural movement (associated above all with Averroism) that put the Scholastic system itself into question. An important feature of this 'new encyclopaedism' is that it existed outside the cultural system of the church and even of the lay culture of the universities, although it did not feel itself to be separated from them, and still less opposed to them. A particularly obvious sign of the times was the growing use of the vernacular, in its many local variants; as it became more and more refined, the *volgare* began to replace both Latin and the French that had developed as a literary tongue even among Italians, such as Aldobrandino da Siena, Rustichello da Pisa, Martino da Canale, and Brunetto Latini, Dante's teacher.

---

[11] See for example, L. De Angelis, 'I trattati di agricoltura', *Archeologia medievale* viii (1981), pp. 83-92; *La Divina Villa di Corniolo della Cornia*, ed. L. Bonelli Conenna (Siena, 1982).

It is worth looking more closely at Brunetto; for he, thanks to his personal characteristics and the importance of his teaching, fully deserves to be taken as an emblematic example of the level now reached by a mature Italian communal culture, before the socio-economic crisis of the 1310s and 1320s which did not and could not fail to affect learning as well. Latini's culture was truly 'lay' and 'communal': not only in a structural and a political sense, but above all because these were the aims which he specifically pursued in his intellectual activities, as a professional, a teacher and a writer. He was a notary, and thus linked to the Bolognese world that we have so often seen to be the motor of communal culture in the twelfth and thirteenth centuries; he then spent six years as a Guelf exile in France, in 1260-66. With these experiences at his back, he offered to his Florentine compatriots an encyclopaedic work in French, *Li livres dou trésor*, in which he intended to communicate to the Florentines a series of reports of historical, ethical, philosophical and political character. This was an encyclopaedia written for a totally civic purpose, that is to say for the cultural development of a dominant or emerging stratum of professionals, notaries, and merchants: none of them were able easily, if at all, to gain a command of Latin, but all of them needed a culture which they avidly desired from anyone who could share with them that kind of bread, or could lay for them that kind of table, to use a metaphor from Dante. The eminently political nature and aims of the *Trésor* are very clear in the part of the work dedicated to the 'podestarial culture', following the traditions we have already seen. Indeed the chronicler Dino Compagni, like Latini a supporter of the *popolo*, described him, in a way that shows how well Compagni had understood his programmes and positions, as 'the founder and master instructor of the Florentines, [aiming] to have them recognised as good speakers and as capable of ruling our republic with political skill'.

The use of French by Brunetto Latini must not only be seen as a result of his long exile beyond the Alps, which might have made him reluctant to use the Florentine vernacular. His choice of French was entirely legitimate and natural at the time; it reflected a long Italian tradition, and also indicated a precise relationship between the writer of a text and the public to which he intended to offer it. His audience was above all constituted by the most conscious and advanced strata of the *popolo grasso*: merchants, bankers, and politicians expert in French affairs, who were at home in the courts of the pope, the Angevin king of Naples, and the king of France himself. But things were changing, and new literary and linguistic needs were developing.

The maturer Brunetto Latini must have posed this same question to himself very explicitly; for, in his next work after the *Trésor*, he chose Florentine as the language in which to set out a culture that was (unlike at least part of the *Trésor*) entirely 'lay' and 'communal'. His *Favolello* was an ethical treatise composed on the basis of the *Amicitia*, a short work by Boncompagno da Signa. The theme was Ciceronian, but it had passed through several filters, one patristic and ascetic, another courtly; for it had attracted the reflections of several centuries of theorists about communal monastic life and chivalric *compagnonnage*. The theme, that is to say, had political and social connotations. This is for now less relevant than the fact that an essentially Ciceronian discourse was being offered to the unlearned laity (who were anyway by now constructing their own culture, and thus ceasing to be unlearned), people who would not in any way have had direct access to the pages of Cicero. Latini did not translate the classics; he reinterpreted and rewrote them, reproposing them in the light of the cultural, civic, political and spiritual needs of his own time. According to some historians, with Latini and the authors of the late thirteenth century we are already at the roots of humanism; it was not chance that the humanists themselves remained for decades uncertain whether to write in Latin or Italian, before choosing the latter.

Latini was not unique; it must not be forgotten that writing at the same time were Guidotto da Bologna, translator of Cicero's *Rhetorica ad Herennium*, and Bono Giamboni, to whom is attributed a translation of the *Trésor* (which also circulated in a verse summary, the *Tesoretto*). Giamboni, another notary, was certainly a tireless translator, and translated works by Lotario da Segni (later Pope Innocent III), Orosius and Vegetius. This role seems to have been much more important than his authorship of an ethical and allegorical tract, the *Libro de' vizi e delle virtudi*, or his translations of other Latin works, if we accept the many attributions of anonymous translations that have been proposed for him.

The question of translation is fundamental for understanding the levels and general objectives of Italian culture in the thirteenth century. This is not only because of the choice of authors and subjects made by translators for their public, but also and especially for the choice of the vernacular itself, an index among other things of a by now widespread ability to procure books and to read, at least at the highest levels of society. Translations into Italian were also texts to be read collectively, to be recited and summarised orally; with them all of communal society, at least at its medium and perhaps even at its lowest levels, found an effective instrument of cultural development.

This brings us back to the question of the written language. As the thirteenth century went on, examples multiply of the vernacular used for rhetorical, philosophical, or scientific purposes. We are no longer restricted to the Italian of the poets and storytellers (though that was itself important); there developed now, with the *Composizione del mondo* of Ristoro d'Arezzo, a scientific language, and, with Dante's *Convivio*, a philosophical language. Dante, who clearly set out the problem of how to establish a 'distinguished' vulgar language in the *De vulgari eloquentia*, could discuss in the *Divina commedia* itself theological problems that normally required the use of Latin – and he did so not only to maintain a cultural position, but also to establish a real technical vocabulary for theology as well. The polemic between Dante and Giovanni Del Virgilio, who criticised him for degrading his genius and culture by writing in vernacular verse, is symptomatic of a changed environment, in which the requirements of a wider diffusion of culture imposed the birth of a new language. The cultural level of Italian was by now much higher than it had been a few decades earlier, when it had simply constituted the language of daily speech, but it still abandoned to Latin and to literary French the expression of more noble and difficult thoughts and concepts. This would be the next conquest of the vulgar tongue in Italy; but the intellectual climate, and intellectuals themselves, would be very different from those of Latini's time when the conquest took place.

3

The Conversion of St. Francis

John Stephens

In religious history sometimes too much is explained and at other times
too little. It is easily assumed that standards of worship differ from age to
age, that definitions of doctrine are brought into line with 'living' faith, or
that heresies or reformed churches supply the failings of a universal
church, but that faith is substantially the same.[1]

Thus the conversion of the pagan barbarians has sometimes been seen
as not a problem to be explained at all – only why it took so long to be
effective. Similarly the appearance of the new monastic orders in the
eleventh and twelfth centuries has been interpreted as a cycle in religious
observance, whilst the conversion of St. Francis is accepted as an act of
grace. At other times historians explain too much. A large part of the
eleventh, twelfth and thirteenth centuries is reduced to an 'evangelical
awakening', with common denominators which are too 'low': a market
economy, the rise of towns, the spread of lay education.[2] These factors
may form the general background of the religious history of the time, but
they are not the common causes, because there is not a universal problem
to be explained. The evangelical symptoms of that age were frequently the
common features of disparate phenomena. Partly for the same reason the
most critical and imaginative work in Franciscan studies has been
diverted either into this evangelical landscape or into a massive
investigation of the texts.

This latter task is a necessary one because there is a 'Franciscan
Question', which is a problem of the sources. The Franciscan Order
evolved in the course of the thirteenth century and, as it did so, the records
relating to St. Francis were altered or suppressed. The problem therefore
has arisen of uncovering the true career, doctrines and beliefs of St.

[1] I am grateful to Dr. Rosalind Brooke and to Dr. Malcolm Lambert who both kindly
read an earlier draft of this.

[2] M.D. Chenu, 'The Evangelical Awakening' in his *Nature, Man and Society in the 12th
Century* (Chicago, 1968); B.H. Rosenwein & L.K. Little, 'Social Meaning in the Monastic
and Mendicant Spiritualities', *Past and Present*, lxiii (1974), 4-32.

Francis, by dating and analysing the few early memorials of his life. There is only one early biography, that of Thomas of Celano, but it has two versions and it is not known from where the author derived his knowledge. Nor is it certain how his sources are related to the other early documents, notably the so-called Anonymous of Perugia and the Legend of the Three Companions. This, very loosely, has been the Franciscan Question, and it has produced an important literature.[3] All the same, it has come to overshadow the tasks for which it was begun.[4]

A chief problem which has been neglected is the conversion of St. Francis. From it followed the special forms of Franciscan spirituality: poverty, romance, and the very direction of his thought and devotion. Very little has been written on the subject, and much of it has been devoted to questionable assumptions or to whimsy. Some biographers have contented themselves with copying out the account in Thomas of Celano's Lives, comparing it to the conversion of St. Paul or declaring it beyond human capacity to explain.[5] Other studies have turned aside from the problem to consider individual incidents in the conversion,[6] or the themes of Celano himself.[7] The general characteristics of St. Francis's spirituality, have rightly received close attention. These include his

---

[3] E.g. *I Fiori dei Tre Compagni*, ed. J. Campbell (Milan, 1967) (cf. E. Pásztor in *Studi Medievali*, ix (1968), 252-64); M. Bigaroni, '*Compilatio Assisiensis' dagli Scritti di Fr. Leone e Compagni su S. Francesco d'Assisi* (Perugia, 1975) (cf. T. Desbonnets in *A[rchivium] F[ranciscanum] H[istoricum]*, lxix (1976), 240-42); D. Lapsanski, 'The Autographs on the "Chartula" of St. Francis of Assisi', *AFH*, lxvii (1974), 18-37; T. Desbonnets, 'La "Legenda Trium Sociorum": Edition critique', ibid., 38-144; idem, 'Généalogie des biographies primitives de S. François', *AFH*, lx (1967), 273-316; idem, 'La Légende des Trois Compagnons, nouvelles recherches sur la généalogie des biographies primitives de Saint François', *AFH*, lxv (1972), 66-106; *St. François d'Assise: Documents écrits et premières biographies*, ed. idem and D. Vorreux (Paris, 1968); J. Campbell, 'Les écrits de Saint François d'Assise devant la critique', *Franziskanische Studien*, xxxvi (1954), 82-109 and 205-64; S. Clausen, *Legenda antiqua S. Francisci* (Studia et Documenta Franciscana, v, 1967); *Scripta Leonis, Rufini et Angeli sociorum S. Francisci*, ed. R.B. Brooke (Oxford, 1970); K. Esser, *Das Testament des heiligen Franziskus von Assisi* (Vorreformationsgeschichtliche Forschungen, xv 1949); idem, *Studien zu den Opuscula des Hl. Franziskus von Assisi* (Subsidia Scientifica Franciscalia, iv, 1973); idem with R. Oliger, *La Tradition Manuscrite des Opuscules de Saint François d'Assise* (Subsidia Scientifica Franciscalia, iii 1972); F. de Beer, *La Conversion de Saint François selon Thomas de Celano* (Paris, 1963); D. Flood, W. van Dijk, T. Matura, *La Naissance d'un Charisme* (Paris, 1973).

[4] Cf. Pasztor, p. 264.

[5] A. Fortini, *Nova vita di San Francesco* ([Perugia], 1959) 1, i, 243; O. Englebert, *Saint Francis of Assisi* (Chicago, 1965), pp. 67-68.

[6] L. Bracaloni, 'Il Prodigioso crocefisso che parlò a San Francesco', *Studi Francescani*, xxxvi (1939); K. Esser, 'Das Gebet des hl. Franziskus vor dem Kreuzbild in San Damiano', *Franziskanische Studien*, xxxiv (1952), 1-11; M. Faloci Pulignani, 'Il Messale consultato da S. Francesco quando si converti', *Miscellanea Francescana*, xv (1914), 33-43.

[7] De Beer, *La Conversion*.

imitation of Christ,[8] worship of the Virgin Mary, theology,[9] the social springs or social message of his teaching,[10] and the relationship of his spirituality to the evangelical movements of the eleventh and twelfth centuries.[11]

The effect of this has been to interpret the conversion and St. Francis's spirituality in terms of its traditional elements. 'The greatness of St. Francis', it has been said, 'consisted in the fact that he had no original idea outside the Gospel and that in essence, he wished to be nothing else than the imitator of Christ'.[12] This is to understand St. Francis too much in the light of his own claims. The words echo those of Francis himself as he later described his vocation.[13] It can be argued that St. Francis was wholly original in his path to God, that its origins lay outside the Gospel, and that conversion determined the direction of his spiritual career. Afterwards his faith was subtly altered as he tried to make sense of it in the light of Scripture. Even after conversion it is hard to accept the notion that Francis had no idea outside the Gospel, that he was merely a 'good' heretic (a common view), that he and his friars drew heavily on the work of hermits, heretics and itinerant preachers,[14] and on the 'evangelical awakening',[15] and that his greatest achievement was to mediate between a learned and popular Christianity.[16] More accurate are the very few estimates which have emphasised his originality, such as the view that for Francis poverty was 'less a flight out of the world than a deliverance of earthly goods and a new way of regarding nature'.[17]

The justice of this can be glimpsed in a story of Francis's last hours. He

---

[8] O. von Rieden, 'Das Leiden Christi im Leben des. hl. Franziskus von Assisi', *Collectanea Franciscana*, xxx (1960), 5-30, 129-45, 241-63, 353-97.

[9] S. Verhey, *Der Mensch unter der Herrschaft Gottes* (Düsseldorf, 1960).

[10] H. Roggen, *Die Lebensform des heiligen Franziskus von Assisi in ihrem Verhältnis zur feudalen und burgerlichen Gesellschaft Italiens* (Mechelen, 1965).

[11] E.g. H. Grundmann, *Religiöse Bewegungen im Mittelalter*, 2nd edn. (Hildesheim, 1961); M. Mollat, 'Pauvres et pauvreté à la fin du XII siècle', *Revue d'Ascétique et de Mystique*, xli (1965), 323; Chenu, pp. 259 ff.; *Povertà e ricchezza nella spiritualità dei secoli XI e XII* (Convegni del Centro di studi sulla spiritualità medievale, viii [Todi, 1967], 1969) esp. the contribution of R. Manselli, pp. 11-41; C. Thouzellier, 'Hérésie et pauvreté à la fin du XIIe et au début du XIIIe siècle', in *Etudes sur l'histoire de la pauvreté*, ed. M. Mollat (Paris, 1974), i, 387.

[12] W. Dettloff, 'La spiritualité de saint François et la théologie franciscaine', *Etudes Franciscaines*, xxxviii (1966), 206, cf. 191.

[13] Desbonnets and Vorreux, pp. 114-16.

[14] Rosenwein and Little, p. 18; the view is found already in E. Scott Davison, *Forerunners of St. Francis* (London, 1928), esp. pp. 276-84.

[15] Chenu, *ubi supra*.

[16] E. Delaruelle, 'Saint François d'Assise et la piété populaire', in *San Francesco nella ricerca storica degli ultimi ottanta anni* (Convegni del Centro di studi sulla spiritualità medievale, ix [Todi, 1968], 1971), p. 155.

[17] B. Bligny, 'Les Premiers Chartreux et la pauvreté, *Le Moyen Age*, lvii (1951), 60.

asked to be stripped of his tunic, his one possession, and to be placed naked on the earth.[18] The attitude implied here to the religious life had what may be called (without irony) an imaginative quality. Francis understood poverty literally and he embraced it literally. He died naked as sometimes he had preached. Francis also surrendered himself to the natural world. Moreover the embrace of poverty and of nature were, as will be seen, conjoined.

The most useful way we can understand this distinctive vision is Francis's conversion. Why did something happen at all? Why did it begin? These questions are associated. In order to comprehend the unusual spirituality of St. Francis it is important to consider its beginnings. Why did he ever set upon his course? Why (and how) did he take his first step? What pressures, and impulses, and motives made him embark upon it?

The Franciscan Question, most broadly understood, has a bearing upon the possibility of answering these questions. It is essential to have confidence in the chief source, the Lives of Thomas of Celano. The older worries can be dismissed that these works contain no more than the commonplaces of earlier saints' lives. There are hagiographical echoes in Celano's work but not of a kind to affect the truthfulness of their factual foundation.[19]

More essential is the relationship of Celano's Lives to the other early records of Francis's life. Something of a scholarly consensus exists, that the latter texts were sources for Celano's Second Life. Besides the writings of Francis himself, the most authentic of Franciscan sources are considered to be Celano's First Life, the Anonymous of Perugia, the Legend of the Three Companions and Celano's Second Life, for certain additional materials which it contains of undecided provenance.[20] Celano's two Lives therefore remain the chief accounts, supplemented by these additional documents. However, the latter tell us little of interest about the conversion itself.

One important problem remains, which is to decide whether Celano himself coloured his Lives with some personal or theological bias. It has been argued recently that the very difference between the two works is to be accounted for by the purposes of Celano.[21] Contrary (it is said) to what

---

[18] *Scripta Leonis*, pp. 294-96.

[19] M. Bihl, 'De S. Francesco praedicante ita, de toto corpore faceret linguam', *AFH*, xx (1927), 196-213; P. Sabatier, *Speculum Perfectionis seu Sancti Francisci Assisiensis legenda antiquissima auctore fratre Leone* (Paris, 1898), pp. xcviii-cix; J.R.H. Moorman, *The Sources for the Life of St. Francis of Assisi* (Manchester, 1940), pp. 66-76.

[20] A. Pompei, 'Francesco da Assisi', in *Bibliotheca Sanctorum* (Rome, Pontificia Università Lateranense, Istituto Giovanni XXIII, 1961-70), v, cols. 1120-28; Desbonnets and Vorreux, pp. 1490 ff.; *La 'Questione Franciscana' dal Sabatier ad oggi* (Atti del convegno internazionale 'Società internazionale di studi francescani', Assisi, Oct. 1973); *Scripta Leonis*, ed. Brooke.

[21] De Beer, *La Conversion*.

Thomas of Celano himself and contemporaries alleged, the Second Life (1246) is not simply a collection of further facts omitted in the First Life (1229). It is, rather, a reworking of the First Life. Each was animated by a distinct theme, the first 'spiritual', the second one 'religious'.

In the First Life St. Francis's conversion was shown to have been effected by God. Francis himself was depicted as a sinner transformed by grace into a state of sinlessness *ex nihilo*. Henceforth he was a new man, constantly reasserting his vocation by efforts of will. In the Second Life by contrast, what is mentioned is the native goodness of St. Francis, and the effects of grace and of his upbringing before conversion. Already in childhood his mother had foreseen that he would be a son of God thanks to his merits. According to this interpretation the conversion in the Second Life was less a sudden rejection by Francis of his old life by a triumph of the will than a change of direction: he still loved delights but now of the spirit, not the flesh, and his conversion was represented as a return to the goodness of nature. In the First Life more attention was given to God; in the Second, more to Christ and the Spirit.

These insights are helpful for an understanding of Celano's Lives, but it is necessary to reassert that, despite the differences, the two Lives do present broadly the same portrait. It is the construction which Celano lends the facts, and the way he reports them, which differ. Celano's two versions also have much in common: the conversion is a very definite event in the Second Life and it is one brought about by divine intervention. This will be plainer if the chief incidents in the two accounts are set forth (see p. 36).

The similarity of the two accounts emerges from this comparison. In each case the general chronology of events is close. Adversity led Francis to amend his life, although in the First Life it was sickness and in the Second it was imprisonment which prompted the change. There are two main episodes (or phases) in the conversion, and their outlines were the same: the abandonment of an expedition to Apulia and the employment of commercial profits to restore the church of San Damiano.

The main differences are that in the Second Life there is reference to Francis being made chief of the revellers in Assisi (3b) and that he kissed a leper (3c). The second of these incidents does however correspond loosely to a story of St. Francis serving lepers which is recorded in Chapter 7 of the First Life after the account of the restoration of San Damiano. There are several minor differences in the Second Life, chiefly the 'evangelical preparation' with which Francis is credited before conversion. Furthermore the dream of glory he would win in Apulia is placed in a palace instead of in his own home, and it is said that he was inspired to restore the church by the miraculous image which spoke to him there.

FIRST LIFE	SECOND LIFE
1. Excessive youthful vanity (cap. 1).	1. Youthful zeal for God (cap. 1).
2. Sickness led to consciousness of vanity, but Francis returned to same (c. 2).	2. Francis imprisoned in Perugia but laughed at his chains, prophesying that he would become a saint, and after was more compassionate to poor. Thus he clothed a poor knight, like St. Martin (c. 1-2).
3. Vision of glory and prosperity (warlike accoutrements) in his house, to be won on expedition to Apulia (c. 2). Refused to go to Apulia speaking of great and precious treasure he had found, and great and noble deeds he would do in Assisi and that he would marry a nobler and fairer bride than any (c. 3).	3(a). Vision of warlike accoutrements and bride in a palace, following which he sought to win knighthood in Apulia, but after second vision, in which spoken to by God, he returned home (c. 2). After this he 'began to be changed into a perfect man' (c. 3).
	3(b). Made chief of the revellers in Assisi, and prepared banquet and sang drunken songs around streets, but Francis drifted apart and suddenly filled with divine sweetness. Gave his clothes to paupers and church ornaments to poor priests (c. 4).
	3(c). Devil tempted him with being made a hideous hunchback unless he gave up goodness: God however told him he must give up what he had loved carnally for spiritual things; and Francis kissed a leper (c. 5).
4. Francis gave the profits of cloth sales to restore church of San Damiano (c. 4). These were also used to feed the poor (c. 6). Francis willingly agreed to father's demands to renounce his inheritance, and even gave back clothes off his back (c. 6).	4. Painting of Christ in San Damiano spoke to him ordering him to 'repair my house' (c. 6). Bishop ordered him to give up money to his father which Francis was planning to spend on San Damiano, and he did so, giving up his clothes also, declaring that henceforth he was no longer son of Pietro Bernardone but of God (c. 7).
5. Francis described himself (to robbers) as the Herald of the Great King and sang aloud praises of the Creator. He later served lepers (Celano here quoting and incorporating Testament dedication). Thereafter Francis attained perfect conquest of himself (c. 7).	

A comparison of the two texts also suggests that the Second Life elaborated the facts of the earlier one. This in certain respects reduces its credibility. Three new strands may be detected in it: there is a definite spiritual message in that Francis was 'foreknown' to God, more concerned with Christ, and his conversion was gradual. Secondly, there are hagiographical echoes: in Chapter 2 Francis is compared to S. Martin;[22] the story of his kissing the leper (who then miraculously disappears) may also have a hagiographical lineage.[23] Thirdly, stories are included probably because they were popular in Franciscan circles around 1246, some twenty years after Francis's death.

There are few other early Franciscan sources which add much to Celano's picture. The chief of them is the so-called Legend of the Three Companions. Broadly it conforms to the story of Francis's conversion in Celano's Second Life, although textual critics consider that the dependence is the other way about – the Legend having been a source of Celano's Second Life. The Legend of the Three Companions supplies three significant facts. It records that it was Spoleto where Francis was stopped by a divine visitation, and from which he returned home rather than continue to Apulia.[24] Secondly, it reveals that when he was 'visited' again in the streets of Assisi, Francis's companions asked if he was thinking of taking a wife and he said that this was so – a bride, 'nobler, richer and fairer than you have ever seen'.[25] The Legend also indicates that the money which Francis wished to give to San Damiano was the profits of a cloth sale which he had made in Foligno.[26] Finally there is one more essential source of the conversion: an account which St. Francis himself placed in his Testament. He says there that before he came to God he was revolted by the sight of lepers and that afterwards he was repelled no more.[27]

Francis's abandonment of the world raises many questions. He was not converted for conventional reasons: it did not happen in a conventional manner, nor to a conventional end. In the ancient world and the early Middle Ages (when it was a question of a change to Christianity from paganism) the common causes of conversion seem to have been the fear of magic and superstition or what may be considered the 'insufficiences' of pagan religion.[28] In the eleventh and twelfth centuries the religious awakenings of the leaders of the New Monasticism were often directed to the improvement or restoration of an existing model of religious life. Most

---

[22] Cf. F. Cardini, 'I primi biografi francescani dinanzi a un modello agiografico cavalleresco: San Martino di Tours', *Studi Francescani*, lxxvi (1979), 51-61.

[23] F.E. Chavin, *Histoire de saint François d'Assise* (Paris, 1841), p. 19.

[24] T. Desbonnets, 'La "Legenda Trium Sociorum"', p. 93.

[25] Ibid., p. 95.

[26] Ibid., p. 102. This fact is also to be found in the *Legenda Major* of St. Bonaventure.

[27] Esser, p. 100.

[28] A.D. Nock, *Conversion* (Oxford, 1933).

of these leaders – St. Norbert, Bernard of Abbeville (or Ponthieu or Tiron), Vitalis of Mortain (or Savigny), Robert of Arbrissel, Robert of Molesmes, Stephen Harding, St. Bruno and Gilbert of Sempringham – were already in orders (many of them were canons) before they sought a more perfect, or austere, spiritual vocation. They seem to have been moved to improve their lives by a desire to imitate the perfect of the past. Robert of Molesmes wished to lead a life of poverty like that of the Apostles.[29] The founders of Cîteaux (Robert again, and Stephen Harding) wished to restore the purity of the Benedictine Rule.[30] Reinfrid and the monk of Winchcombe, who led the effort to re-establish monasticism in northern England in the late eleventh century, seem to have been moved by reading Bede's stories of the early Anglo-Saxon saints and by the desolation of Whitby, one of the monasteries described by him.[31] These religious figures of the twelfth century were also assailed by different doubts from those troubling St. Francis. The latter, according to Celano and Francis himself, was disturbed by the fear of deformity and disease; the monastic reformers, if we believe their biographers, were attacked by the Devil,[32] or this is how the reformers saw fit to interpret the event.

St. Francis, then, was not converted for the usual reasons. Nor did it come about in a customary manner. Unlike Peter Waldo, the founder of the Waldensian sect, he was not affected by a sermon. He was not moved, either, by the bad example of the church. In contrast to St. Bruno, the founder of the Carthusians, he did not flee from a church that was too worldly for his tastes.

Francis also pursued unorthodox ends. He was not led to seek God in the monastic life and his renunciation of riches was more extreme than that of any monk because he renounced corporate as well as individual wealth. There had been heretics before him who had wandered, preached and begged, but he was alone in his unusual attitude to poverty and nature.

Francis's conversion is also much more reliably documented than those of the religious leaders of the previous age. The life of Robert of Molesmes for example was written more than a century afterwards,[33] the account of the conversion of St. Norbert is obviously based on that of St. Paul and is

---

[29] 'Vita S. Roberti', ed. P.K. Spahr, *Das Leben des hl. Robert von Molesmes* (Freiburg, 1944), pp. 10-11.

[30] D.J. Othon, 'Les Origines Cisterciennes', *Revue Mabillon*, xxii (1932), 134, 241-43.

[31] D. Knowles, *The Monastic Order in England* (Cambridge, 1963), pp. 165-66.

[32] Cf. Stephen of Fougères, 'Vita Sancti Vitalis', (*Analecta Bollandiana*, 1882), Bk. I, chap. 13, p. 369; Bernard of Tiron, 'Vita', *Acta Sanctorum*, Aprilis II, 1866, pp. 220 ff.

[33] M. Séraphin Lenssen, 'Saint Robert Fondateur de Citeaux', *Collectanea Ordinis Cisterciensium Reformatorum*, iv (1937), 6-8.

laced with other uncertainties,[34] while there is no early life of St. Bruno at all. Other lives, it is true, like that of Bernard of Tiron, are early,[35] but they record little of the springs of religious convictions. This applies to the biographies of those lay leaders of the religious revival of the twelfth century who were most like St. Francis. The biographer of Herluin, the founder of the abbey of Bec in Normandy, gives little information about his conversion and it may be suspected that he knew little.[36] Stephen of Muret, the founder of Grandmont, had been converted (it was said) by meeting the Greek hermits of southern Italy,[37] whose model he sought to imitate. But in fact this life has so many chronological confusions that the reliability of the factual information that it contains is cast into doubt.[38]

There is one partial exception in Bernard of Clairvaux. Like Francis he was a layman and his influence was similarly great. There is a hint that Bernard's spiritual progress was impelled initially by no conventional influence nor directed to a restoration or perfection of any older form of spiritual life. According to one source, when a contemporary observed St. Bernard and his companions shortly before they entered Cîteaux and asked if they were crusaders bound for Jerusalem, Bernard affirmed that they were, but destined not for Jerusalem where Christ once was, but for the one where he was now.[39] This story suggests that St. Bernard and his companions, who all seem to have come from the knightly class, may have seen their abandonment of the world as a development, rather than a rejection, of their old worldly values.

The conversion of St. Francis was unconventional in its manner as well as in its end. The one thing explains the other. How then had it come about? The key lies in the direction of Francis's life at the time. It is necessary to consider how far he was turning away from something and how far he was directed towards something else.

In Celano's picture the process happened by stages. In the Second Life these were presented as a series of visitations from God: Francis had a vision, he was filled with divine sweetness, a crucifix spoke. In the First Life the pattern is the same, although there is less reference to divine intervention. It is possible to grasp the drift of Francis's mind if the context of these episodes and his mental 'trajectory' are defined. What was Francis doing when these episodes occurred?

---

[34] P. Lefèvre, 'L'Episode de la conversion de S. Norbert et la tradition hagiographique du *vita Norberti*', *Revue d'Histoire Ecclésiastique*, lvi (1961), 813-26.

[35] J. von Walter, *Die ersten Wanderprediger Frankreichs* (Leipzig, 1906), pp. 123 ff.

[36] 'Vita Herluini', ed. J. Armitage Robinson, *Gilbert Crispin, Abbot of Westminster* (Cambridge, 1911), pp. 88 ff.

[37] Gerardus, 'Vita S. Stephani', cap. 6, ed. E. Martène, V. Durand, *Veterum Scriptorum Amplissima Collectio* (Paris, 1724-33), vi, 1052-53.

[38] H. Platelle, 'Stefane di Muret', in *Bibliotheca Sanctorum*, xi (1968), 1406-8.

[39] E. Vacandard, *Vie de St. Bernard* (Paris, 1910).

In the first incident he was journeying to fight in Apulia; in the second, he was revelling in the streets of Assisi; whilst in the third he seems to have been embarking upon a commercial tour to Foligno. These stages in Francis's religious conversion were not fulfilments or developments of something which had already begun. Francis was not on pilgrimage or (except possibly during the last incident) engaged in prayer. These events represent arrested worldly activities; they are also renunciations. In the first case Francis abandoned his expedition to southern Italy. In the third he gave away the profits of commercial selling. Arguably in the second episode as well he was renouncing something (or seeing its irrelevance). As renunciations these stories show that Francis's conversion was much more a turning away than a turning towards something new. He came back from Spoleto with no clear purpose other than to do great deeds in Assisi. In the Second Life he is shown to have been distracted from the revels by the thought of a 'nobler, richer, fairer' bride. Only when he renounced commerce was it for a clear end, of repairing a church, but this was a temporary one.

In the first case, Francis had set out for Apulia after he had dreamt of his house (a palace in the Second Life) filled with arms and a beautiful woman – a dream of knighthood and its rewards of glory and the love of courtly women. The importance to him of chivalry and romance may be glimpsed here. This fits with what we know of his tastes. He was called Francesco because of his father's interest in French affairs and Francis himself when excited would talk in French or sing French songs.[40] In seeking to restore the church of San Damiano by using the profits of a sale of his father's cloth, Francis was rebelling against the career which his father had planned for him. In the story his father, having discovered what his son was doing, tried to recover the money, whereupon Francis made a final break with him: saying that henceforth he was the son, not of his father Pietro Bernardone, but of his father in Heaven. The second episode is more obscure. Francis and his companions seem to have been serenading the girls of Assisi. The immediate reaction of his companions when Francis drifted apart was that he had been 'struck' by love for a woman and he admitted that he had. Historians usually interpret this lady as Lady Poverty, but it is possible that he was discovering his sentimental attraction to Creation.

Francis, then, was rejecting the secular goals of his old life: the things which had excited his hope and ambition and made sense of his life. Arguably it was not just what Francis was doing at the time of his conversion which was significant, but the sequence of his rejections. He gave up chivalry, love, and finally trade. He seems to have abandoned the avenues of expectation in the reverse order to that in which they had come to him. First he rejected those ambitions most extraneous to someone

---

[40] Thomas of Celano, *Vita I*, cap. 7.

sprung from the merchant class of northern Italy – French chivalry. Then he put aside the consolations of his fellows and last the ambitions of his own father. It is noteworthy also that Francis when he had been converted seems to have gone through a 'swing-door': his conversion was less a renunciation of his old values than their reversal. In the first episode, abandoning the road to Apulia, he said he would embark instead on great and noble deeds at home.[41] In the Second Life he was warned by God to exchange what he had loved carnally and vainly for spiritual things.[42] His conversion, in short, was an exchange. From fighting for honour he fought for Christ; from loving women he loved creation and from liking money and display, he came to seek poverty and simplicity. His conversion was a rejection of his own values – not of worldly values as others might have defined them.

This may highlight the course of Francis's conversion, but not its cause. There are, however, clues in Celano and a clear message in Francis's own Testament that it was triggered by a horror of destitution, disfigurement and disease. Celano records that even before he came to God Francis performed acts of mercy to the poor.[43] In the Second Life he says that Francis was told by the Devil that he would be made a hideous hunchback unless he gave up goodness, while God warned him that he must exchange carnal for spiritual love. It was following this that Francis kissed a leper.[44] There are hints here that Francis was convinced of a curious equation: that beauty was evil, and deformity good.

Francis's Testament shows that this was no accidental association. There Francis reveals that it was his attitude to lepers which was the central feature and the start of his conversion:

> This is how God inspired me to embark upon a life of penitence. When I was in sin, the sight of lepers nauseated me beyond measure; but then God himself led me into their company, and I had pity on them. When I had once become acquainted with them what had previously sickened me became a source of spiritual and physical consolation for me. After that, I did not wait long before leaving the world.[45]

Why should conversion be prompted by a horror of deformity or disease? These miseries threaten life or a stable expectation of it, and the central Middle Ages with their expanding and insanitary towns were fouled by filth and disease, horrors with which the friars associated themselves. In later thirteenth-century England the Grey Friars' house at Exeter stood six feet from an open sewer. When the earl of Hereford once stayed there

---

[41] Ibid., cap. 3.
[42] Ibid., *Vita II*, cap. 5.
[43] Ibid., cap. 2.
[44] Ibid., cap. 5.
[45] Esser, p. 100.

he reported that nine of the friars had died in the previous two years.[46] In the early days it was the policy of friars to settle in such places. Probably the population of the central Middle Ages was more vulnerable to disease than that of the early Middle Ages had been. But the latter period, on the other hand, was overwhelmed to a greater extent by poverty and death, and this had not then led men to God. Moreover, the north Italian cities of the twelfth and thirteenth centuries are unlikely to have been more assailed by disease than the teeming cities of antiquity, when the fear of it had not been a significant prompter of conversion.

St. Francis himself was not a typical convert, although the loathing of material things which is to be seen in many currents of spiritual life in the preceding age is analogous to his own. Nevertheless, Francis's conversion was distinctive in that he was primarily turning away from something. So strong was the pull of his old values that they moulded his new ones. This may suggest that what leprosy and deformity had undermined were the old values, for it was them that he abandoned. It was chivalry, romance and commercial enterprise or the hopes they carried that seem to have been threatened by misfortune.

Was disease especially horrible in the thirteenth century not because there was more of it but because there were inadequate psychological defences? The ancients had been better defended by the ecstatic religion or consolatory philosophies accepted at the time. The Dark Ages possessed an heroic Christianity, which made life into a defiance of death. In both ages religion was concerned with accepting or confronting misfortune in a way that the central Middle Ages was not, with its 'Greenhorn' philosophies of glory, love and money. Was this related to the admiration which came to be felt for lepers in the twelfth century, for the reason that they had paid already in this world for their sins? Certainly it began to be thought then that it was a virtuous act to care for lepers, because they had achieved an early redemption.[47]

Poverty and disease particularly confronted the worldly values in which Francis had been educated, and he accommodated them by abandoning worldly ambition. For him accepting God was the same as accepting the human condition. This set the tone for Francis's spirituality upon conversion. The sources recall that from the first he praised the Creator and that his earliest follower, Bernard of Quintavalle, heard him secretly intone in the night 'Meus Deus et omnia' ('My God and all'). From this time also St. Francis began to be 'consoled' by lepers. Later he came to possess a sense of fraternity with all creation, speaking of 'Brother Sun' and of flowers as 'our sisters'. Embracing God seems to have meant for Francis embracing all that was God's. Hence he came to abandon

---

[46] A.G. Little, *Studies in English Franciscan History* (Manchester, 1917), p. 12.
[47] R.I. Moore, *The Formation of a Persecuting Society* (Oxford, 1987), pp. 60-61.

prudence and accept all that mercy brought him. He made no plans to earn or eat; he advocated having no thought for the morrow and taking nothing with one on a journey.

The religious convictions of St. Francis have something about them which is at once Italian and distinctively personal. The curious amalgam of chivalric and commercial attitudes, which we sense in his background, could not have been formed outside a north Italian city. A seer in the ancient pleasure-gardens of Carthage or Milan or the monks and hermits of Celtic Ireland or Romanesque Burgundy were not shaken into faith at the sight of diseased beggars. So fervent was Francis's embrace of misfortune, and so close was his equation of beauty with evil and of goodness with deformity and disease, that the idea suggests itself of there having been at the heart of his spirituality a personal vision that God was the world.

4

A Blood-Feud with a Happy Ending: Siena, 1285-1304

Daniel Waley

The tale to be related in the following pages concerns two Sienese families of no great wealth, power or fame. If it has some importance for historians this is because the figures involved were not themselves important. The participants were, on the one side, Cione Picchiati and his four sons Guerra, Pone, Meo and Sozzino, of the *popolo* of S. Lorenzo, and, on the other, Piero Cacciamonici and his two sons Mino and Bindo. The two families knew each other well and were closely related.[1] However, a quarrel arose between them, for reasons which are not recorded, and as a result of this Cione Picchiati was killed by Mino di Piero Cacciamonici. The date of the murder is not known, but it happened before 1285, perhaps some time before.[2] There was an interval of at least seven years before revenge was taken. Guerra, who was the eldest son of the victim, decided that he must avenge his father's death. In 1292 or shortly before, he 'caused to be killed' Mino, his father's murderer – or possibly he himself killed him, since the phrase in his own account (*fecit occidi*, rather than *occisit*) might be a euphemism. Clearly he accepted (or, as the newspapers now say, 'claimed') responsibility. The role of the three younger brothers is less clear, but it seems that they were not directly involved in this murder.

All four brothers then fled the city. It must have been well known who were Mino's enemies, and indeed after committing a serious crime it was normal to take flight to one of the more distant and inaccessible areas of the Sienese *contado*.[3] The brothers were then condemned *in absentia*, Guerra to be executed and to suffer confiscation of all his property, the others to fines of 3,000 *lire* each or imprisonment in the event of non-payment. They

---

[1] The source of all information given here is, unless otherwise stated, the petition printed as an Appendix to this article, from A[rchivio] [di] S[tato,] S[iena], Consiglio Generale, Deliberazioni, 65, fos. 99-102v.

[2] Cione was dead when his sons made tax payments in 1285 (ASS, Biccherna, Entrata e Uscita, 88, fo. 87v; 90, fo. 95v).

[3] P.R. Pazzaglini, *The Criminal Ban of the Sienese Commune 1225-1310* (Milan, 1979), p. 108.

doubtless heard of their condemnation as 'contumacious', and all then left
Sienese territory and settled at Viterbo. This was a city which traded a
good deal with Siena[4] and had the advantage, for the brothers, of being
neither too close nor too distant. The two places are 120 km. apart, but
Viterbo was the next city of any commercial importance that a traveller
from Siena would meet on a journey to Rome. Sozzino, one of the younger
brothers, died at Viterbo but the other three traded and 'made good'. The
nature of their business is not recorded in the surviving material known to
me.[5]

At some stage Guerra, Pone and Meo, from their Viterbese base, made
contact with the surviving brother in the other party to the vendetta,
Bindo, and reached an agreement or 'pacification' with him. In doing so
they were taking the step advocated in all legislation and treatises on the
subject of the blood-feud, but naturally such a pacification did not in itself
secure for them a pardon from the Sienese commune. As they wished to
return to their native city, their only hope seemed to lie in an approach to
the ruling officials, the Nine, accompanied by the offer of a financial
settlement. Hence the formulation of a petition which was read to the
main Sienese council on 22 August 1304 and is the principal source of
information for this note.[6] The brothers proposed that a joint payment by
them of 1,000 *lire* should secure for them all (including Sozzino, the
deceased brother) a full pardon for the condemnation of twelve years
before. Moreover they asked to enjoy the full rights of Sienese citizens.
The 1,000 *lire* offered would be paid promptly in ready money if the
petitioners' proposal was accepted.

There was a brief discussion in the council, opposition to the settlement
proposed being expressed by the *Maggior Sindaco* whose obligatory task it
was 'to object to any proposals that might derogate the rights and honor of
the commune, and thus to oppose any measure that contradicted existing
statute, whether procedurally or substantively'.[7] A motion that the
proposals made in the petition be put fully into effect then passed by a
large majority, of 226 votes against twenty-one. Since the petitioners had
assured the Nine that their return would secure for Siena 'five men and
merchants', it would seem that to the three survivors of one generation
had been added two members of a new one. After the success of their

---

[4] See, for example, W.M. Bowsky, *A Medieval Italian Commune, Siena under the Nine, 1287-
1355* (Berkeley and Los Angeles, 1981), pp. 239, 243.

[5] A charter relating to the house of the Teutonic Knights at Monticchiello near
Montepulciano (ASS, Diplomatico, Archivio Generale dei Contratti, 16 May 1299)
mentions a purchase of land by them. Investigation at Viterbo might yield more
information.

[6] See Appendix.

[7] Bowsky, p. 42: for a fuller treatment of the subject v. idem, 'The Constitution and
Administration of a Tuscan Republic in the Middle Ages and Early Renaissance: The
'Maggior Sindaco' in Siena', *Studi Senesi*, lxxx (1968), 7-22.

petition their return must be presumed and fuller search among Sienese material might provide information about their subsequent activity.

* * *

So much for *l'histoire événementielle*. What is to be learned from it? One may begin with the attitude of the Sienese commune towards the institution of the feud. This was ambiguous and, if law was to reflect opinion, could not have been otherwise. The perpetuation of the vendetta was clearly a menace to the social welfare of the city, yet it had to be recognized that a self-respecting citizen could not be expected to accept his father's murder – failing judicial action by the city's court, which was rarely effectual – without attempting revenge. The vendetta was not merely an institution that had to be tolerated; failure to carry it on was liable to be thought despicable. Hence the statutes of the Italian communes tend to reflect the view that the feud should when possible be limited, through the encouragement of formal pacifications and above all by inhibiting its lateral extension within the families concerned – and yet, when it came to direct revenge, it was only realistic to proclaim 'killing no murder'.

Sienese law recognised the blood-feud in a clause authorising the grant of a licence to wear armour (*arma defensibilia*) to those known to have 'capital enmities' (*qui haberent et notorium esset ipsos habere inimicitias capitales*).[8] There were also regulations concerning the surety to be offered by men swearing on oath that they had 'particular enmities'.[9] The crucial aim of legislators was to restrict the feud to the 'principals' originally involved. Hence the statute establishing that whenever 'a Sienese takes revenge (*fecerit vindictam*) against another Sienese for a crime not committed by that person' the punishment was to be triple that normally due.[10] Nevertheless a clause in the vernacular constitutions of 1309-10 did much to undermine such restraints by proclaiming that a man taking revenge on his known enemy (*chi fa vendetta di suo nimico pubblico*) could not be accused of murder, this being extended to include revenge against a relation up to the third degree: first and second cousins, as well as brothers.[11] Whatever the intention of this measure, it recognised the privileged position of the man committing homicide in the pursuance of a feud.

This was the attitude characteristic of most of the communes, as it had to be when the conventional view was that 'he who fails to avenge a wrong

---

[8] Constitution of 1262, v. i, ed. L. Zdekauer in *B[ollettino] S[enese] [di] S[toria] P[atria]*, ii (1895), 141: repeated in *Il costituto del comune di Siena volgarizzato nel MCCCIX-X*, ed. A. Lisini (Siena, 1903) (hereafter *Costituto*), ii, 230.

[9] Ibid.

[10] Constitution of 1262, v, ccxxxviii in *BSSP*, iii (1896), 89; repeated in *Costituto*, ii, 362.

[11] *Costituto*, ii, 405.

commits a wrong' (*ingiuria fa chi ingiuria non vendica*).[12] Florentine law did not prohibit the vendetta as such, but insisted that revenge should be appropriate (*condecens*), i.e. not exaggerated. Thus a man using an iron or wooden implement as a weapon in avenging an injury inflicted manually was to suffer a double penalty. Florence also had measures designed to check the lateral extension of the feud. If the 'principal' offender was alive, revenge could be taken only against him; defiance of this law involved exceptional penalties, the killing of a 'non-principal' being punished by death and the confiscation of the offender's entire property, which was allocated as compensation to the victim's heirs. Also revenge could only be licit if undertaken by a relative, within the third degree, of the victim.[13]

Much of the interest of the petition printed here lies in the way in which the petitioners saw and presented their case. The original family quarrel is, of course, regretted and attributed to the devil, 'the sower of discords and of all evils'; he was the 'bad angel' who 'in the beginning brought about discord between relatives'. The pacification between the two parties is, in contrast, the work of a 'good angel' (unidentified!) who has installed (*misit*) 'concord and peace'. If the vendetta was, in the first place, the work of the devil, the brothers concede that one of them, Guerra, was guilty of the killing of Mino di Piero Cacciamonici, or at least of having brought it about. They state that Guerra alone merited conviction on this charge and that the younger brothers, 'as God knew', were innocent.

The petitioners straightforwardly give as their motive for wishing to return to Siena *amor patrie*. Their affairs in Viterbo are proceeding satisfactorily and they are liked there (*bene faciant facta eorum . . . et diligantur ibidem*). But 'love of their fatherland' compels (*cogit eos redire*), and this plea was doubtless heard with sympathy and belief. Love of the native city must have been strongly felt, yet it was rarely stated or recorded in such plain words as early as 1304, merely because circumstances rarely elicited them or caused them to be preserved.

Whatever the 'compulsion', and however considerable the brothers' commercial success at Viterbo (*lucrati sunt*, they state roundly), they had to balance against their assertion of financial well-being the need to negotiate a reasonable price for their readmission and pardon. Carefully pitching their offer, and accompanying this with the assurance that 'although they have made money, they are not so rich that they could pay the full amount of the fines' levied in 1292, they assert that payment of 1,000 *lire* in respect of Guerra's merited condemnation would use up all the profits of their Viterbese years. They had started out at Viterbo with

---

[12] G. Salvioli, *Storia del diritto italiano*, viii (Turin, 1921), pp. 704-6, a good summary.

[13] *Statuti della Repubblica Fiorentina*, ed. R. Caggese: *Statuto del Capitano del Popolo (1322-5)*, (Florence, 1910), pp. 272-73; *Statuto del Podestà (1325)*, (Florence, 1921), pp. 202-3, 207-12, 278. See A.M. Enriques, 'La vendetta nella vita e nella legislazione fiorentina', *Archivio Storico Italiano*, xci (1933), 85-146, 181-223.

no capital. If their offer were accepted, they would begin again at Siena twelve years later 'having become poor' once more (*volunt effici pauperes et lucrari a capite*). Siena would be making a good bargain since it would receive five merchants 'who live by their own labour and industry' (*v homines et mercatores qui de suo labore et industria vivunt*), as well as 1,000 *lire*. Justice would be done. The guilt of the aptly-named Guerra was admitted, but the other brothers had been young at the time and their condemnation to a monetary rather than a personal penalty was surely – the petition suggested – a recognition that the *podesta*'s court held them guilty of contumacy rather than involvement in Mino's murder. The petitioners looked on themselves as citizens of Siena and would risk their persons and lives in defence of the city (*reputant se cives et pro defensione civitatis personas suas exponerent ad vitam et mortem*).

The payment proposed by the petitioners was considerable and the decision to accept it unsurprising. The commune periodically offered general amnesties in return for payment of much reduced penalties, as the brothers must have known. Such amnesties had been declared in both of the years preceding 1304, the sums accepted as 'compositions' often amounting to no more than 10 or 15 per cent of the original condemnation. These amnesties were an important source of revenue, that of 1302 yielding a total of over 30,000 *lire*.[14] The brothers' tender and its acceptance may indeed be considered late products of the 1302-3 amnesties, particularly since pacification with the injured party was often a precondition of such compositions.

It has already been remarked that the families involved in the vendetta discussed here were not of great wealth or social importance. They are not among those declared *casati* (magnates) by the Sienese legislation of the late thirteenth century, nor do they figure among prominent councillors or office-holders. The payments of *dazio* (direct taxation) by the 'sons and heirs of Cione Picchiati' in 1285 were 3*l*. 11*s*., in respect of a levy of ⅟₂₀th and 2*l*. 16*s*. 10*d*. in respect of a ⅟₂₅th. This places them in the top 20 per cent of the tax-payers in terms of assessment, but only just within it. In the case of the former tax the average (arithmetic mean) payment was 2*l*. 18*s*. 10*d*., but some 80 per cent of the payments fell below that average.[15]

The standing of these people is of importance, since it has been implied by some writers that the vendetta was a near-monopoly of the magnates and aristocrats, an indication of social grandeur. The revenges of the prominent were certainly more likely to be recorded by memorialists and

[14] Pazzaglini, pp. 87-89.

[15] ASS, Biccherna, Entrata e Uscita, 88, fo. 87v; 90, fo. 95v (see note 2 above). For these tax payments see D. Waley, 'Project for a Computer-assisted Analysis of Sienese Tax Payments in 1285', *Florence and Italy: Renaissance Studies in Honour of Nicolai Rubinstein*, ed. P. Denley and C. Elam (London, 1988).

chroniclers. On account of their political implications and the threat to
public order presented by the serjeants, familiars and clients of the great,
such vendettas were a matter of greater moment to the commune. The so-
called 'anti-magnate legislation' was brought about by magnate
vendettas: these laws have recently been well defined as 'iniziative dirette
a rafforzare l'autorità giurisdizionale del comune per una migliore
salvaguardia dell'ordine pubblico'.[16] Nicolai Rubinstein, in his
penetrating essay on the subject, was surely right in seeing the *faide*
(feuds) of the non-noble classes as less politically important, yet he may
have been misleading when he also described them as 'negligible in
number'.[17]

Guerra di Cione Picchiati carried out his act of revenge because 'he
could not bear the great sorrow of his father's death' (*non potens substinere
tantum dolorem de morte patris*). Such feelings are not the monopoly of
aristocrats or 'magnates'. Professor Bossy's doubts about whether the
feud had 'at any time so exclusively aristocratic an image as is often
suggested' are surely justified, as is his warning against 'underestimating
its force at any level of the population at any period of the history of the
West'.[18] Blood feuds were characteristic of a society in which men and
women had recourse to violence with some readiness, though it must be
borne in mind that Guerra himself waited seven years or more before
taking his revenge. There is some temptation to bring Guerra and his
story into a consideration of the famous Jonesian generalisation about an
'ennobled bourgeoisie'.[19] but this must be resisted. The 'bad angel' which
inspired the quarrel of these two families is not a factor in the *mores* of
nobles and magnates only. Rather, anticlimactically, the tale is relevant to
human, and not only to aristocratic, nature.

[16] S. Collodo, in *Istituzioni, Società e Potere nella Marca Trevigiana e Veronese (sec. XIII-XIV): Sulle tracce di G. B. Verci*, ed. G. Ortalli and M. Knapton (Rome, 1988), pp. 35-36.
[17] N. Rubinstein, *La lotta contro i magnati a Firenze*, ii. *Le origini della legge sul 'sodamento'* (Florence, 1939), pp. 17-57: 'le faide degli altri ceti (*sc.* of the non-nobles) . . . erano, veduta la cosa nel suo complesso, quantità trascurabili' (p. 32).
[18] *Disputes and Settlements*, ed. J. Bossy (Cambridge, 1983), p. 288.
[19] P.J. Jones, *Storia d'Italia, Annali*, i.*Dal feudalesimo al capitalismo* (Turin, 1978), p. 258 (and in idem, *Economia e società nell'Italia medievale* (Turin, 1980), p. 75).

Appendix

Siena, Archivio di Stato, Consiglio Generale N. 65,
fos 99r-102v

Super petitionem filiorum Cionis Picchiati.
In nomine domini amen. Anno domini millesimo ccciiii.to. Ind. secunda die xxii.o mensis agusti. Congregato generali consilio campane communis Sen' et quinquaginta per terzerium de radota in palatio dicti communis ad sonum campane et per bannum missum more solito de mandato nobilis militis domini Manentis de Esio dei gratia honorabilis potestatis Sen'. Facta prius inposita de infrascriptis de conscientia et consensu dominorum Camerarii et duorum de iiii.or provisoribus dicti communis apud palatium dicti communis secundum formam statuti Sen'. Sapiens et discretus vir Andreas olim Guidi de Campi nunc prior dominorum Novem defensorum et gubernatorum communis et populi Sen' de voluntate et assensu dicti offitii dominorum Novem proposuit in dicto consilio et ab ipso consilio consilium petiit. Quia cum audiveritis legi in presenti consilio per me Fonem notarium de Sancto Geminiano notarium communis Sen' ad consilia colligenda quandam petitionem exibitam et porrectam coram dictis dominis Novem pro parte Guerre, Ponis et Mei fratrum filiorum quondam Cionis Picchiati que talis est.
Videlicet: Coram vobis discretis et sapientibus viris dominis Novem gubernatoribus et defensoribus communis et populi Sen' proponunt et dicunt Guerra, Pone et Meus fratres et filii quondam Cionis Picchiati de populo Sancti Salvatoris quod inter ipsos et patrem eorum ex parte una et Pierum Cacciamonici et Minum et Bindum filios eius ex parte altera fuit parentela propinqua et stricta sed diabolo procurante qui est seminator discordiarum et malorum omnium dictus Minus filius dicti Pieri occidit (*sic*) dictum Cionem Picchiati patrem eorum. Unde ipse Guerra non potens substinere tantum dolorem de morte patris dictum Minum fecit occidi. Qua de causa processum fuit per accusam contra dictum Guerram quia fecit occidi dictum Minum. Et ipso non comparente fuit condempnatus quod si quo tempore veniret in fortiam communis Sen' quod sibi caput amputari debetur ita quod moriretur. Et quod bona sua deberent destrui. Item dictus accusator accusavit se Ponem, Meum et Sozzinum defuntum qui erant valde iuvenes et erant sine culpa similiter

quod debuerunt facere interfici dictum Minum qui dubbitantes curiam non comparuerunt. Unde de dicto malleficio fuerunt condempnati quilibet eorum in tribus milibus libris et quod si non solverent dictam condempnationem deberent stare in carcere communis cum catenis donec eam solverent. Qui sic deus novit non fuerunt culpabiles de dicto malleficio. Et hoc patet ex condempnationibus factis de eis quia Guerra fuit accusatus quod fecit occidi et fuit condempnatus in capite et de destructione bonorum et ipsi similiter fuerunt accusati quod fecerunt occidi et fuerunt condempnati in avere solum. Ita quod propter contumaciam condempnati fuerunt. Tamen potestas sciens ipsos non esse culpabiles gravavit eos condempnando in pecunia sed eos noluit condempnare in persona. Unde dicta de causa tunc pauperes recesserunt et iverunt Viterbium et facti sunt mercatores et lucrati sunt. Et sic angelus malus a principio commisit discordiam inter coniuntos. Nunc angelus bonus misit concordiam et pacem et fecerunt pacem cum Bindo fratre dicti Mini. Qui quantumcunque bene faciant facta eorum in civitate Viterbii et diligantur ibidem amor patrie cogit eos redire quod placeat eorum communi, verumtamen licet lucrati sint non sunt tam divites quod pro quolibet eorum possent solvere secundum ordinamenta facta. Credunt tamen quod summa ordinata pro persona Guerre qui fuit culpabilis de predictis sit conveniens quod solvatur que est mille libre et hoc erit eis grave quia xii anni sunt quod discesserunt et nichil habebant et fecerunt sibi et eorum familie expensas ita quod si m. libras ultra lucrati fuerunt satis fecerunt. Tamen ut sint cives Sen' iterum volunt effici pauperes et lucrari a capite. Ideo supplicant vobis humiliter quod solvendo mille libras communi Sen' in pecunia numerata sine aliquo sconputo quod omnes quattuor computato Sozzo defuncto rebanniantur et eorum condempnationes cancellentur. Et quod Camerarius et quattuor provisores dicti communis possint et teneantur et debeant ipsas condempnationes facere tolli et cassari et cancellari de libris clavium et aliis libris communis Sen' sine aliqua alia solutione pecun'. Non obstantibus ordinamentis dicti communis factis et approbatis super facto exbannitorum et condempnatorum dicti communis publicatis manu ser Andree ser Fuccii notarii que in hac parte et predictis terminis sint cassa et remota et absoluta et nullius efficatie vel valoris. Recuperabitis v. homines et mercatores qui de suo labore et industria vivunt et commune Sen' habebit mille libras. Reformabitur iustitia quia in veritate unus solus silicet dictus Guerra fuit culpabilis in predictis quicquid inde fiat reputant se cives et pro defensione civitatis personas suas exponerent ad vitam et mortem.

Quid sit super dictam petitonem et super hiis que in dicta petitione continentur agendum utilius pro communi Sen' in dei nomine consulatis.

Dominus Nerius Ranaldi super articulo dicte proposite et super hiis que in dicta petitione et proposita continentur dixit et consuluit quod ita sit firmum procedatur fiat et executioni mandetur ad plenum sicut in supradicta petitione et proposita continetur. Et quod facta solutione librarum mille communi Sen' sine aliquo sconputo in pecunia numerata a supradictis in dicta petitione contentis eorum condempnationes et banna tollantur et cancellentur de libris clavium et aliis libris communis Sen' sine aliqua alia solutione pecunie facienda communi sicut in supradicta petitione et proposita plenius continetur. Et quod ipsi Guerra Pone et Meus restituantur et sint ad benefitia communis Sen' sicut sunt alii cives et ita habeantur et teneantur et tractentur in communi Sen' sicut habentur et tractantur alii cives civitatis Sen'.

Dominus Gentile de Reate maior sindicus communis Sen' contradicendo dixit quod nichil fiat de contentis in petitione predicta.

Summa et concordia dicti consilii fuit voluit et firmavit per duas partes et ultra dicti consilii secundum formam constituti Sen' super articulo dicte proposite et super hiis que in dicta petitione et proposita continentur cum dicto et consilio supradicti domini Neri Ranaldi. Et fuit dictum consilium in concordia hoc modo quod facto et misso solempni et diligenti scruptineo ad bussolos et palloctas secundum formam statuti Sen' misse fuerunt per consiliarios in dicto consilio existentes et se concordantes ad predictam in bussolo albo del si ccxxvi pallocte et in bussolo nigro del no in contrarium misse fuerunt xxi pallocte et sic dictum consilium fuit et est obtentum et reformatum secundum formam statuti Sen'.

5

A Monastic Clientele? The Abbey of Settimo, its Neighbours and its Tenants (Tuscany, 1280-1340)

Charles M. de la Roncière

Florentine research, which as the years have passed has taken on a more American tinge, has come more and more to pursue the study of families, lineages (following Philip Jones) and clienteles; scholars have tended to focus their researches in this area, which is one where they had all already gathered some information.[1] The problem that has faced me, after going through numerous rural notarial registers, is that of investigating whether clienteles survived or were developing in the countryside as well as in the city. In this article, rather than discussing the feudal lords of the Appennines or the magnates of the *contado*, on which my research is in progress, I propose to look at the issue in the light of Philip Jones's own work on the Cistercian abbey of Settimo, just outside Florence.[2] Here, the monks leased out their landed properties; and, thanks to the monastic archives, we know a good deal about their tenants (*fittaiuoli*), in particular for the first half of the fourteenth century. To what extent did these people, as part of a larger but less well-documented entourage, constitute for the monks a 'clientele' (or its core, or its beginning, or its remnants)?

In the thirteenth century, as Jones so expertly showed, rural lordship around Florence had changed considerably, and the lands of Settimo illustrate clearly its new form at the beginning of the fourteenth. Direct exploitation by the monks had been restricted to a subordinate role there,

---

[1] P.J. Jones 'Florentine families and Florentine diaries in the fourteenth century', *Papers of the British School at Rome*, xxiv (1956), now translated into Italian in idem, *Economia e società nell'Italia medievale* (Turin, 1980). Philip Jones was preparing in Florence his contribution to the second edition of the *Cambridge Economic History* volume I when I began as a scholar at the Archivio di Stato. I was quickly put in contact with this expert, whose knowledge and breadth of reading, already legendary, had by no means extinguished his sense of humour. Some of his articles were already known to me, and his work on the finances of the abbey of Settimo (see below n. 2) was one of the most appropriate recent works for the guidance of a beginner in the inexhaustible collections which that impressive archive holds for rural affairs.

[2] Idem, 'Le finanze della badia cistercense di Settimo nel secolo XIV', *Rivista di storia della chiesa in Italia* x (1956), now in idem, *Economia e società*.

and perpetual tenure had almost everywhere disappeared. In their place came long-term *livelli* and *affitti* (for twenty years or more) linked to buildings and to the plantation of vineyards, and, above all, short-term (roughly three-year) *affitti*, by far the most numerous contracts in the neighbourhood of the monastery. These latter were either for fixed rents (*affitti* in their technical sense) or 50 per cent share-cropping agreements (*mezzadria*).[3] The spread around the monastery of these new types of lease put at the disposition of the monks new frameworks of dependence, capable, at first sight, of prolonging or reviving the local influence which previous seigneurial relationships had given to the abbey. Because of the distribution of monastic lands, scattered as they were across the territories of the surrounding parishes (*popoli*), we find the tenants or share-croppers of the abbey, the *laboratores*, in all these parishes (those of the *pieve* of Settimo, the monastery itself, S. Colombano, S. Michele a Gangalandi, S. Martino la Palma, and S. Angelo a Legnaia). There were a lot of them. The surviving leases of the years 1310-48 (and many are lost) list 22 in the *popolo* of the *pieve*, 36 in that of the monastery, 31 at S. Colombano; these figures represent for each village between 15 and 50 per cent of the male population.[4]

One group of people, when observed more closely, seem to have been attached to the monks fairly tightly, in several separate ways. The lands leased to several of them consisted of an individual holding (*podere*), reasonably sized (the average area of such a *podere* is 100 *staiora*, or 5.25 ha), normally with a house on it. Each of these would have needed the entire labour-time of its *laborator* to exploit it properly. If the lease was in *mezzadria*, as sometimes at Settimo (and always at S. Martino la Palma), it was accompanied by very detailed clauses in which the abbey claimed the right to watch over its observance; these clauses can be found in fixed-rent leases (*affitti*) too. The second point to note is that, although the contracts are for brief periods, the same tenant, through frequent renewals, could remain in the service of the abbey for a considerable time. Examples of this stability are numerous. It could often happen that several brothers were tenants of the monks at the same time, and one can find cases of families who remained dependent on the monks for several generations. Thus, for example, in 1318 Fede Donati, together with his brother Cione, took in lease for nine years a *podere* situated 'nel donicato' (in the parish of the

---

[3] Cf. Jones, 'Finanze'; also idem, 'From Manor to Mezzadria: a Tuscan Case-study in the Medieval Origins of Modern Agrarian Society', in *Florentine Studies*, ed. N. Rubinstein, (London, 1968), now in *Economia e società*.

[4] These figures come from the following sources in the Archivio di Stato, Florence: C[ompagnie] R[eligiose] S[oppresse], 480, 481, 482; Dipl[omatico], Cestello, *passim*; San Paolo [de'] Conv[alescenti]; and the following notarial registers: Not., A 937, B 2166-67, B 2559, G 585, J 97, M 39, M 293, M 458-59, M 478, O 56, R 159. In what follows all other sources are in Archivio di Stato, Florence, unless otherwise noted.

monastery); his sons Donatino and Piero renewed the lease in February 1323, and then again, together with their cousin Lapo, son of Cione, in 1327. In 1337 Piero and Lapo, sons of Donatino, had succeeded their father in a *podere* which was probably the same holding, and in 1377, forty years later, Donato di Lapo di Donatino di Fede di Donato was still in place as tenant of the ancestral holding, though it was now slightly smaller.[5] Links as long-lasting as this necessarily reinforced a personal relationship between the monks and their peasants, which could be older still, and which other forms of contact could both create and consolidate. When in 1310 Ricco Gherardi and his children (one of whom at least was later a monastic tenant, in 1337-38) made peace with a nearby *consorteria* of eighteen men from S. Martino la Palma (some of these worked for the abbey too), the two parties appealed to the abbot and one of his monks, perhaps the authors of the reconciliation, to witness the agreement in a nearby church.[6] Conversely, when the abbey was in dispute with its neighbours or dependants, it might ask for the arbitration of third parties; monastic leaseholders could well be among the chosen experts.[7] Between the monks and their tenants, lasting links of collaboration and trust could then become established. This relationship could bring about, inside the peasant milieux around the monastery, the creation of a durable clientele of friends, protégés and the devout, eventually susceptible across the generations to the development of the spiritual influence of the community.

It must, on the other hand, be recognised that families like these, in close and privileged contact with the monastery, were not very numerous, and did not by any means include all the *laboratores* of the abbey of Settimo. Over the peasants that surrounded and depended on the monastery, the power of the monks (at least their temporal power) was fairly restricted, and this was as true for tenants as it was for their neighbours. For a start most of the *laboratores* of the abbey were attached to it in much more temporary ways than those we have just seen. In the three parishes of the *piviere* of Settimo containing the largest proportion of monastic land (the *pieve*, the monastery and S. Colombano), 70 per cent of known tenants between 1318 and 1338 (58 out of 84) only appear once in the monastic records, for a single lease. Even taking account of the documents that are

---

[5] CRS, 480, fos. 58v (1328), 168v (1333), 137v (1327); Estimo, 240, fo. 23 (1377); Jones, 'Finanze', Appx. n. 25. Also in 1377 another son of Donatino, Niccolò, held from the monks part of the *podere* of Donato di Lapo. Other examples of stability are provided by Fanuccio Doni Broli in the parish of the abbey (1327, 1334, 1337) and Bensi Bugli in the *pieve* (1322, 1332, 1337). See also Jones, 'Finanze', in *Economia e società*, p. 324. For brothers in the abbey's service at the same time: CRS, 480, fos. 63v, 172, 178v; Dipl. Cestello, 3 July 1334; etc.

[6] Not., M 39, fo. 44v (June 1310).

[7] Dipl. Cestello, 9 July 1329.

lost, this figure is high.[8] These leases furthermore were for very variable amounts of land, ranging from whole *poderi*, through houses with a few fields, to isolated plots. The average amount of land rented to a single individual is not higher than 2 ha in any of the three villages; in the parish of the *pieve* it is only 1.32 ha. Perhaps over half the tenants must, in order to survive, have had more resources than this: personal property, wage-labour (though this does not appear in our sources), or, probably most often, leases from elsewhere.

What most limited the power of the abbey over its own tenants and over other villagers, quite directly in fact, was that of the other proprietors of the region, even in the villages where monastic power was most firmly rooted. Nothing distinguishes the estate-management of the monks from that of the lay proprietors of the *piviere* of Settimo: there is the same elimination of traditional manorial lordship (no more perpetual tenures, demesnes restricted to a garden or a vineyard); the same predominance of short-term leases; the same types of contracts.[9] The abbey did not have any sort of supplementary authority (such as seigneurial justice) to superimpose over that of the neighbouring large landowners. These large landowners, mostly urban, were numerous and had their own tenants. As in the case of the monastery, these tenants often remained linked to their patron for some time: Chiaro Giuntini, tenant of the hospital of S. Paolo de'Convalescenti in the *pieve* of Settimo, was its dependent between 1314 and 1340 without a break.[10] Around foundations like S. Paolo, or the lay families of Nerli, Pulci, or Rinucci, stable groups of tenants were assembled, groups which at times begin to look like clienteles: once again, one finds patrons intervening in the disputes of their protégés and guaranteeing their reconciliation.[11] Inside these groups the temporal authority of the abbey was non-existent.

Not all dependent peasants were fully part of these groups of 'clients'. Many individuals were simultaneously, or in rapid succession, tenants of different lords, and this dispersal seems more common still if we look at families, whose individual members were frequently subject to many different patrons. This situation is clear for many tenants, or families of

---

[8] In the three villages, out of 64 *laboratores* of the abbey named between 1318 and 1334, only 9 were still in the abbey's service in 1337: inventory of 1337 published by Jones, 'Finanze', Appx.

[9] For very numerous examples, especially from the *popolo* of the *pieve*: Not., 0 56, fo. 2 (*mezzadria* grants by the Nerli and Capponi, 1310); Not., L 38, fo. 37 (*mezzadria* grant by Ser Ricupero Benvenuti of Florence, 1319); Dipl., Dono Rinuccini, 21 July 1320 and 23 Aug. 1327; CRS, 482 (last fo.).

[10] San Paolo Conv., 976, fos. 83v, 102v, 105, 107.

[11] A member of the Pulci family (Florentine merchants, former Guelfs and *popolani*) intervened in a reconciliation between some *contadini*, of whom at least one was his tenant: Not., M 39, fo. 41 (25 Mar. 1300); CRS, 482, fo. 66. On the Pulci, cf. S. Raveggi et al., *Ghibellini, guelfi e popolo grasso* (Florence, 1978), pp. 46, 85.

tenants, dependent on the monks. Puccino Salimbeni, tenant of the monastery in 1334 (for 43 *staiora* of a larger *podere*) and also in 1338 (three plots of land, making 15 *staiora*), had already successively leased from a notary of Settimo in 1313 and a Florentine of the parish of S. Frediano in 1323; by 1348, his son Colombano had had links for several years with another Florentine, of the parish of S. Jacopo Oltrarno.[12] Another example is that of the seven Fancelli brothers. Dono, *laborator* of the monastery in 1319, had previously in 1312 leased a *podere* from a Florentine of S. Piero Scheraggio; Berto worked the lands of Bindo Machiavelli until 1311, and never seems to have been a monastic dependent; Fancello worked a field belonging to the monastery for five years starting in 1334, together with Dono; and only at that date did the other brothers, Giovanni, Piero, Lorenzo and Bonaiuto, previously tenants of the Nerli, begin to lease from the monks.[13]

Serving several masters means being able, when necessary, to pass from one protector to another, and to participate simultaneously or successively in several clienteles. When in 1310 two family groups from S. Colombano, both of seven members, made peace in front of a notary, it was a member of an important local lineage who presided over the reconciliation. Although three of the fourteen participants later became *laboratores* of the abbey (notably the faithful Cione Donati), the latter did not intervene; its authority over them was not, or was not yet, comparable to that of a local notable.[14] Also in 1310 it was a *consors* of the Pulci, another powerful local lineage, who determined the dowry that Dono Fancelli should give to his daughter; Dono, as we have just seen, was part of a family linked simultaneously (or nearly so) to the Nerli, the Pulci and the monastery, that is to the three largest clienteles of the area.[15] To rent from several patrons meant not to depend very closely on any one of them, especially when the links with each were capable of being untied so quickly at the end of short-term contracts. It is most likely that the lease was the most important issue, and that, at the moment of the contract, the tenant chose to rent a given plot of land rather than to be linked to a given patron. The diffusion of short-term leases, the incompleteness of *appoderamento* (the creation of compact tenures) and the mobility of landed property tended to scatter the local clienteles, which the increasing power of urban jurisdiction – especially so close to the city – had already begun to undermine.

Despite their economic dependence, the peasants of Settimo also had

---

[12] Not., M 39, fo. 193v (1313); B 2166, fos. 5, 7 (1323); CRS, 482, fo. 114 (1334); Dipl. Cestello, 28 Dec. 1338; Podestà, 340, fo. 53 (1348).

[13] Not., O 56, 28 Feb. 1311; A 937, fo. 100 (1311); CRS, 480, fos. 172 (1334), 202, 204v; Dipl. Cestello, 3 July 1334.

[14] Not., M 39, fo. 46 (1310); CRS, 480, fos. 114v (1324), 137 (1327), 171 (1334).

[15] Not., A 937, fo. 47v (1310).

social relationships which allowed them to consolidate their personal autonomy with respect to the powerful. The most effective of these relationships was certainly formed by the communities in which they lived, that is to say the family and the parish. This was very clearly the case for the peasants who lived near and served the monastery.

What one sees first of all when one looks at peasant families is their quarrels, sometimes leading to violence and even murder, which caused tenacious enmities between them. Family clans were built up as a result. These disputes, which happened at Settimo like anywhere else, could involve monastic *laboratores* on both sides. It is quite certain that, if there was a clientele around the monastery, its unity and its cohesion were weakened by these tensions.[16]

What one also sees when one looks at these local peasant families is their alliances. These could be very wide-ranging. Even from families many of whose members long remained in monastic service, children often married outside the circle of the tenants (whether habitual or occasional) of the monastery. Let us take for example the Broli family: after Brolio's death, three of his sons (of whom two had worked or would work for the monks) married off five of their daughters between 1309 and 1313. Although the future sons-in-law were all from immediately neighbouring villages (Monticelli, the *pieve* of Settimo, Brozzi), none of them seems to have been linked, either personally or via his family, to the abbey, at least as a *laborator*.[17] The same is true of the Fancelli brothers: their three daughters whose marriages are documented married in the neighbouring villages, but outside the circle of those who worked for the monks. The networks of wider alliance that were thus constituted around family nuclei (whether conjugal or patriarchal) went beyond the surviving frameworks of the local clienteles and weakened them. The clienteles thus competed with each other and weakened each other mutually inside the same family grouping.[18]

Village communities had their role to play as well. They were very active; their assemblies took place regularly under the direction of their rectors. The *laboratores* of the abbey each participated in his own parish; but they were in a minority everywhere, in that they were dispersed across the parishes.[19] Indeed some of the village communities, the more powerful and more independent ones (that of the *pieve* of Settimo for example),

---

[16] The notarial acts of Maffeo di Settimo (M 39) contain a good dozen disputes among hostile families and groups in the villages of the *piviere* between 1305 and 1320; for involvement of tenants: fo. 46 (1310).

[17] Not., M 39, fos. 37 (1310), 43 (1310), 73v (1313); A 937, fos. 51v (1309), 211v (1314).

[18] Dono Fancelli (to say nothing of his brothers) was apparently tied either at the same time or successively to the Florentine Rinuccio Lapi, owner of the *podere* he worked (Not., 0 56, 28 Feb., 1311/12), to Metto Pulci, and to the abbey (at least after 1319).

[19] In the parish of the *pieve*, which contained around 190 men in 1310-13 (according to

apparently carried on their deliberations without any monastic pressure: no monk at least ever appears as a witness to their activities. Since their concern was to debate administrative and financial problems that had nothing to do with the abbey, one can conclude that the social relationships created among the members of each of these communities, through their deliberations and their mutual involvement, undermined the local influence of the monastery (which was absent from the debates, except in cases of dispute), and weakened what remained of the clientelar solidarity between the *laboratores* and the monks.[20] The powerful had not lost all local influence or authority over the peasants; but the influential people were now above all laymen, great families important in Florence, who could offer financial help and political mediation. Even the parish community of the village around the monastery (the *popolo della badia*) seems to have been quite independent of the monks.[21]

Among the *laboratores* of the monastery one can also find prosperous people, notables. This was not a general rule. Most tenants were poor; their difficulties forced them into debt, and even to the sale of part of their personal property, sometimes to the abbey.[22] All the same, some people were better off. The Broli brothers owned at least four land plots by the Arno; and if Dono Broli had to sell a field in 1309, he bought another in 1312, for three times as much.[23] The dowries the Broli gave to their daughters, at an average value of 134 *lire*, are among the highest in the *piviere* of Settimo.[24] The Fancelli brothers were less well off (their average dowry is 65 *lire*), but we know of at least four land plots owned by them as well. We know that some other tenants lent money, too, up to 18 florins.

It can clearly be seen that despite the up-to-date care with which an abbey like Settimo ran its property, one that was in all respects analogous to that of the urban bourgeoisie, it did not have any really lasting power or authority over its dependent peasants, other than a very small group. Monastic tenants were sometimes well-off, based in stable and solid

the lists of those present at six assemblies in those years), there are only 22 tenants of the abbey recorded 1318-38.

[20] The most frequent business debated related to the imposition of Florentine taxes and infantry levies, to roads, and to expenses and loans: Not., M 39, fos. 99-v, 179, 188, 193v; A 937, fos. 5v, 17v, 19, 24v, 25, 39, 60, 64-v, 66, 71, 72v, 74, 100, 104, 123v, 136, 195v, 217. Abbey tenants were involved in village administration: in the parish of the *pieve* between 1309 and 1313, 4 served as *massari* and 2 as councillors deputed to levy taxes: Not., A 937, fos. 50, 64-v, 104, 133v.

[21] No monk appeared at assemblies, even as a witness, whereas monastic tenants were very active in village administration, providing three of the five rectors, 1309-13 and one or two *massari* every year.

[22] Not., M. 39, fos. 47, 50; B 2567, fo. 65v; A 937, fos. 51v, 139v, 182v; for a sale to the abbey: Dipl. Cestello, 17 July 1323.

[23] Not., A 937, fos. 115v, 166, 174; Dipl. Cestello, 20 Aug. 1329.

[24] Of 45 dowries from the years 1306-19, the median value was 88 *lire* and there were 5 greater than 134 *lire*.

communities (family and parish), and detached from exclusive service to the monastery by the multiplicity of contracts that the richest lay proprietors of the area offered to them; they probably considered the monastery above all just as a landlord. As a result their attitude to the monastery must have been similar to that of their neighbours, with a touch of difference among the most faithful tenants, but with all of them showing (sometimes very acutely) the sense of hostility that could set the local peasants against the monks. There was no shortage of reasons for friction between monks and peasants.

Neighbours could not avoid having relations with an institution like Settimo, even if the abbey did not have either power or jurisdiction over them. These relations could be tense, in two ways in particular: over the collective use of monastic properties such as river-ports or mills; and over the buying-up of land, which the monastery, like any rich and prudent proprietor, engaged in. In these two contexts we can find signs of ill temper among the peasants. In 1289 three men of S. Martino la Palma injured the monastic miller and said menacing things about the monks and their properties.[25] In 1294, in order to safeguard a wood belonging to it at S. Martino, the abbey had an old wall that surrounded it restored, and built other enclosures; six peasants of the village (of whom several, or else their sons, would later be monastic *laboratores*) broke down these enclosures and made a hole in the wall, claiming that they blocked access to their own neighbouring woodland. At the end of a long court case the peasants lost; one can imagine their resentment against the monks.[26] As well as these general problems, the *laboratores* of the monastery had their own reasons for discontent; one does not always know the exact causes, but there are conflicts referred to in the sources. In 1329 the sharecroppers of a *podere* of S. Martino la Palma broke their contract with the abbey; their anger was so great that one of them menaced the monks with death.[27] Hostility towards the monks had deep roots at S. Martino for, apart from the disputes already cited, the villagers there had already set themselves against the abbey at least twice before, in 1266 over the election of the parish priest and in 1282 over the question of tithes, the latter dispute reaching as far as the pope.[28] The administration of its temporal properties thus involved the monastery in actions that angered the neighbouring peasants; this reinforced the solidarity and autonomy of the latter as well as sharpening the tensions that they already had with the monastery as its *affittuari*.

[25] This dispute was pacified through the abbot's arbitration: CRS 481, fo. 253; Dipl. Cestello, 23 June 1289.

[26] CRS 481, fo. 203; Dipl. Cestello, 27 Aug. 1294.

[27] Dipl. Cestello, 9 July 1329, 18 May 1294. For a claim that the monks 'mentiebant per gulam': Podestà, 182, fo. 2 (June 1347).

[28] C.C. Calzolai, *La storia della Badia a Settimo* (Florence, 1976), pp. 70, 84.

The abbey of Settimo was principally a religious centre; this was, after all, its proper role. It is quite possible, if the community showed itself to live a pious and regular life, that it could, at the level of the care of souls, find the influence that it had gradually lost, at the level of social and material life, over its ex-dependents – who no longer recognised themselves as dependents, if indeed they had ever done so. The disputes over priests and tithes mentioned above only seem to have affected one village, S. Martino la Palma, where they may have lessened across time.[29] The monastery, on the other hand, under a series of able abbots showed a real spiritual vitality that brought to its monks between 1280 and 1310 a variety of responsibilities: that, for example, of taking over monasteries in decline in order to reform them, such as Camaldoli, Monte Amiata (1320), and Buonsollazzo (1322). One can also find the lay faithful ceding to Settimo their patronage rights over parishes, as in 1323. Proofs of the esteem the monks were held in do not stop there; for the Florentine government entrusted to them various financial and administrative tasks, showing that it, too, had confidence in them.[30]

Did the peasants of the area share this flattering vision of the abbey? In the 1330s probably not, for in those years the serenity of the monks was broken by a series of internal disputes about the level of debt owed by the monastery. In 1333 some of the monks protested to their abbot, Andrea, who had apparently made these debts worse.[31] In 1337, at Andrea's death, the trouble flared up again; it took eight months and considerable agitation to get rid of an undesirable candidate for the succession (June 1338).[32] On the other hand, the years before 1330 seem to have been relatively peaceful for the monastery, despite growing concern about its chronic debt; and even the disputes of the 1330s soon calmed down. It is then possible that its local spiritual influence survived its authority as a lord. This is something I think can be tested, given our documentation, in three ways: by analysing name-giving; by looking at local confraternities; and through a discussion of the wills of the Settimo area.

I have tried to show elsewhere the importance of the changes in the system of first names in Tuscany in the years 1300-40. Instead of the traditional names that had hitherto dominated in the region (based on diminutives, names that conveyed good luck, and Germanic personal names), name-giving came to be taken above all from the saints (such as Giovanni, Pietro, or Francesco), thus showing that a new religious value

[29] Not completely, however: CRS, 481, fos. 214v (1277), 216 (1323/4) show disputes about the running of the parish.

[30] Calzolai, pp. 75, 83, 93.

[31] Jones, 'Finanze', in *Economia e società*, p. 329.

[32] It was the papal candidate who triumphed: Calzolai, pp. 97-100.

was becoming attached to the forename.[33] In the specific case of Settimo, we could test, when looking at the names of people in the neighbouring villages, the popularity of monastic personal names, in particular Benedetto, Bernardo, and Salvatore, and thus, as a result, the local popularity of the monks. This enquiry has proved negative. Among 420 men born between 1300 and 1348 only two or three bore each of these three forenames, which therefore only come thirtieth in the list of the most popular names (the first, John, had 45 citations). Lorenzo is more frequent (eleven examples), but this is the name of the patron of the parish, S. Lorenzo, not the monastery. No name seems to give evidence of the attachment of local inhabitants to the monastery as a spiritual centre, except for a handful of families, although this was by now an environment in which devotion to the saints and choice of first name was clearly linked.

The second test concerns what is known of the confraternity founded in 1288 by the parishioners of S. Lorenzo di Settimo.[34] This confraternity, also dedicated to S. Lorenzo, set down its statutes between 1288 and 1324, of which 25 chapters survive, and began a register on 7 January 1324. Chapter 5 stated that the confraternity was open to all men, including monks; and one of the four councillors who ran it had to be the *cappellano* (curate) of the parish. (This priest was very closely linked to the monastery, and could even be a monk himself, as for example in a text of November 1338).[35] The members of the confraternity grew rapidly (there were 42 in 1323, but 60 others joined later, plus 22 strangers to the village); among them in 1323 were at least 16 recent or current *laboratores* of the abbey. A female confraternity matched it; it was as popular as its male counterpart, for it had 41 members in 1323 (others followed), including several wives of tenants. The two corporations could be seen in this way as an extension and an echo of the spiritual influence of the monks. While this influence was quite probably there, it was at the same time limited and circumscribed. The surviving text of the statutes does not mention, apart from in Chapter 5, either monks or monastery. The devotions set out there – solidarity in face of death and poverty; devotion to the Virgin and to the Eucharist – are not specifically monastic. The first monks of Settimo to join did not do so before 1360, following Abbot Pietro Cambini, who was elected in that year. The picture most clearly presented by the evidence is one of a coherent *parish* community, receptive to the

[33] C.M. de la Roncière, 'Orientations pastorales du clergé, fin du XIII-XIV s.: le témoignage de l'onomastique toscane', *Comptes rendus des séances de l'Académie des Inscriptions et Belles-Lettres*, Jan.-Mar. 1983.

[34] Biblioteca Nazionale, Florence, Cl. xxxii, cod. 44.

[35] Calzolai, p. 101 (1338). The links between the parish of San Lorenzo and the abbey were particularly close: according to an amicable agreement between the priest of the *pieve* and the abbot in 1287/8, the parish was released from obligations to the *pieve* regarding participation in services and the obligation to invite the *pievano* to the parish festival: CRS, 481, fo. 71v.

models of solidarity and devotion offered by the pastoral care practised by the friars (and by some priests). The specific contribution of the monks, in liturgy, devotion, or participation in prayers, was nil. If the curate, who was certainly linked to the Cistercians, involved himself in the confraternity, it was only in the context of these atypical pastoral concerns. This at least is the conclusion suggested by the incomplete statutes.

Wills, with their pious legacies that testators, here as elsewhere, did not fail to include, provide us with our third test. I have been able to assemble about thirty of them for the Settimo area from the years 1290-1330. In these wills, legacies were scattered among many people and institutions; the monastery was a beneficiary seven times, five times from its neighbours, whether noble or peasant, and twice from Florentines. Two of these bequests were really substantial, and included several plots of land; their authors were a *conversus* who came originally from Settimo (S. Colombano), and an inhabitant of Monticelli.[36] Four other people, from the *pieve* and from Florence, left small properties (such as a field), or small sums of money (5 to 10 *soldi*), or conditional gifts; a fifth will, from S. Colombano, has a single clause that designates a monk as its executor. These acts confirm in their own way what one has now come to expect: that there was around the monastery a handful of the devout, whether individuals or families, who were particularly attached to it, might sometimes take the habit, sought its intercession and its prayers, and showed to it considerable generosity.[37] Such devout people (two in these texts) were, however, a dispersed minority, and did not coincide either in their persons or in their domiciles with the group of monastic tenants; they only represented, it seems, a very small proportion of monastic neighbours. One can add to them the authors of the smaller bequests, which show some devotion, but a limited one. Such devotion was shared with other institutions, for these legacies are mingled with others, often many others. But the majority of testators have not a word for the monastery; they ignore it or dismiss it. To the spiritual mediation of the monks among their neighbours, other mediations and devotions were added or superimposed at the moment of death, and these weakened, marginalised and ended up by eliminating it.

[36] Fra Guido di Cione and Jacopo del Brolio di Benincasa: CRS, 480, fo. 153v (1330/1); Dipl. Cestello, 7 Feb. 1292.

[37] In Feb. 1287/8, one of the points at dispute between the monks and the *pievano* of Settimo was the administration of the sacraments to the inhabitants of the neighbouring parishes (the *pieve*, San Colombano). Eventually, the monks undertook to administer them, even to those who had declared an intention to be buried at the abbey. The dispute reveals that the abbey's faithful were at least important enough to arouse the opposition of the nearby parish clergy (though only, it seems in these two parishes): Dipl. Cestello, 15 Feb. 1287/8.

There were other, more important, spiritual resources. Local religious centres and institutions are the most often cited in the wills. The parish churches (including the *pieve*) were particularly important to testators, but the confraternities, the hospitals, and nearby hermits and recluses had their faithful too. Although lessening in importance, the churches and religious houses of Florence, such as the Augustinians, the Carmelites and some monasteries, had a few followers here and there in the countryside. The mendicant movement was also beginning to have an effect. The institutions closest to the faithful, those which best represented either their communities (*pieve*, parish churches), or their solidarity and compassion (hospitals), or their ideal of Christian life (confraternities), were those that mattered most to local consciences at the moment of truth that is death. Whatever spiritual influence the abbey of Settimo had was weakening, and its clientele of devout was pared down even among its neighbours and dependants.

Around the abbey of Settimo one can perceive that a small nucleus of peasant families leased its lands for long periods, showed it spiritual devotion (notably on the deathbed), sought the arbitration of the abbot, let their sons enter the community as *conversi* or join it as servants, and formed around it a circle of friends (*amici*). But however small, how stable was this nucleus?

The monastery had ceased to play the role of lord and master, a role which it had anyway only taken on partially and belatedly, and whose contours we can barely see. The new patterns of estate management that it had like many others adopted, did not favour the establishment or maintenance of a real group of faithful. Other competing forces opposed this. The families of the local aristocracy, or the Florentine bourgeoisie now implanting themselves outside the city walls, had other farms and fields to let, in addition to what they could offer as rich and powerful patrons: loans, guarantees, other contracts, witnessing, arbitration. They did so without necessarily establishing lasting links of patronage, for contracts were short-term on their lands too (five years or less), and were often for tiny fields; peasants were frequently forced to rent land from several different patrons, simultaneously or successively, in order to live. Each of them chose their new landlords each time as they wished, or as they could, without necessarily having to follow the example of their fathers or brothers. Family labour in the countryside was as precociously fragmented as in the city – perhaps more so, if one thinks of the family-based commercial companies of Florence.

Other peasant solidarities persisted despite everything: that of the family (even outside work); that of personal alliances, carefully established with neighbours; that of religious devotion, sustained from 1300 or so by male and female confraternities, which were already flourishing in and around the parishes; that of compassion, focussed on the hospital and the poor of the area; that of village administration, shaped in the assemblies, where everyone took on their share of responsibilities. But these solidarities in great part escaped any kind of seigneurial control. They crystallised around strictly local places (churches, hospitals, communal centres) or powers (curates, local councils). Certainly external influences (of nobles, bourgeois, monasteries) continued to exist, whether long-lasting or intermittent; nevertheless, being so close to the city walls, it was above all from Florence that they came, and from the leading institutions based there – the mendicant orders, the innumerable craft guilds, and the whole apparatus of administration and justice. Although the word clientele is not always the most suitable for the city context, it is probably there that one should look to find its new ties and supports.

6

Civic Religion and the Countryside in Late Medieval Italy

Giorgio Chittolini

In the study of religious festivals of the cities of late medieval and Renaissance Italy, light has often been thrown in recent years on aspects of civic ritual which are apparent in many of them, in various forms and periods, along with the civil and political meanings they expressed. These values and meanings were especially apparent on certain special occasions: the festivals of the city's patron saint, for example (or of the one patron saint out of several whose cult had especial significance) or the festival of the Virgin Mary (as protectress of the city) or other religious festivals (for example, Corpus Christi) that were adopted as community festivals.[1] The public and civic character of such ceremonies is found especially in their culminating moments, that is, in the procession of all the constituent parts of the community, of the whole social body, in honour of their heavenly protector, with gifts of candles, cloths (*palii*) and other offerings, to the saint. But little attention has been paid in general to the role in these urban rituals of the inhabitants of the countryside (*comitatini*) or their representatives, whose presence was often required.[2] We must await the broader and deeper research which will enable us to trace the history and geography of this phenomenon, but the pages that

---

[1] H. Peyer, *Stadt und Stadtpatron im Mittelalterlichen Italien* (Zurich, 1955); R. Trexler, *Public Life in Renaissance Florence* (New York, 1980); E. Muir, *Civic Ritual in Renaissance Venice* (Princeton, 1981); A.M. Orselli, 'Vita religiosa nella città medievale italiana tra dimensione ecclesiastica e "cristianesimo civico": una esemplificazione', *Annali dell'Istituto storico italo-germanico in Trento*, vii (1981); A.I. Galletti, 'Sant'Ercolano, il grifo e le lasche: note sull'immaginario collettivo nella città comunale', in *Forme e tecniche del potere nella città, secoli XIV-XVII, Annali della Facoltà di Scienze Politiche* (University of Perugia) xvi (1979-80); A. Vauchez, 'Patronage des saints et religion civique dans l'Italie communale à la fin du Moyen Age', in *Patronage and Public in the Trecento*, ed. V. Moleta (Florence, 1986); P. Ventrone, 'Le forme dello spettacolo toscano nel Trecento: tra rituale civico e cerimoniale festivo', in *La Toscana nel secolo XIV. Caratteri di una civiltà regionale*, ed. S. Gensini (Pisa, 1988).

[2] Some indications in S. Bertelli, *Il potere oligarchico nello stato-città medievale* (Florence, 1978), p. 150; Trexler, p. 257 ff; and see especially the abundant documentation in 'Il

follow offer a first outline of these ceremonies, especially as regards the participation of *comitatini*.

The festivals were important occasions of solemn celebration. Regulated by urban statutes and decrees, described by chroniclers, illustrated in the *laudationes urbium*, they are well known. There is no need here to rehearse in detail their more picturesque aspects, such as the town criers who, in the days beforehand, would announce the coming of the festival and who were despatched round the *contado* so that everyone could make preparations; the proclamations for the shops to close; the interruptions of work and of judicial sessions; the orders to clean the streets and squares; the equipment and decoration of houses, of public and private palaces and of religious buildings; the torches and peals of bells. Goro Dati, the early fifteenth-century Florentine chronicler (to take only one example) described in emotional terms the image of the piazza in Florence on the morning of the festival of San Giovanni: it was 'a magnificent, triumphal affair, marvellous, such that it almost overwhelms the spirit'. He records the 'one hundred towers, which seemed to be made of gold, some of them carried on carts, others by hand. They were called *ceri* (church-candles) and were made of wood, paper and wax, with gold and other colours and with painted figures'; and continuing, he describes the armed horsemen, the foot-soldiers with lances and shields, the young girls dancing *a rigoletto* (rounds) and the banners of fur or velvet or of 'taffeta edged with silk, which were marvellous to behold'.[3]

Scenes similar to this, if not always as splendid, formed the background to patronal festivals in many other cities. The sources offer us extraordinarily rich and varied pictures of them: games of various sorts (races, jousts, balls) would continue for several days; fairs might last for weeks; sometimes unusual ceremonies are recorded (the killing of a bull or of a cock) or grotesque and outlandish games (races for prostitutes or asses). 'Profane' elements were thus not lacking; nor, as elsewhere in Europe, was the expression of protest and subversive sentiments, or of

territorio per la festa dell'Assunta: patti e censi di Signori e Comunità dello Stato', ed. L. Nardi et al., in *Siena e il suo territorio nel Rinascimento*, ed. M. Ascheri and D. Ciampoli (Siena, 1986). These festivals received greater attention in the past: cf. A. Gianandrea, 'Festa di S. Floriano martire in Jesi . . .', *Archivio storico marchigiano*, i (1879); L. Mariani, 'La cavalcata dell'Assunta in Fermo', *Archivio della Società romana di storia patria*, xiii (1890); C. Lozzi, 'Le feste dei comuni italiani e in ispecie del Santo patrono di Ascoli e del tremuoto', *La Bibliofilia*, vii (1905-6). And cf. L.A. Muratori, *Antiquitates italicae medii aevi* (Milan, 1738-42), v, Diss. 58, coll. 1-60.

[3] G. Dati, *Istorie di Firenze . . . dall'anno MCCCLXXX all'anno MCCCCV* (Florence, 1735), pp. 652-53. C. Guasti, *Le feste di San Giovanni Battista in Firenze* (Florence, 1908) lists the more important descriptions of this festival from the thirteenth century to the eighteenth.

animosity between civic groups or districts – aspects which the civic authorities were always trying to contain and control.[4]

As these festivals and ceremonies acquired a more explicit place in civic ritual, however, the cruder and more violent episodes tended to be refined, controlled and exploited (for some of the most vulgar, profanatory elements were used to denigrate and ridicule those outside the city or its social body, such as enemy factions or rival cities).[5] Conversely, there was an emphasis on those aspects which exalted, in a solemn and splendid manner, the character of a grand civic celebration, calculated to magnify the commune and the city. The sources thus record various types of ceremony, ritual act and liturgy in the cathedral or in the 'city church': some of these were common to many cities (for example, the release of prisoners from gaol), others were more specific (at Pisa, a large silver belt was drawn all the way round the cathedral).[6] Almost everywhere the most solemn ceremony, the most significant episode, was the great procession in honour of the saint or of the Virgin and the offerings made.

The procession would be crowded and magnificent. It would follow a precisely set route, thus giving symbolic and ritual value to civic spaces.[7] The main destination was the church of the patron saint (which rarely coincided with the cathedral, for the practice of changing a city's patron saint was widespread). Sometimes the church had been specifically constructed by the commune.[8] The composition and order of the procession was regulated in detail: the communal magistrates and their supporters, representatives of the quarters and the military companies, representatives of the professional associations and guilds, all according to a precise hierarchy, the religious companies, and so on.[9] The ceremony of the offering, which sometimes ended the procession and sometimes came the previous day, shows similar features. Decorative candles, banners or, more simply, candles, faggots and carts full of stones, were presented by the communal magistrates, by various civic bodies, by

[4] J. Heers, *Fêtes des fous et Carnavals* (Paris, 1983); W. Heywood, *Palio and Ponte* (London, 1904).

[5] Heers, pp. 261 ff.; for some Tuscan communes, Ventrone, pp. 502-8 and the bibliography there.

[6] P. Vigo, *Una festa popolare a Pisa nel Medio Evo: Contributo alla storia delle costumanze italiane* (Pisa, 1888), pp. 37-39.

[7] See references in S. Carandini, 'Teatro e spettacolo nel Medioevo', in *Letteratura italiana*, ed. A. Asor Rosa, vi, *Teatro, musica, tradizione dei classici* (Turin, 1986), pp. 44-48.

[8] J. Larner, *Culture and Society in Italy, 1290-1420* (London, 1971), pp. 65-75; M. Ronzani, 'La chiesa del comune nella città dell'Italia centro-settentrionale (secoli XII-XIV)', *Società e storia*, vi (1983).

[9] The composition and arrangement of the procession, as regards the order of precedence appointed for the various guilds, is examined in A.I. Pini, 'Le arti in processione; professioni, prestigio e potere nelle città-stato dell'Italia padana medievale', in idem, *Città, comuni e corporazioni nel Medioevo italiano* (Bologna, 1986).

groups and individuals. Many statutes or decrees refer to offerings to be made specifically for the construction or upkeep of the church, especially when the festival emphasised the commune's particular oversight of the church of the patron saint and the importance of its Board of Works (*Opera* or *Fabbrica*).[10]

In such ceremonies, the elements of civil celebration are obvious and easily distinguishable from those ceremonies with a more specifically religious content.[11] Participants and protagonists were not only the faithful and the people, but above all the citizens, in their public capacities as members of the various social bodies or of the commune. The citizenry, led by its magistrates, ranked variously according to profession or class, gathered together to celebrate their common civic values. The figure of the patron saint or of the Virgin Mary,[12] with their local attributions, symbolised these ideals and values, which were both religious and civic or political. In these the city saw reflected its own identity and its past. The procession and the offering were intended to renew the city's pledge to its heavenly protectors. The splendour of the ceremony reflected the grandeur of the commune, its prosperity, power and devotion. The harmoniousness of the celebration signalled, in Italy as elsewhere in Europe, the cohesion of the commune.[13] Hence the participation, in Italy, of rural communities and (sometimes) of feudatories. Their presence and their offerings were intended to underline the tight bonds uniting the city and its surrounding territory. For the close union of city and territory was, as is known, one of the striking features of the Italian city, contrasting it, in political shape and development, to those of northern Europe.[14] From the twelfth century the city communes had begun to expand their control over their *contadi*, often reaching the borders of their dioceses. In the course of the thirteenth century this control was finally established throughout north and central Italy, and the city-states were born. Urban political ideology, in the form given it by communal chanceries, used various

[10] As mentioned in M. Fanti, *La fabbrica di San Petronio in Bologna dal XIV al XX secolo* (Rome, 1980), pp. 81 ff.

[11] For which, it should be noted, the participation of priests and faithful from the countryside was required: P. Gios, *L'attività pastorale del vescovo Pietro Barozzi a Padova, 1487-1507* (Padua, 1977), p. 144; *Le carte dell'Archivio capitolare di Savona (1067-1398)*, ed. V. Pongiglione (Turin, 1913-34), p. 186 (episcopal synod of 1388).

[12] As is known, the saint could change, as the civic and religious ideals that the patron had to express and symbolise changed. For the promotion of civic cults for 'new' saints, see Vauchez, *ubi supra*; also, for an earlier period: P. Golinelli, 'Istituzioni cittadine e culti episcopali in area matildica', in *Culto dei santi, istituzioni e classi sociali in età preindustriale*, ed. S. Boesch Gaiano and L. Sebastiani (L'Aquila, 1984).

[13] Cf. (for example) M. Jones, 'Ritual Drama and Social Body in the Late Medieval English Town', *Past and Present*, xcviii (1983); J. Rossiaud in *Histoire de la France urbaine*, ii, *La ville médiévale*, ed. J. Le Goff (Paris, 1980), pp. 591-603.

[14] P.J. Jones, *Economia e società nell'Italia medievale* (Turin, 1980), pp. 4 ff.

images to underline the naturalness of the ties between city and territory: the city was the mother, the rural communities daughters; or the city was the head, the villages the members. The figure of the patron saint, from the beginning, acted as a sign and guarantee of this unity. Sometimes, for example, an act of submission of a village to the urban commune was symbolically rendered into the hands of the patron saint, perhaps to mitigate the sense of political subjection, certainly to sacralise the new relationship and to underline the common subordination of city and territory to one divine lord and protector. Often even the very terms of submission ordained that this act of homage be repeated every year, on the patron's feast-day (or on other days, of similar import).[15] In following centuries too, the representatives from the *contado* continued to be present at the chief civic celebrations of the city-states.

The participation of the rural communities in such ceremonies is attested from many cities,[16] especially in the regions of Tuscany, Umbria and the Marche, on account of their dense urban pattern and robust, enduring municipal institutions; they do not seem to be recorded, however, in some of the major cities of the Po valley, of Lombardy and the Veneto, for example Milan, Verona, Padua or (more understandably) Genoa or Venice. References are rarer, too, in the Alpine and Appennine areas. Conversely, even relatively small towns in the more urbanised areas could require the presence of their *comitatini*: thus Crema in Lombardy (a 'new' city with a rather small district, by Lombard standards), Ivrea in Piedmont, Cortona and San Gimignano in Tuscany, Ancona, Senigallia, Jesi, Camerino and Fermo in the Marche and Todi in Umbria.[17] Even towns (*borghi*) and castles, which had jurisdiction over a small piece of surrounding territory, sought the participation of their rural communities: Bassano from its 'suburbs'; Carpi to celebrate its role as capital of the tiny principality of the Pio family; and Tolentino from its only two dependant castles (Colmurano and Urbisaglia).[18] Alongside

---

[15] Bertelli, pp. 27, 30, 150.

[16] See the following notes, esp. nos 17-21 (which make no claim to completeness).

[17] F.S. Benvenuti, *Storia di Crema* (Crema, 1949), pp. 191-92; G. Mancini, *Cortona nel Medioevo* (Florence, 1897), pp. 175-76; L. Pecori, *Storia della terra di San Gimignano* (Florence, 1853), p. 343; *Statuti del Comune di Ivrea*, ed. G.S. Pene Vidari (Turin, 1968-74), iii, 223-24; M. Natalucci, *Ancona attraverso i secoli* (Città di Castello, 1961), i, 426, 516; G. Boccanera, 'Antico folclore nella festa patronale di S. Venanzio a Camerino (secoli XIII-XVII)', *Atti e Memorie della Deputazione di storia patria per le Marche*, ser. 7, ix (1954); G. Ceci, *Todi nel Medioevo* (Todi, 1897), i, 291; Mariani, p. 3, n. 1 refers also to Fabbriano, Fossombrone, San Severino, San Genesio, Senigallia and Orvieto.

[18] O. Brentari, *Storia di Bassano e del suo territorio* (Bassano, 1884), p. 277; *Statuta civitatis Carpi annis MCCCLIII et MCDXLVIII* in *Memorie storiche e documenti sulla città e sull'antico principato di Carpi*, viii (Carpi, 1905), pp. 405-8; D. Cecchi, *Storia di Tolentino* (Tolentino, 1975), pp. 215-16, 243-45 (fifteenth century).

representatives of peasant villages were sometimes those of lordly families and feudatories (where such existed).[19]

The forms of participation and the content of offerings varied greatly in different cities and on different festive occasions; they also probably changed with the passage of time and of political regimes. But some features were common: a concern that peasants take part; the coercive nature that this participation eventually took; the coercive nature too of the offerings (which made them more like homage); the reassertion of the city's sovereignty over the *contado* and, consequently, of the subjection of rural communities to the city.

The requirement of *contadini* and rural lords to take part and to make offerings was often created at the moment of their submission to the city commune and was included in acts of submission.[20] It was then reiterated by ordinances of the urban consuls or *podestà*, by decrees of the city council, by the city statutes.[21] These also provided penalties for non-observance: mostly money fines, but sometimes greater penalties at the discretion of the *podestà* or consuls. At Ascoli the statutes went as far as to

[19]Cf. *Statuta civitatis Novariae* (Novara, 1583), pp. 231, 234 (a list of 'feudatarii communis Novariae' dating probably to the later fourteenth century); *Consuetudini e statuti reggiani del secolo XIII*, ed. A. Cerlini (Milan, 1933), p. 39; *I capitoli del comune di Firenze*, ed. C. Guasti, i (Florence, 1866), p. 452 ff. (acts of submission or *accomandigia* by rural lords requiring participation and offerings for S. Giovanni); *Ephemerides urbevetanae*, *RIS*[2], XV, v/i, 322-33 (a list of lords of the *contado* of Orvieto, 1290); Gianandrea, pp. 56-59; 'Il territorio per la festa dell'Assunta', *passim*; the obligation to participate of the vassals of the bishop of Bergamo perhaps dates to an earlier period: G. Ronchetti, *Memorie istoriche . . .* (Bergamo, 1805-39), v, 179.

[20] *Capitoli del comune di Firenze*, *passim*; *Regestum reformationum comunis Perusii ab anno MCCLVI ad annum MCCC*, ed. V. Ansidei (Perugia, 1935), p. 133; Boccanera, pp. 24-25; *Carte diplomatiche iesine*, ed. A. Gianandrea (Ancona, 1884), pp. 109, 111, 126, 132 etc; 'Il territorio per la festa dell'Assunta', *passim*.

[21] *Statuta civitatis Novariae*, pp. 233-34; *Statuta civitatis Cremonae . . .* (Cremona, 1583), p. 125, rubr. 412; *Laudensium statuta seu jura municipalia* (Lodi, 1586), fo. 180; *Statuta communis Parmae digesta anno MCCLV*, ed. A. Ronchini (Parma, 1855), p. 114 (addition of 1264); *Statuta civitatis Mutine anno 1327 reformata*, ed. C. Campori (Parma, 1864), p. 280; *Statuto del comune di Lucca . . . dell'anno 1308 . . .*, ed. S. Bongi and L. Del Prete (Lucca, 1867), pp. 36-42; *Regestum reformationum communis Perusii*, p. 133; *Statuti di Perugia dell'anno MCCCXLII*, ed. G. Degli Azzi (Rome, 1913-16), i, 211-17; ii, 62-64; *Statuta communis Fulginei*, ed. A. Messini and F. Baldaccini (Perugia, 1969), ii, 288-89; *Statuti di Ascoli Piceno dell'anno MCCCLXXIII*, ed. L. Zdekauer and P. Sella (Rome, 1910), pp. 325-26; *Codice diplomatico della città d'Orvieto . . .* ed. L. Fumi (Orvieto, 1884), p. 765 n.; *Statuti di Spoleto del 1296*, ed. G. Antonelli (Florence, 1962), pp. 51, 53; *Statuta civitatis Aquilae*, ed. A. Clementi (Rome, 1977), p. 366 ff. (May 1434). For other regulation of festivals and processions: G. Mantese, *Memorie storiche della chiesa vicentina*, III, i, *Dal 1404 al 1563* (Vicenza, 1958), pp. 423-24, 439-43; Heywood, pp. 55-62; G. Vaccai, *La vita municipale di Pesaro sotto i Malatesta, gli Sforza e i Della Rovere* (Pesaro, 1928), p. 127; Mariani, *ubi supra*; A.F. Giachi, *Saggio di ricerche storiche sopra . . . Volterra . . .* (Volterra, 1887), pp. 78, 79; G. Volpe, *Toscana medievale* (Florence, 1964), p. 132 etc.

declare defaulting communities as rebels and to outlaw their inhabitants.[22] Such legislation also suggests that offerings were more tribute than homage. For the offerings from the *contado* were regulated in greater detail than those of other participants (for instance the quality of wax, the value of the *palio*, the type of cloth).[23] Offerings were sometimes calculated according to criteria similar to those used for taxation: according, that is, to the *estimo* of the subject communities or the number of their inhabitants.[24] The *podestà* (or other officials) was responsible for checking the offerings and would be punished if he did not. Sometimes it was ordained that rural communities should have citizen guarantors. For those who failed to make offerings, penalties were laid down, often a fine equal to twice the value of the offering. Compositions, money payments in place of the offerings, were not always accepted, in order to avoid a reduction or loss in the ritual and symbolic character of the ceremony.[25] Nor was it always acceptable for rural communities to send offerings, but not to be present: they had to send the required representation (consisting of the consul, the *massaro*, and some others to accompany them). All were to be 'suitably, indeed honourably, dressed'. Various statutes reserved to the *podestà* and the civic *anziani* the right to fix the number and condition of men whom each village should send; and it was suggested, or rather ordered, that these should assemble in the city singing and playing instruments, in attitudes expressing feelings of joy and festivity.

These aspects of the ceremony, and the very proliferation of rules that were more rigid and coercive than for other participants (guilds, confraternities), show clearly that rural communities barely identified with the values that the ritual was meant to celebrate. The patron saint belonged to the city;[26] he was not a spontaneous object of rural devotion,

[22] *Statuti di Ascoli Piceno*, p. 326.

[23] *Statuta civitatis Novariae*, pp. 233-34 (fixing the weight of 'good-quality' wax to be offered by each commune); likewise at Pisa and Orvieto: Vigo, pp. 17-18; *Codice diplomatico d'Orvieto*, p. 765. Sometimes a minimum amount, for all communities, was fixed: *Statuta civitatis Aquilae*, p. 367; *Statuta communis Parmae*, p. 114. For the value of the *palio*: *Statuti di Ascoli Piceno*, p. 326.

[24] For example, in the Bresciano in the early fifteenth century, every hearth had to contribute 6 ounces of wax; when the number of taxable hearths was reduced in 1430, this was increased to 15 ounces, though subsequently reduced to 12 in 1432, after protest by the inhabitants: Zanelli, pp. 6-8. In the Pisano in the mid-fourteenth century, the amount of wax due depended on the size and importance of the territory: Vigo, p. 18. Cf. also *Statuta communis Fulginei*, p. 289; *Statuta civitatis Carpi*, p. 405; Gianandrea, pp. 53-55. For payment of large sums of money, in conjunction with offerings of *palio* and wax: Heywood, p. 55; 'Il territorio per la festa dell'Assunta', *passim*.

[25] Ibid.; Zanelli, p. 10.

[26] The countryside, deprived of importance as a site of religious devotions (Trexler, pp. 3-4), lacked any forms of religious or civil celebration that extended beyond the limited bounds of village or *borgo*. On the insignificance of patrons of the diocese and their cult: Galletti, pp. 213-14.

he did not arouse in *contadini* feelings of 'civic religiosity', nor could he
easily be accepted by them as a symbol of unity and concord. Their act of
homage to the saint was essentially another act of subjection, a new
tribute, to the urban centre; yet another burden, like so many others
(fiscal, jurisdictional, administrative) that the *contado* daily sustained.

The ceremony therefore, took on in practice the function of reaffirming
urban supremacy over the territory and rural dependence on the city. The
procession and offering, according to the statutes of Ascoli Piceno, were
established 'to do honour and reverence to the cathedral of the city of
Ascoli and to blessed Emindio and to conserve the rights of the commune
and people of the city and the cathedral'.[27] In Florence the variously-
coloured silk banners and the models in wood and paper of the city and
castles, 'which are called *ceri*', were seen as 'symbols of submission' of the
communities that offered them ('veluti servitutis indicia donant
quotannis').[28] Sometimes the ritual of the ceremony and the form of
offering seem to have been intended to underline the tribute and
subjection of rural communities: at Bologna, on the eve of the feast of San
Petronio, the *vicari* of the *contado*, accompanied by one man from each
community and 'cum tubis vel aliis instrumentis ante eos pulsantibus',
had to appear before a platform on which stood the *gonfaloniere* of the city,
at least three of the *anziani*, four *gonfalonieri del popolo* and four guild *massari*.
Each vicar, on making his offering, had to turn to the *anziani* and say:
'These are your servants, the men of such-and-such a district, who
commend themselves to San Petronio and to your dominion'. And the
statute ordering this continued: 'This offering will signify to *contadini* the
loyalty and obedience which they are obliged to have towards your
commune'.[29] Indeed so much did participation in processions become a
sign of subjection that it was used, even much later, as sufficient proof
when the dependence of a village or fief on a city was in dispute. As late as
the eighteenth century, Pompeo Neri based a claim that the county of
Carpegna belonged to the Grand-duchy of Tuscany on offerings of *palii*
which the counts had made in Florence since the end of the fourteenth
century. On the same grounds, the Sienese claimed that the so-called 'fief
of the bishopric' (*Vescovado*) belonged to their city.[30]

The long history of these ceremonies, stretching from the moment of

---

[27] *Statuti di Ascoli Piceno*, p. 325.
[28] G. Mancini, 'Il bel San Giovanni e le feste patronali di Firenze descritte nel 1475 da
Pietro Cennini', *Rivista d'Arte*, vi (1909), 223; cf. 'Il territorio per la festa dell'Assunta', pp.
91 ff.
[29] Fanti, pp. 52-55.
[30] Pompeo Neri's text is in *Voto a favore della Toscana nella vertenza con la S. Sede sulla
sovranità delle antiche contee di Carpegna e di Scavolino* (Florence, 1860), pp. 68-72; N. Mengozzi,
Il feudo del vescovado di Siena (Siena, 1911), p. 144.

consolidation of city control over its territory in the second half of the thirteenth century to the modern period, did of course see expressions of discontent and episodes of resistance. A cruel signal of rural hostility was made in the late thirteenth century by the mountain-dwellers of the Garfagnana, who cut off the right hand of a local notary who had taken a candle to the festival of Santa Croce in Lucca.[31] It was especially from the later fourteenth century to the early fifteenth that such episodes became relatively numerous (or at least are referred to more frequently in the sources).·At Lodi, for example, in 1391 the obligation on *contadini* to make the usual offering in honour of S. Bassiano had to be reiterated.[32] In 1392 Fiorenzuola obtained from Gian Galeazzo Visconti exemption from the usual offerings in Piacenza on the festivals of S. Antonino and of the Assumption of the Virgin Mary; and other places in the territory of Piacenza probably obtained a similar concession (or at least followed Fiorenzuola's example), for in 1421 the directors of the *Fabbrica* of Piacenza cathedral denounced for default not only Fiorenzuola, but also Borgonuovo, Castell'Arquato and Compiano.[33] In 1438 various communities of the Cremonese, who claimed to be immune, had to be vigorously commanded to fulfil their obligations.[34] In the Novarese the early years of Sforza rule provide various references to non-fulfilment by communities which had obtained privileges and concessions during Francesco Sforza's conquest there.[35] In the territory of Parma it was chiefly Borgo San Donnino (now Fidenza) which led resistance to the tribute of one wax candle for the festivals of S. Ilario and the Assumption; with the result that Parma at one point ordered the arrest of Borghigiani who, for whatever reason, came to the city (Borgo replied with a similar order for the immediate arrest of Parmigiani there).[36]

There are references to resistance also from Tuscany (the territories of Pistoia in the early fifteenth century and of Cortona some decades later) and from the Venetian *Terraferma*.[37] At Brescia, around 1430, a dispute

[31] G. Tommasi, *Sommario della storia di Lucca dall'anno MIV all'anno MDCC* (Florence, 1847), p. 77.

[32] *Laudensium statuta, ubi supra.*

[33] E. Ottolenghi, *Fiorenzuola e dintorni: notizie storiche* (Fiorenzuola, 1903) pp. 50, 54, 65, 68. Cf. P.M. Campi, *Dell'historia ecclesiastica di Piacenza* (Piacenza, 1651-52), iii, 137.

[34] Archivio di Stato, Milan, Archivio visconteo, Carteggio, 10 Aug. 1438; L. Cavitelli, *Annales* (Cremona, 1588), p. 180.

[35] *Statuta civitatis Novariae*, p. 235 (Francesco Sforza's letter of 8 Feb. 1451); cf. F. Cognasso, *Storia di Novara* (Novara, 1971), pp. 362-63. The list of communities obliged to make offerings (*Statuta*, pp. 233-34) did not include Vigevano, which was already politically autonomous; while at Mortara, the ceremonial breaking-up of the candle by the *populus*, after it had been formally requested, is probably a record of an older dispute.

[36] A. Pezzana, *Storia della città di Parma* (Parma, 1837-59), iv, 172, 218.

[37] *Cronache di Ser Luca Dominici*, (Pistoia, 1933-9), ii, ed. G.C. Gigliotti, p. 131; Mancini, p. 309.

broke out between the city and its territory over the amount of wax that
the *contado* owed, which the *contadini* wanted reduced. Despite a
provisional agreement here, the conflict continued for several years and in
1446 the civic festival was disrupted by a noisy episode when, during the
palio race, a representative of the *contado* presented, instead of a banner of
velvet bearing the arms of the Venetian officials, 'a nasty, dirty blanket'.[38]

Is this quickening of references accidental? Or is it a sign of a general
crisis in these years in the relations between city and *contado*? This was of
course the period when regional states throughout north and central Italy
were consolidating their power: the duchy of Milan in Lombardy, Venice
in its *Terraferma*, the Florentine state encompassing new centres and
territories in Tuscany. As a result the hegemony of city over countryside,
successfully imposed in the period of the city states, had now to readjust to
the new administrative, fiscal and jurisdictional order of the regional
states. The regional states, though unable and unwilling to ignore the
political weight of the cities in their new territorial structures, were
nevertheless not averse to giving room and recognition to the demands
from *contadini* for emancipation. The regional states looked for both a
wider basis of consent and a reappraisal of the political aspirations of the
old city communes. As a result these decades saw new measures being
taken: some tax rebates for the countryside, administrative reorganisation
aimed at reducing the power of urban magistrates, and the grant of
privileges of autonomy to small centres (*borghi* such as Vigevano, Borgo
San Donnino, Treviglio and Legnago).[39] The possibility seemed to open
up within regional states of a new, less oppressive relationship between
city and territory; or, at least, rural communities were now aware of the
prince or the regional capital as possible allies against the excessive power
of the city.

In such a context the general ferment of protest allowed challenges to
the ancient customs in the matter of ceremonies and processions. The
coincidence is sometimes exact. The threat, by the Pistoiese communities
in July 1402, not to send *palii* to the festival of S. Giacomo came only
shortly after a Florentine reform creating new *podesterie* (administrative
districts) in the *contado* of Pistoia, which were removed from Pistoia's
jurisdiction and subjected directly to Florence. Similarly the resistance of
villages and *borghi* in the Milanese state intensified in the very decades in
which many of them obtained new fiscal, administrative and
jurisdictional autonomy. The episode at Brescia occurred when Venetian
control of the city, recently threatened by the Visconti, seemed poised

[38] Zanelli, pp. 8-11; C. Pasero, 'Il dominio veneto fino all'incendio della Loggia (1426-
1575)', in *Storia di Brescia* (Brescia, 1961-64), ii, 87.

[39] G. Chittolini, 'Le "terre separate" nel ducato di Milano in età sforzesca', in *Milano
nell'età di Ludovico il Moro* (Milan, 1983), i, 115-28.

between recognition of Brescia's traditional supremacy and the grant of wide privilege to the *borghi* and valleys of its territory.[40] The festival of the patron saint, which cities had intended should reflect and solemnly sanction their organic relationship with the countryside, underwent the same instability in the early fifteenth century as that relationship itself.

Whether the episodes of resistance and protest recorded above had lasting consequences is not easy to ascertain. Sometimes the governments of regional states were apparently inclined to entertain the requests of rural communities, releasing them from obligation to contribute offerings (either through explicit privilege or by a simple rejection of the city's protest). More often the rights of cities to receive offerings from their subject communities were confirmed – especially after the formative period of the regional states, when the definition of relations between their constituent parts could not but sanction the preponderant power of the cities. In the Milanese state the duke intervened repeatedly, at Novara and Cremona, to ensure observance of the old customs, and he ordered his officials to recall reluctant rural communities to their duty.[41] Nevertheless the civic spirit of these festivals, as has been variously shown,[42], was progressively weakened. In particular the assertion through the festival of the city's authority over 'its' territory was less in evidence as the territory slowly became a mere province of a larger state. The regional states staged their own celebrations – in republican regimes, such as Florence, these still took the form of an offering and procession, but now involving the communities of the whole state – in which, however, the festive, rather than ceremonial, elements tended to predominate. This is the case in the festival of S. Giovanni, and even more so in the celebration of the reigning dynasty in the principalities, as in Milan under the Visconti or Sforza or in Florence under the Medici.[43] Eventually, during the sixteenth century,

---

[40] Idem, *La formazione dello stato regionale e le istituzioni del contado* (Turin, 1979), xv-xix and pp. 295 ff.; D. Parzani, 'Il territoro di Brescia intorno alla metà del Quattrocento', *Studi Bresciani*, iv (1983).

[41] Cf. *supra*, notes 32-36. The duke of Milan insisted on the obligation of rural communities to make offerings to Cremona (1438) and Novara (1451) notwithstanding their privileges of 'separation'. Immediately following Francesco Sforza's death in 1466, Cremona presented a series of requests to his widow, including a demand that all communities in the Cremonese territory be returned to full subjection to the city and that, as a result, they be obliged to attend the festival of the Assumption with the required *palio*, wax and other offerings (the duchess approved this request): Biblioteca Trivulziana, Milan, cod. 1428, 'Decreta ducalia pro Cremona', fo. 158.

[42] Ventrone, pp. 500-1, 516-17; Galletti, p. 215.

[43] See, for example, E. Garbero Zorzi, 'La festa scenica: immagini e descrizioni', in *Il costume nell'età del Rinascimento*, ed. D. Liscia Bemporad (Florence, 1988), pp. 194-98 (the festivities for the wedding of Cosimo de' Medici and Eleonora di Toledo in July 1539: these included a dance-scene involving 48 characters, including personifications of Tuscan towns, though also of rivers and hills).

there was a reassertion of more religious values: especially during the Counter-Reformation many of these celebrations came under the influence of the church authorities, under whose direction they moved away from their original civil character.[44] Of some festivals all record is lost at this point.[45]

In some centres, aspects of the old ceremony survived. In the eighteenth or nineteenth centuries we can still find in diaries and chronicles descriptions of these processions, of the rural representatives who participated, and of the sense of civic festival that they still retained.[46] In civic ceremony, as in economic, fiscal and administrative spheres, the old tradition of urban supremacy over the countryside was preserved into the modern age.

[44] On the *a posteriori* regularisation of the cult of many saints, beatified or canonised during or after the sixteenth century: A. Vauchez, *La sainteté en Occident aux derniers siècles du Moyen Age* (Rome, 1981), pp. 488-89.

[45] Lozzi, p. 331.

[46] G.B. Biffi, *Diario (1777-1781)*, ed. G. Dossena (Milan, 1976), pp. 91-94; Boccanera, pp. 74, 77; Gianandrea, pp. 58-59.

7

'Honour' and 'Profit': Landed Property and Trade in Medieval Siena

Giuliano Pinto

Siena has been described by Philip Jones as 'the southernmost capital' of the commercial revolution of the Middle Ages:[1] almost no other city of medieval Italy shows such a clear and wide contrast in its social and economic fabric between its period of greatest prosperity and the early modern period. In the second half of the thirteenth century, Siena was a star of the first order in the European economic sky.[2] Sienese merchant and banking companies operated on a large scale in many parts of western Europe. They were prominent in the exchanges leading to the fairs of Champagne; and they had a strong presence in England, Germany and southern France (though less so in Flanders, Spain and the Levant). In Italy Sienese merchants had warehouses and sizable business at Pisa, Genoa, Venice and Naples (though their numbers were fewer in Sicily,[3] which is indicative of their lesser interests in and contacts with the Mediterranean area).

For almost the entire thirteenth century, the Sienese families of the Piccolomini, Tolomei, Salimbeni, Bonsignori and Gallerani constituted, with only a few other Italian companies, the mercantile and banking aristocracy of Europe. Their good relations with the papal court – they served for a long time as papal bankers – brought them profitable financial operations and increased their prestige. The great Sienese companies were well-organised internally, were endowed with ample funds, were

---

[1] P.J. Jones, *Economia e società nell'Italia medievale* (Turin, 1980), p. 27.

[2] The bibliography on Siena's thirteenth-century economic expansion is substantial; it suffices to record the works of Bourquelot, Patetta, Zdekauer, Chiaudano, Astuti, Sayous, Bautier, Sapori, Bowsky and English. For recent statements, see M. Tangheroni, 'Siena e il commercio internazionale nel Duecento e nel Trecento', in *Banchieri e mercanti di Siena* (Rome, 1987), and M. Cassandro, 'La banca senese nei secoli XIII e XIV', ibid.

[3] G. Petralia, 'Sui Toscani in Sicilia tra Due e Trecento: la penetrazione sociale e il radicamento dei ceti urbani', in *Commercio, finanza, funzione pubblica: Stranieri in Sicilia e in Sardegna nei secoli XIII-XV*, ed. M. Tangheroni (Naples, 1989), esp. Appendix I, tab. c, p. 209. The Sienese merchants were outnumbered by those from Lucca, Pistoia and San Gimignano, to say nothing of those from Florence and Pisa.

able to draw on the combined capital of their partners and enjoyed the confidence of their depositors and of the rulers, churchmen and businessmen with whom they had dealings.[4] Siena's trading peak largely coincided with its period of greatest political power, which culminated in the victory over Florence at the battle of Montaperti in 1260. The same years saw the beginning or the completion of major building projects in Siena which had a lasting effect on the face of the city.[5]

Two centuries later the picture had altered drastically.[6] Siena's population had fallen to around 15,000, one third (more or less) of its level in the early thirteenth century. The city seemed a sleepy provincial town,[7] despite the fact that it governed a vast (if little populated) territory of 7,000 sq. km. and 80,000 inhabitants in central-southern Tuscany.[8] One of the few sparks of life in the city, and the only one that gave it a cosmopolitan air, was provided by the university and its crowd of foreign students.[9] The documentary and literary sources are agreed on the character of Siena's economy and society in the fifteenth and sixteenth centuries. The more well-to-do citizens, who also participated actively in political life, based their wealth almost exclusively on landed property and on livestock.[10] Their tax-returns consist of lists of farms and houses, rarely of warehouses. Only a small group of families – a few dozen – were engaged in banking or in trade (in wool, silk, linen, leather), but their investments were modest (rarely exceeding 1,000 florins) and were accompanied by large investments in land. According to the records of a fiscal levy (*lira*) in 1453, the trading and manufacturing investments of the wealthier families amounted to less than a quarter of their total wealth. Government bonds formed another 10 per cent; and the rest, around two-

---

[4] E.D. English, *Enterprise and Liability in Sienese Banking, 1230-1350* (Cambridge, Mass., 1988).

[5] D. Balestracci and G. Piccinni, *Siena nel Trecento; Assetto urbano e strutture edilizie* (Florence, 1977), pp. 103-12; L. Bortolotti, *Siena* (Rome & Bari, 1983), pp. 13-56.

[6] Cf. A.K. Isaacs, 'Popolo e Monti nella Siena del primo Cinquecento', *Rivista storica italiana*, lxxxii (1970); G. Fioravanti, *Università e città: Cultura umanistica e cultura scolastica a Siena nel '400* (Florence, 1981), pp. 34-39; D.L. Hicks, 'Sienese Society in the Renaissance', *Comparative Studies in Society and History*, ii (1960), 412-20; idem, 'The Sienese State in the Renaissance', in *From the Renaissance to the Counter-Reformation*, ed. C.H. Carter (New York, 1965); idem, 'Sources of Wealth in Renaissance Siena: Businessmen and Landowners', *Bullettino senese di storia patria*, xciii (1986); G. Cherubini, 'I mercanti e il potere', in *Banchieri e mercanti di Siena*, pp. 168-70; G. Pinto, 'I mercanti e la terra', ibid., pp. 280-86. On Siena's territory: M. Ginatempo, *Crisi di un territorio: Il popolamento della Toscana senese alla fine del Medioevo* (Florence, 1988).

[7] Cherubini, p. 165.

[8] Ginatempo, p. 461 (1532).

[9] Cf. *I tedeschi nella storia dell'Università di Siena*, ed. G. Minnucci (Siena, 1988), pp. 159-65, for bibliography; and references in A. Brilli, *Viaggiatori stranieri in terra di Siena* (Rome, 1986), pp. 147-71.

[10] Isaacs, pp. 73-75; Hicks, 'Sources of Wealth', pp. 16-37; Pinto, 'I mercanti e la terra', pp. 264-86.

thirds, was derived from land.[11] Even neighbouring cities such as Pisa and
Arezzo (to say nothing of Florence) had much more pronounced trading
and manufacturing contours;[12] and *they* were subject cities, not capitals of
vast territories, and were also still recovering from the crisis of Florentine
conquest. As a region, the Sienese state was a producer mainly of raw
materials (grain, livestock, metals) for the major markets of the Florentine
state, and Florentine businessmen were active in Sienese markets, often
supplanting local merchants.[13]

Although this picture has many obscurities which still need to be
clarified, it gives greater credibility and force to the numerous comments
of observers, from both inside and outside Siena, who underlined the fact
that high-ranking *Senesi* generally lived off landed rents and the salaries of
office and showed detachment, if not distaste, for the world of business.[14]
The memory of the great thirteenth-century mercantile era hardly seemed
to survive. The last great Sienese banker, Agostino Chigi, was Sienese
only by birth and spent most of his life in Rome, which was the centre of
his commercial and financial activities, and he retained with his native
town ties that were little more than sentimental.[15]

This transformation, or rather crisis, of the Sienese economy seems to
have been quite rapid, and perhaps without parallel in contemporary
Italy. By the 1320s the space of little more than one generation had seen
Siena's international position contract substantially.[16] This followed the
failures of the *Gran Tavola* of the Bonsignori (1298) and of the larger
company of the Tolomei (1313), and the rapid decline of the fairs of
Champagne (to which Sienese commerce was umbilically linked) as the
major centre of commercial and financial exchanges in Europe.
Emblematic was the absence of *Senesi* from the Avignon markets during
the Papacy's period there.[17] The (sporadic) appearance of Sienese
companies in some parts of France in the mid fourteenth century[18]

---

[11] Hicks, 'Sources of Wealth', p. 21.

[12] Ibid., n. 32; and generally, D. Herlihy and C. Klapisch-Zuber, *Les toscans et leurs
familles* (Paris, 1978), pp. 249-55. Cf. G. Pinto, 'Per la storia della struttura sociale delle
città toscane nel Trecento: la distribuzione della ricchezza a Firenze e a Siena', in *La
Toscana nel secolo XIV. Caratteri di una civiltà regionale*, ed. S. Gensini (Pisa, 1988).

[13] Idem, *La Toscana nel tardo Medioevo: Ambiente, economia rurale, società* (Florence, 1982),
p. 89.

[14] Isaacs, pp. 64-65; Fioravanti, p. 39, n. 1; Cherubini, pp. 164-65.

[15] F. Dante, 'Chigi Agostino', in *Dizionario biografico degli Italiani*, xxiv (Rome, 1980), pp.
735-43. The Spannocchi family (in particular Ambrogio di Nanni) also built their fortune
far from Siena, in Naples, Venice and especially in Rome; their eventual return to Siena in
the early sixteenth century coincided with their abandonment of business: U. Morandi,
'Gli Spannocchi: piccoli proprietari terrieri, artigiani, piccoli, medi e grandi mercanti-
banchieri', in *Studi in memoria di F. Melis* (Naples, 1978), iii, 91-120.

[16] Cassandro, pp. 121-50.

[17] Cherubini, p. 169 (referring to the studies by Y. Renouard and B. Guillemain).

[18] Tangheroni, pp. 54-56.

signifies little, especially in relation to the overall picture of Italian commercial activity there, which is by now well documented.

The last two decades of the fourteenth century brought a further crisis of Siena's banking and commerce, following Charles of Durazzo's sequestration of foreign traders' goods at Naples and, above all, as a result of Siena's war with Florence during Gian Galeazzo Visconti's lordship of Siena.[19] In the course of a century, the cycle was complete: from having been a great European economic centre, Siena now had a role that was little more than regional. Siena thus represents perhaps the earliest and clearest example of the process of marginalisation which was advancing up the peninsula and by the end of the Middle Ages had affected many towns of central Italy.[20] But it should be noted that the so-called 'fourteenth-century crisis' seems not to have had a decisive role in Siena, save insofar as it accentuated tendencies already present for some decades.[21]

In attempting to explain this general picture, historians have used a variety of interpretations and evidence: the limits and inherent weaknesses of Sienese economic expansion; structural conditions and constraints; or the emerging difficulties of international trade. These, though unexceptionable in themselves, have, when put together, appeared insufficient or incomplete, as we shall see. Historians have noted how the scarcity of Sienese companies in commercially strategic areas such as the Levant, Sicily, Catalonia and Flanders brought to Siena's international economic relations deficiencies and disequilibria which exposed it to greater cyclical dangers.[22] The markedly financial role of Sienese companies constituted a further restriction, and explains their non-involvement in certain areas. The Sienese economy also suffered from some basic flaws: distance from the sea and the lack of a port of its own (a port was an almost indispensable resource for the development of trade: the port of Talamone, acquired by Siena in 1303, never took off);[23] and the shortage of water, which prevented the growth of textile manufacture, thus depriving Siena of that conjunction of manufacture, banking and trade which alone was able to give life and weight to the urban economies

---

[19] Cherubini, pp. 168-69.

[20] M. Ginatempo and L. Sandri, *L'Italia delle città: Il popolamento urbano tra Medioevo e Rinascimento* (Florence, 1990), pp. 139-47.

[21] For the effects of the 'crisis' on the *contado*, see Ginatempo, *Crisi*.

[22] Tangheroni, pp. 101-3.

[23] But the lack of a port of its own did not prevent Florence's great commercial development; nor did Lucca suffer unduly from the inactivity of its outlet on the Tyrrhenian Sea at Motrone. There is no full study of the port at Talamone, but it came alive only when used by foreign merchants, Florentines especially: L. Banchi, 'I porti della Maremma senese durante la Repubblica', *Archivio storico italiano*, x-xii (1870); G. Pinto, *Il Libro del Biadaiolo: Carestie e annona a Firenze dalla metà del '200 al 1348* (Florence, 1978), pp. 84-85.

of the interior, as it did at Milan and Florence, or, at a lower level, Verona, Padua, Cremona, Bologna, Prato, Arezzo and so on.[24] Instead the Sienese wool industry, already modest in 1300, declined further; silk production struggled to survive, despite public subsidies; and cotton production never prospered, in contrast to that of neighbouring cities (which suggests too, that shortage of water is not a sufficient explanation).[25]

Historians have also noted that the economic conjuncture of the late thirteenth century damaged Siena's economy, bringing first the crisis in the Champagne fairs and then loss of the leading position in papal finance owing to Florentine competition. Here it has been underlined how the coining and international diffusion of the gold florin created difficulties for Sienese bankers used to dealing in their own silver *soldi*.[26] But what is surprising is that bankers as experienced as the Sienese did not plan to create their own gold currency, as happened at Genoa and Venice. It has further been claimed that political and military events – Siena's abandonment of the imperial party after its defeat at Colle Val d'Elsa in 1269 and its adherence to the Guelf party, but in subordination to Florence – marked the start of both economic and political decline, as if the destiny of the city was doubly bound to that of the Empire.[27]

All of these arguments can, to a large degree, be accepted. Nevertheless, underlying explanations for many of them are lacking, and they end up, in the manner of a serpent eating its own tail, by begging the essential question. It would therefore seem more profitable to call attention to some internal peculiarities of Sienese society and economy in the thirteenth and fourteenth centuries. Recent historiography has not overlooked the deep bond between Sienese ruling groups and landed property.[28] Around 1320, 2 per cent of citizen families owned one third (by value) of all urban and rural property. Four great families (the Gallerani, Salimbeni, Tolomei and Malavolti) held almost 20 per cent of all landed wealth.[29] This situation had arisen from an interest in land already at least a century old. In the course of the thirteenth century, the major families directed their economic energies in two quarters: to international

[24] P.J. Jones, 'La storia economica: Dalla caduta dell'Impero romano al XIV secolo', in Einaudi *Storia d'Italia*, ii (Turin, 1974), pp. 1706-28.

[25] S. Tortoli, 'Per la storia della produzione laniera a Siena nel Trecento e nei primi anni del Quattrocento', *Bull. senese di storia patria*, lxxxii-iii (1975-76), 220-38; L. Banchi, *L'Arte della seta in Siena nei secoli XV e XVI* (Siena, 1881); Pinto, *La Toscana*, p. 88; B. Dini, *Arezzo intorno al 1400: Produzioni e mercato* (Arezzo, 1984), pp. 53-69.

[26] Tangheroni, p. 103; Cassandro, pp. 151-52.

[27] P. Cammarosano, Introduction to *Caleffo vecchio del Comune di Siena*, (Siena, 1988), p. 15 (referring to Zdekauer and Schneider).

[28] G. Cherubini, *Signori, contadini, borghesi: Ricerche sulla società italiana del basso Medioevo* (Florence, 1974), pp. 231-311; Pinto, 'I mercanti e la terra'; S.K. Cohn, *Death and Property in Siena, 1205-1800* (Baltimore and London, 1989).

[29] Cherubini, *Signori*, pp. 247-51.

expansion, especially in the banking sector, and to the massive acquisition of lands and castles, with corresponding seigneurial rights.[30] They became at one and the same time great merchant bankers and great landowners and lords of castles, more so than the major families of other Tuscan cities, which had smaller territories and stronger rural aristocracies.

This planting of roots in the Sienese *contado* took place only shortly after the period of great international successes; it suffices to recall only the main phases of the process.[31] The Piccolomini, who in the early thirteenth century had banks in many European cities and were linked both to ecclesiastical and to lay potentates, in the same period obtained local fiefs from Frederick II in exchange for services to the Empire. The Salimbeni in the course of the thirteenth century took advantage of Siena's expansion to create a large power base in various parts of the *contado*; in 1275 they acquired, from the commune of Siena itself, in repayment of a debt, castles with attached seigneurial rights in the Val d'Orcia, the upper Val d'Elsa and the Val d'Ombrone. The Malavolti, in the decades around 1200, built up a strong core of properties around Monteriggioni, owing in part to their connections of alliance, and perhaps of marriage, with the major aristocratic family of the area (the Soarzi, lords of Staggia). The Bonsignori concentrated on an area further south, in the territory of the Ardenghesca, where they obtained rights over various castles. This agglomeration of great landed estates seems to involve motives and purposes beyond mere economic calculation. Investments in landed property in the countryside (rarely in the city) were not intended to diversify sources of wealth, nor to create a balance among different economic activities, but were a means of legitimising rapid social advance and of consolidating the power of individual clans (*consorterie*) through the possession of solid bases in the countryside and of huge agricultural surpluses, so as to provide armed men and faithful clients for use at opportune moments.[32]

All this assumes special importance in the light of Paolo Cammarosano's recent, fundamental studies on Sienese society in the

[30] Research has still to ascertain whether individual *consorterie* practised any division of trading tasks, inside and outside the city (but see E.D. English, *Five Magnate Families of Siena, 1240-1350*, University of Toronto Ph.D. thesis, 1982).

[31] For what follows, see A. Lisini and A. Liberati, *Genealogia dei Piccolomini di Siena* (Siena, 1900), p. 5; P. Cammarosano, 'Le campagne senesi dalla fine del secolo XII agli inizi del Trecento: dinamica interna e forme del dominio cittadino', in *Contadini e proprietari nella Toscana moderna*, i, *Dal Medioevo all'età moderna* (Florence, 1979), p. 193, n. 82; idem, *Monteriggioni: Storia, architettura, paesaggio* (Milan, 1983), pp. 43, 50; A. Verdiani Bandi, *I castelli della Val d'Orcia e la repubblica di Siena* (Siena, 1926), pp. 61, 67; Cherubini, *Signori*, p. 291.

[32] For evidence from chronicles and record sources: Pinto, 'I mercanti e la terra', pp. 233-34; and, in general, Jones, *Economia e società*, pp. 43-47.

twelfth and thirteenth centuries. We now know that the great merchant families did not descend from the ranks of the rural aristocracy, even less from the comital houses. They arose within the city walls: 'It was not the aristocracy which made the communal city, but the communal city which created an aristocratic class'.[33] If some families (for example, the Malavolti) appeared on the political stage in the period of the consular commune, most of them emerged later, at the end of the twelfth century, if not in the early thirteenth.[34] Their strong roots in the *contado* were not therefore inherited from previous generations, but the outcome of a deliberate choice; and the cultural models of the traditional aristocracy would have conditioned that choice. This is shown by the marriage relationships which soon bound these prominent urban families to the old nobility of the *contado*, and by the fact that the urban families not infrequently succeeded to the nobles' estates and seigneurial rights, or acted as intermediaries between the great dynasties of the territory and the commune of Siena.[35]

Mercantile and aristocratic culture coexisted in Sienese society in the thirteenth and early fourteenth centuries, as in most cities of north and central Italy.[36] At Siena, however, the noble model acquired a particular attraction with the growth in importance of military and aristocratic forces during the city's constant warfare with its powerful neighbours.[37] The noble model, at first perhaps only outwardly imitated, was later fully absorbed into urban life and enthroned among the aspirations and aims of the major families. The latter increasingly detached themselves from the popular traditions within which they had arisen, and created a *de facto* aristocratic class that was distinguished as much by its wealth (in trade and property) as by its attitudes and behaviour.[38] At the same time mercantile culture failed to establish deep roots, or to become the common property of the higher social strata, or to be transmitted from generation to generation. It is symptomatic that a second generation of great merchant bankers did not come forward to fill the places of the great companies that had failed or disappeared in the years around 1300.[39] The

[33] Cammarosano, pp. 34-35.
[34] Ibid., pp. 57-60, 68, 78. The claim of ancient origins for families of the thirteenth-century mercantile oligarchy was made in the imaginative reconstructions of modern genealogists, which were groundlessly adopted by historians from the late nineteenth century on.
[35] Ibid., pp. 78-80.
[36] W.M. Bowsky, *A Medieval Italian Commune. Siena under the Nine, 1287-1355* (Berkeley, 1981), pp. 260-98; Cherubini, 'I mercanti e il potere', pp. 163-64, 180-81; and, in general, Jones, *Economia e società*, pp. 70-96.
[37] Cammarosano, pp. 65-66.
[38] Cherubini, 'I mercanti e il potere', pp. 176-77; F. Cardini, 'L'argento e i sogni: cultura, immaginario, orizzonti mentali', in *Banchieri e mercanti di Siena*, pp. 312-33.
[39] English, *Sienese Banking*, pp. 113-14.

failure of international companies was of course not altogether extraordinary in the later Middle Ages: companies' lives were always short, and their fall sometimes noisy;[40] but other trading companies would take their place, as new businessmen (*gente nuova*) emerged into the international limelight. This happened in many cities of communal Italy; but not in Siena, where the opening of the fourteenth century closed an era. Perhaps Siena's precocious development was, in the last analysis, a weakness. If (to use Lopez's expression) it is an exaggeration to talk of a false start in the light of the successes that had been achieved, it was certainly the case that a rising curve had been suddenly broken and that Siena was thus brought fully into line with the division between the Middle Ages and the Renaissance once proposed by Armando Sapori.[41]

Faced with their first great difficulties – both structural and conjunctural – the Sienese commercial aristocracy showed no resistance, nor any will to respond. A return to the land, in terms of vast landed estates and seigneurial rights, seems to have been totally congenial to their mental patterns and ideals. Did they perhaps see in it an assertion of identity against the ruling classes of neighbouring cities? A more or less conscious desire to stand out and to create an identity would indeed seem to explain 'archaic' behaviour among the Sienese aristocracy: the large expenditure on clothes and banquets, the taste for ceremony and festival, the cult of courtesy, the fine facades (and they were only facades) of the patrician palaces, the grandiose and unrealistic architectural projects, and the strong spirit of faction (manifested in the peculiar local subdivision into *Monti*).[42]

In the management of the large estates, the more practical methods of the thirteenth century were slowly replaced by the detachment typical of rentiers.[43] This was responsible, at least in part, for the economic decline in the fifteenth century of some families from the old urban aristocracy whose wealth had by then long been identified with the land.[44]

The mercantile mentality and the world of business (*negotia*) seemed,

[40] At least until the rise of holding companies (F. Melis, *Aspetti della vita economica medievale: Studi nell'Archivio Datini di Prato* (Siena, 1962), pp. 125-34).

[41] A. Sapori, 'Il Rinascimento economico', in idem, *Studi di storia economica (secoli XIII-XIV-XV)* (Florence, 1955), pp. 619-52.

[42] Many examples of these Sienese peculiarities (which gave rise to well-known literary clichés) may be found in Cardini, 'L'argento', pp. 298-312.

[43] For example the adoption, common from the second half of the thirteenth century, of the contract of *mezzadria* on the farms of great landowners: Cherubini, *Signori*, pp. 295-301; Pinto, 'I mercanti e la terra', pp. 251-63.

[44] G. Catoni and G. Piccinni, 'Alliramento e ceto dirigente nella Siena del Quattrocento', in *I ceti dirigenti nella Toscana del Quattrocento* (Florence, 1987), pp. 454-55. Only detailed research on the management of great estates between fourteenth and sixteenth centuries can reveal the pace and course of this decline; but such research is impeded by lack of records.

from at least 1400, largely alien to the prevalent culture among the upper
strata of Sienese society. Such activities became dishonourable for
gentlemen, for whom living off the profits of the land or of public office was
more appropriate.[45] Indeed among the great families the concept of
honour was often connected to the management of property.[46] We should
not be deceived by references in the fourteenth and fifteenth centuries to a
lively trading sector in the city:[47] Siena, after all, remained an important
city (the second in Tuscany), with a large territory, and it continued to
offer notable opportunities to small and middling traders operating at a
local or regional level. But they remained small and middling merchants.
Evidence pointing in the opposite direction is much more frequent in the
sources.[48] The contrast with Florence is striking: there trade continued to
be praised as 'that which alone can make cities rich from its many
profits'.[49]

If we return to the first half of the fourteenth century, we can now
reconsider the 'bourgeois ideology' of the great frescoes of Good
Government in Siena and of the preambles to public measures taken
under the goverment of the Nine.[50] In both cases what is expressed is the
mentality, the ideals and the political credo of the class then in power, that
is to say the merchants of the 'middling people' (*mezzana gente*), who
distinguished themselves from the merchant-banking aristocracy. This
mezzana gente, or a sort of *popolo grasso*, was largely composed of merchant
bankers active at a regional level (or at most within Italy), of rich wool
craftsmen, of spicers, goldsmiths, retailers and so on. They were
distinguished, too, from the artisans, shopkeepers, small traders and wage
labourers below them.[51]

Even among the families of the Nine, the aristocratic model was not
slow in establishing itself. At the beginning of the fourteenth century, they

[45] Isaacs, pp. 63-65; Fioravanti, pp. 35-36.

[46] There are numerous examples in the tax declarations of 1453 and 1509, for example:
Archivio di Stato, Siena, *Lira*, 234, declarations of Alessandro Bichi and Crescenzo
Borghesi. The concept was also not infrequently expressed at a collective level: M.
Ginatempo, 'Motivazioni ideali e coscienza della 'crisi' nella politica territoriale di Siena
nel XV secolo', *Ricerche storiche*, xiv (1984), pp. 293, 298.

[47] Cf. Cherubini, 'I mercanti e il potere', pp. 166-68.

[48] Ibid., p. 170. Note also S. Bernardino's sermons, which are full of references to the
merchant class, but which also reveal that it was characteristic of Sienese gentlemen not to
engage 'in any business' ('in niuno esercitio'), in contrast to those in other cities.

[49] '. . . que sola potest reddere civitates multis proventibus opulentas': D. De Rosa,
Coluccio Salutati: Il cancelliere e il pensatore politico (Florence, 1980), p. 38. In general, see C.
Bec, *Les marchands écrivains: Affaires et humanisme à Florence, 1375-1434* (Paris, 1967).

[50] Cf. L. Carbone, 'Note sull' ideologia e la prassi politica di una oligarchia borghese del
'300 (I Nove di Siena, 1287-1355)', Tesi di laurea, University of Florence, Facoltà di
Lettere e Filosofia, 1976-77; C. Frugoni, 'Il governo dei Nove a Siena e il loro credo politico
nell'affresco di Ambrogio Lorenzetti', *Quaderni medievali*, vii-viii (1979); Cherubini, 'I
mercanti e il potere', p. 191.

[51] Bowsky, p. 20; Cherubini, 'I mercanti e il potere', pp. 178-79.

already held considerable landed property;[52] and later, in the fifteenth, they took a leading part in a further expropriation of peasant and common land in the *contado*.[53] By the mid fifteenth century, tax returns show the families of the Nine to be richer on average than families of the other urban *Monti*, including that of the *Gentiluomini*.[54] Their wealth was predominantly composed of land. At the same time they fully adopted aristocratic behaviour. Thus one of the Borghesi family could calmly write in his tax-return that 'it is not proper for a knight to seek after profit', in order to justify a lifestyle beyond his means.[55] This success of the aristocratic model in penetrating the rising middle groups was also assisted by the lack of social replacement in the city: in the fourteenth and fifteenth centuries there was little immigration of *gente nuova* from the subject territory.[56]

Late medieval Siena represents a rare example of the accelerated development of processes and phenomena which in the rest of Italy had a slower pace and achieved their outcome only in the early modern period.[57] Siena saw both a rapid and dazzling expansion and similarly rapid turning in on itself. The mercantile upswing and ideology were suddenly interrupted, before they could fully develop; they gave way to a brisk aristocratisation of society and to a recovery of traditional values. In the triumph of these values the close and 'stifling' relationship with the land played a decisive part. The case of Siena thus provides material to reconsider two contradictory interpretations of late medieval Italy: one which exalts the role of the emergent bourgeoisie and one which speaks of the 'myth of the bourgeoisie'.[58] Italian society between the twelfth and

---

[52] Cherubini, *Signori*, p. 249, n. 19 (referring to the works of Bowsky).

[53] A.K. Isaacs, 'Le campagne senesi fra Quattro e Cinquecento: regime fondiario e governo signorile', in *Contadini e proprietari nella Toscana moderna*, pp. 377-403; and, in general, Ginatempo, *Crisi*.

[54] Catoni and Piccinni, pp. 454-58.

[55] Ibid., p. 453.

[56] Thus, for the fourteenth century: G. Piccinni, 'I "villani incittadinati" nella Siena del XIV secolo', *Bull. senese di storia patria*, lxxxii-iii (1975-76). The case of the Spannocchi in the fifteenth century, migrating from a small town of the Val di Merse, would seem exceptional.

[57] Jones, *Economia e società*, pp. 50-69, 172-89. Piacenza's development between thirteenth and fourteenth centuries was similar: P. Racine, 'Verso la Signoria', in *Storia di Piacenza*, ii. *Dal vescovo conte alla signoria (996-1313)* (Piacenza, 1984), pp. 301-14.

[58] See the debate initiated by Jones, *Economia e società* (the introductory section of which first appeared in 1978 in the *Annali* of the Einaudi *Storia d'Italia*): S. Polica, 'Basso Medioevo e Rinascimento: rifeudalizzazione e transizione', *Bullettino dell'Istituto storico italiano per il Medio Evo*, lxxxviii (1979); M. Nobili, 'L'equazione città antica – città comunale ed il "mancato sviluppo italiano" nel saggio di Philip Jones', *Società e storia*, x (1980); P. Cammarosano, 'L'economia italiana nell'età dei Comuni e il modo feudale di produzione: una discussione', ibid., v (1979); R. Bordone, 'Tema cittadino e 'ritorno alla terra' nella storiografia comunale recente', *Quaderni storici*, lii (1983).

sixteenth centuries revolved around two opposite poles. On the one hand were the innovative elements, new economic activities (trade, banking, manufacture), and a different concept of society, of institutions and of relations between men and between groups. These elements, naturally gathered within cities, were promoted or adopted by largely new classes and represented a break with established values. On the other hand were the elements of tradition: the seigneurial world, the role of land as a sign of power, a more clearly hierarchical concept of society, all of which were expressed in particular styles of behaviour.[59] From the dialogue between these two poles – but sometimes from the combination of individual elements – proceeded the diversity of social, political and institutional conditions in the Italian city communes.[60] Siena, though showing a highly individual development, did not fall outside this general pattern.

[59] Both elements are discussed by Jones, *Economia e società*, esp. pp. 122-25.

[60] For the application of this method to a specific case, see S. Collodo, 'Il ceto dominante padovano, dal comune alla signoria (secoli XII-XIV)', in *Istituzioni, società e potere nella Marca trevigiana e veronese (secoli XIII-XIV)* (Rome, 1988), p. 27.

8

Governments and Schools in Late Medieval Italy

Peter Denley

At the beginning of the fifteenth century[1] the Dominican preacher and reformer Giovanni Dominici, in a book of advice to a Florentine gentlewoman on the bringing-up of children, had this to say about schooling:

> The world being as it is, you would place your son in great danger if you sent him to learn with the religious or with clerics; they are a motley crew, and he would learn little . . . If you send him to the common school where the rabble congregates, wretched and uncontrollable as they are, prone to evil and resistant to good, I fear he would lose in one year what he has laboured to gain in seven.[2]

This cavalier dismissal of two of the available forms of public teaching is often quoted, and rightly so. The first comment, all the more surprising coming from an ecclesiastic, would have found an echo with the majority of parents. Ecclesiastically-organised teaching of the laity was very much in eclipse in late medieval Italy, victim of upheavals and changes of emphasis within organised religion and overshadowed by a burgeoning demand for secular education.[3] The second comment is probably more

---

[1] Earlier versions of this article were read as papers to the London Medieval Society and to Nicolai Rubinstein's seminar on Medieval Italian History at the Institute of Historical Research, University of London. I am grateful to those who commented at that stage. Paul F. Grendler's book *Schooling in Renaissance Italy: Literacy and Learning, 1300-1600* (Princeton, 1988) was published when this article was at an advanced stage; I have incorporated many valuable points from this work, which helped to clarify my thinking without substantially altering the main argument. My chief debt of gratitude, however, is to Philip Jones who as my research supervisor first aroused my interest in the history of Italian education.

[2] G. Dominici, *Regola del governo di cura familiare*, ed. D. Salvi (Florence, 1860), p. 134 (my translation).

[3] For fuller discussion, Grendler, pp. 6-11; see also C. Frova, 'La scuola nella città tardomedievale: un impegno pedagogico e organizzativo', in R. Elze and G. Fasoli (eds.), *La città in Italia e in Germania nel Medioevo: cultura, istituzioni, vita religiosa*. Annali dell'Istituto storico italo-germanico, Quaderno viii (Bologna, 1981), pp. 121-22 and nn. 7, 8.

particular to Florence, where a vein of patrician distrust of public schooling is clearly in evidence. Elsewhere in Italy a revolution was taking place in the way in which education was organised. State intervention was increasingly extending into this area as it was in others.[4] Patterns were established largely with the assistance of government legislation; modes and the content of teaching, the salaries and conditions of the teachers, and by the sixteenth century the behaviour of the taught, were all gradually becoming more defined and regulated. This essay will examine the growth of the government's role in pre-university education, and will discuss the extent to which governments could be said to have shaped the educational system of Renaissance Italy.

In the high Middle Ages, Italy was the chief home of what classical and juridical tradition called 'public schools', that is schools which were open to all who were willing to pay,[5] though it would be fanciful to suppose the secular urban schools of medieval Italy to be direct descendants of the public schools of late antiquity.[6] The transition from these 'public' schools to the communal schools of the late Middle Ages and early Renaissance, and ultimately to the communally-supported schools in which teaching might be free to the pupil, occurs in the 'long fourteenth century', but is gradual and complex to trace. There are many shades of communal involvement before the emergence of the fully-salaried teacher. Towns could commission, protect or assist teachers without actually paying them. When they did pay them, it was rare for that to be the sole source of the teacher's income; student fees were still regularly part of the arrangement.

In the small- and medium-sized towns of Italy a pattern can be detected. Many of them yield evidence, for the thirteenth century or earlier, of the presence of the occasional teacher of grammar; some towns, like Arezzo and Siena, already had several teachers, either at the same time or in rapid succession. 'Public' or state assistance to such teachers often began in response to difficulties in which the teachers found themselves. In the 1259 statutes of Bassano, the commune reinforced the teacher's position, not only by granting him a monopoly of teaching in the town, but also by declaring that students who had attended classes for

---

[4] The terms 'state' or 'government' are inadequate generic terms used here to underline the point that, in educational policy as in many other areas, the similarities between republican and princely administration far outweigh the differences. In this I follow the historiographical tradition that derives from Philip Jones's seminal article 'Communes and Despots: the City-State in Late-Medieval Italy', *Transactions of the Royal Historical Society*, 5th series, xv (1965).

[5] Cf. Grendler, p. 5, nn. 19, 20 on terminology, which I follow here.

[6] G. Arnaldi, 'Students and Professors in Thirteenth-Century Italy', *Italian Quarterly*, xlix (1982), 78; Italian version: 'Studenti e professori nell'Italia del secolo XIII: la prospettiva degli studi "in terra aliena"', *La Cultura*, xx (1982), 420.

eight days had to pay fees for the whole month, even if they dropped out of the class.[7] A century later (1365) the town of Montagnana, in hiring a teacher, and again in giving him a monopoly, guaranteed him sixty scholars or, in the event of a shortfall, the equivalent income from communal funds.[8] Tax exemptions were often given, as were exemptions from military service,[9] and other incentives or rewards such as the granting of citizenship to immigrant teachers.[10] Another regular form of subsidy was assistance with the renting of premises. This is mentioned in a Sienese deliberation of 1268,[11] and in the 1270s the Veronese, when hiring a grammarian, gave him free use of a house.[12] It reappears in Pistoia in 1332,[13] and in Lucca in 1334,[14] and soon became a regular element in teachers' contracts. Later, in several towns a house was actually given to the teacher: in Vigevano in 1377, in Cuneo in 1434 and in many Lombard and Piedmontese towns in the mid and late fifteenth century.[15]

The growth of salaried appointments is not easy to trace. Communally-paid grammar teachers first appeared in the thirteenth century, but it is

[7] Ibid.; cf. provisions in Bra (1357): F. Gabotto, *Lo stato sabaudo da Amedeo VIII al Emanuele Filiberto* (Turin and Rome, 1895), vol. iii, 309-10, tr. in C. Frova, *Istruzione e educazione nel medioevo* (Turin, 1973), p. 112. Arnaldi speculates that the intention may have been to protect the teacher from seasonal fluctuations in the student attendance in a small urban community with strong rural and agrarian connections. In 1297 this provision was strengthened: a student who dropped out after a month had nonetheless to pay six months' fees: Arnaldi, *ubi supra*. In Cuorgnè in 1416 the law was even fiercer: a student who attended the communal school for fifteen consecutive days had to pay the whole year's fee: Frova, *Istruzione*, p. 113.

[8] P. Sambin, 'Un maestro di grammatica condotto dal comune di Montagnana nel 1365', in L. Gargan, P. Sambin and G. Zanato, 'Note e documenti per la storia dei maestri e delle scuole di grammatica', *Quaderni per la Storia dell'Università di Padova*, ii (1969), 78-81. A monopoly is further stipulated in Ivrea: G. Manacorda, *Storia della scuola in Italia. Il medioevo* (Palermo, 1914, repr. Florence, 1980), i, 173.

[9] E.g. in 1332 a Pistoiese master was given exemption from all taxes except the *gabella* for five years: A. Zanelli, *Del pubblico insegnamento in Pistoia dal XIV al XVI secolo* (Rome, 1900), pp. 9, 115-16. Manacorda, i, 175 gives examples of this from Brescia, Ferrara and Genoa; for a Sienese example see *Chartularium Studii Senensis*, ed. G. Cecchini and G. Prunai (Siena, 1942), doc. 13, pp. 10-11 (1262).

[10] For example in Siena one Simone da Campiglia was granted citizenship because 'intentio sui est pueros docere et scolas retinere cum ipse sit bonus gramaticus': A[rchivio di] S[tato], S[iena], *Consiglio Generale*, 172, fo. 45, 21 Apr. 1365. Cf. Zanelli, *ubi supra*. In fifteenth-century Palermo citizenship was on two occasions given to all foreign grammar teachers: S. Tramontana, 'Scuola, maestri, allievi', in *La cultura in Sicilia nel Quattrocento. Mostra, Messina, Salone del Comune, 1982* (Rome, 1982), p. 42.

[11] *Chartularium*, doc. 18, p. 13 (Apr. 1268).

[12] Grendler, p. 4.

[13] Zanelli, *ubi supra*.

[14] P. Barsanti, *Il pubblico insegnamento in Lucca dal secolo XIV alla fine del secolo XVIII* (Lucca, 1905, repr. Bologna, 1980), p. 108.

[15] Manacorda, i, 175.

not always clear at what level they were to teach.[16] Part of the reason for this difficulty is the fact, not previously emphasised, that all the evidence to date has been found in university towns or towns which were attempting to establish a university. It seems at least possible that the appearance of salaried grammar teachers is connected with the growth of salaried lectureships at university level – in which Italy led the way in the thirteenth century.[17] Verona's appointment of a grammar teacher in the 1270s coincides with the town's attempts to establish a *studium generale*.[18] Another contemporary example arose out of the rivalry between Arezzo and Siena over teachers. Maestro Tebaldo, a Sienese, is found teaching in Siena from the 1240s and, incidentally, helping the commune in its attempts to lure teachers and students of the higher subjects to the city in a bid to establish a *studium generale*.[19] In 1262 statutes Tebaldo, now described as 'fons vivus gramatice facultatis', was offered privileges, and a 'salarium sive feudum', if he would return from Arezzo where he was being 'held' to the shame of the Sienese.[20] By 1268 his rent was being paid, and in 1269 he was in receipt of a communal salary of 7 *lire* 10 *denari* for six months.[21] In the 1270s a Maestro Fantino, teacher of grammar, was hired,[22] and by 1278 Maestro Guidotto da Bologna was also teaching rhetoric for public remuneration.[23] By 1287, with the hiring of Bandino d'Arezzo to teach grammar, Siena was getting its revenge on the Aretines for their poaching of Tebaldo.[24] Paolo Nardi's imminent work on the first century of the Sienese *studio* may well establish which of these teachers was active at elementary level; in the meantime the strong possibility must be that at

[16] *Pace* Grendler (pp. 23-24 ff.), there are many cases where terminology is used imprecisely; a late example from Siena reads 'Maestro Antonio di ser Salvi da San Gimignano maestro di gramaticha chondotto a legiare *ne lo studio* di Siena a legiare et insegnare gramaticha et autori' (ASS, *Biccherna*, 460, fo. 12v (1388): my italics), which defies Grendler's categorisation. The fact that university towns included some schoolmasters under their university administration does not help; it also raises the question of how distinct the two groups actually were. Some teachers may well have taught at both school and higher levels.

[17] A.B. Cobban, 'Elective Salaried Lectureships in the Universities of Southern Europe in the Pre-Reformation Era', *Bulletin of the John Rylands Library of Manchester*, lxvii (1985), 663.

[18] R. Avesani, 'Il preumanesimo veronese', in *Storia della cultura veneta*, ii, *Il Trecento* (Vicenza, 1976), p. 112; Grendler, p. 4.

[19] *Chartularium*, docs. 2 (pp. 4-5, 13 Sept. 1241) and 5 (p. 7, Sept. 1248).

[20] *Chartularium*, doc. 13, p. 11.

[21] *Chartularium*, docs. 18-20 (p. 13, Apr. and Sept. 1268, June 1269).

[22] *Chartularium*, docs. 22 (p. 15, March 1275), 28 and 29 (pp. 20-1, March and Dec. 1276).

[23] *Chartularium*, doc. 30, p. 21. Cf. F. Novati, 'Le epistole dantesche', in his *Freschi e Minii del Dugento* (Milan, 1908), pp. 329-61, esp. pp. 335-42.

[24] *Chartularium*, doc. 63 (p. 44, 3 Oct. 1287), and docs. until 126, p. 106 (1310).

least some of them were.[25]

We are on firmer ground by the fourteenth century, where from the first decade onwards a number of non-university towns began to hire grammar teachers.[26] If we use the first known date of a salaried appointment in a town as a crude but workable measure, we can gain a rough impression of the pace at which the movement grew. The list is of course not exhaustive, but includes the more important ones. In 1308 Ivrea hired a grammar teacher,[27] followed by San Gimignano in 1314,[28] Treviso in 1316,[29] Turin in 1327,[30] Pistoia in 1332,[31] Savona in 1339,[32] Moncalieri in 1347,[33] Lucca in 1348,[34] Bassano in 1349.[35] Spoleto resolved in 1347 to hire a grammar teacher, as did Rieti in 1349, though in both cases it is over a decade before we have firm evidence that the decisions were implemented.[36] In the second half of the century the pace is maintained: Bra (1357);[37] Feltre (1364);[38] Vigevano (1377);[39] Chioggia (by the 1380s);[40] Sarzana

[25] Forthcoming in the series *Orbis Academicus: saggi e documenti per la storia dell'Università di Siena*, ii (1990).

[26] An unusual precursor to the communally-sponsored communal school is found in the famous contract of Portovenere, where in 1260 a private citizen, Giovanni di Filippo Nasi, hired a teacher to keep open school; it appears from the contract that only pupils from outside the town had to pay fees, though Giovanni retained the right to veto pupils from the town itself: Frova, *Istruzione*, pp. 107-9.

[27] Manacorda, i, 173.

[28] J. Vichi Imberciadori, 'L'istruzione in San Gimignano dal sec. XIII al sec. XX', *Miscellanea storica della Valdelsa*, lxxxvi (1980), 61.

[29] Grendler, p. 12; A. Serena, *La cultura umanistica a Treviso nel secolo decimoquinto*. Miscellanea di storia veneta, ser. 3, iii (Venice, 1912), p. 49.

[30] Manacorda, i, 172-73, and ii, 329; D. Sassi, *L'istruzione pubblica in Torino dal 1300 al 1880* (Turin, 1880), p. 14, preceding Grendler's reference (p. 12) to one in 1337.

[31] Not 1322 as Grendler has it (p. 12). Zanelli, pp. 9, 115-16. The contract is given as a result of a petition 'pro parte scolarium volentium se instrui in arte gramatica, loice et dictaminis'.

[32] G. Petti Balbi, *L'insegnamento nella Liguria medievale. Scuole, maestri, libri* (Genoa, 1979), p. 131.

[33] Manacorda, i, 173.

[34] Barsanti, p. 50.

[35] G. Chiuppani, 'Storia di una scuola di grammatica dal Medio Evo fino al Seicento (Bassano)', *Nuovo Archivio Veneto*, n.s., xxix (1915), 85; Grendler, p. 12.

[36] L. Fausti, *Le scuole e la cultura a Spoleto* (Spoleto, 1943), pp. 29-30; A. Sacchetti-Sassetti, 'I maestri di grammatica in Rieti sullo scorcio del medioevo', *Bollettino della R. Deputazione di Storia Patria per l'Umbria* vii (1901), 467-68. The first salary known to be paid in Spoleto was in 1361; Rieti's first surviving payment dates from 1360 (Fausti, p. 31).

[37] Manacorda, *ubi supra*.

[38] L. Gargan, 'Un maestro di grammatica a Padova e a Feltre nel secondo Trecento', in Gargan, Sambin and Zanato, pp. 71-77, esp. pp. 71-74.

[39] Manacorda, *ubi supra*.

[40] V. Bellemo, 'L'insegnamento e la cultura in Chioggia fino al secolo XV', *Archivio Veneto*, n.s., xxxv (1888), 283; cf. Grendler, p. 12.

(1396);[41] Modena (1397);[42] Udine (1400).[43] Early fifteenth-century in-
augurations include Recanati (1405);[44] Faenza (1410);[45] Novara (1412);[46]
Bergamo (1430);[47] Brescia (1432).[48] Thereafter the phenomenon is
ubiquitous; in Liguria, Piedmont, the Veneto, the Marches, and
particularly in Sicily,[49] all medium-sized towns, many small ones and not
a few rural communities were appointing teachers, and continuing to do
so on a regular basis.

The clear acceleration of state sponsorship of education in the
fourteenth and fifteenth centuries is very much in tune with the findings of
historians who are looking at state provision for medicine, public health
and other aspects of civic government in the period.[50] But the evidence
adds little that is conclusive to the current revived debate about the role of
the Black Death itself in transforming education and the state's attitude to
it. The example of Lucca is often cited: in 1348 Maestro Filippo requested
the authorities in Lucca to give him assistance, since the plague had
reduced the number of scholars below the level at which he could live off
their fees. He was granted a salary, the first in Lucca's history, and taught
there until 1354.[51] Later in the fourteenth century the salaried teaching
post was revived at Lucca,[52] and it is found throughout the fifteenth
century on an almost continuous basis. But such continuity is found right
across Italy, and the list of first appearances confirms that the movement
was well in motion before the first epidemic.

[41] Petti Balbi, pp. 118-19.

[42] G. Bertoni and E.P. Vicini, 'Gli studi di grammatica e la rinascenza a Modena', *Atti
e memorie della R. Deputazione di Storia Patria per le Provincie Modenesi*, ser. 5, iv (1906), 168-69.

[43] D. Ongaro, *Le scuole pubbliche in Udine nel secolo XV* (Udine, 1885), p. 2.

[44] R.M. Borraccini Verducci, 'La scuola pubblica a Recanati nel secolo XV', *Università
di Macerata. Annali della Facoltà di Lettere e Filosofia*, viii (1975), p. 125.

[45] P. Zama, *Le istituzioni scolastiche faentine nel medio evo (sec. XI-XVI)* (Milan, 1920), pp.
53-55.

[46] Manacorda, *ubi supra*.

[47] F. Chiappa, *Una pubblica scuola di grammatica a Palazzolo nella seconda metà del 1400*
(Brescia, 1964), p. 30.

[48] A. Zanelli, 'Gabriele da Concoreggio ed il Comune di Brescia', *Archivio Storico
Lombardo*, ser. 3, xi (1899), 63-64.

[49] Tramontana, *ubi supra*.

[50] Cf. Vivian Nutton, 'Continuity or Rediscovery? The City Physician in Classical
Antiquity and Medieval Italy', in *The Town and State Physician in Europe from the Middle Ages
to the Enlightenment*, ed. A.W. Russell, Wolfenbütteler Forschungen, xvii (1981), pp. 9-46,
esp. pp. 24-34; Richard Palmer, 'Physicians and the State in Post-Medieval Italy', ibid.,
pp.47-61, esp. pp. 47-49; cf. Grendler, p. 14: 'The schoolmaster took his place alongside
the communal physician and surgeon as a public servant providing services for the public
good'. Among the common features might be mentioned the obligation, by the fifteenth
century, on many communally paid teachers to take in poor without payment – just as the
medico condotto was usually obliged to treat the poor without charge: Nutton, pp. 32-33.

[51] Barsanti, pp. 50-51, 195; also Grendler, p. 13.

[52] Barsanti, pp. 51, 109.

This universal appearance of communally-appointed and salaried grammar teachers in small towns was by no means uniformly echoed in the larger cities. Here the role of state intervention was much delayed and much weaker. The scale of large towns, and the reasons for which they achieved that scale, meant that independent, private teaching was well embedded long before communal appointments became fashionable. For Florence, Giovanni Villani's famous description of 1338 tells of 8,000 to 10,000 boys and girls *a leggere*, of 1,000 to 1,200 boys attending six abacus schools, and of 550-600 attending four schools for grammar and logic. Whatever conclusions one reaches about his statistical reliability, the message of a high level of literacy must be accepted,[53] and this is supported by more objective evidence from fiscal rcords in the fifteenth century.[54] Less exaggerated, perhaps, but also impressive is Bonvesin de la Riva's description of Milan, which according to him boasted eight grammar and over seventy elementary teachers.[55] For Venice, more solid evidence is available: for the period 1300 to 1450 Bertanza and Dalla Santa's trawl through the archives in the late nineteenth century identified 850 teachers present in Venice at one stage or another.[56] In Genoa the numerous private teachers went so far as to establish a college or guild in 1298, through which thirteen regent masters effectively controlled all aspects of teaching in the city. The research of Giovanna Petti Balbi has reconstructed for us the workings of this guild. The many private contracts between teachers show the extent to which schools were set up and operated as commercial enterprises, while the guild provided a means of repelling intruders, regulating the number of pupils in each school, resisting competition from the clergy and defending the financial interests of the regent masters and those who taught under them.[57]

[53] See now Grendler, pp. 71-74 for a thorough if mechanistic refutation of the figures; and A. Frugoni, 'G. Villani, "Cronica", XI, 94', *Bullettino dell'Istituto Storico Italiano*, lxxvii (1965), pp. 229-55 (esp. pp. 251-52) for a consideration of the problem in relation to the whole passage. For a more positive assessment of the value of Villani's description of Florentine schooling, G. Ricuperati, 'Università e scuola in Italia', in *Letteratura italiana*, i (Turin, 1982), *Il letterato e le istituzioni*, p. 985.

[54] D. Herlihy and C. Klapisch-Zuber, *Les toscans et leurs familles: une étude du catasto florentin de 1427* (Paris, 1978), pp. 563-64 suggest that a substantial proportion of declarations from subject towns had children at school, although the *catasto* is not very helpful on school attendance generally (on Florentine education generally, pp. 563-68). A. Verde, *Lo studio fiorentino 1473-1503. Ricerche e Documenti*, iii: *Studenti, fanciulli a scuola nel 1480* (Pistoia, 1977), ii, 1005-206, has published the relevant material from the 1480 declarations; for an analysis see Grendler, pp. 74-78.

[55] Bonvicinus de Ripa, 'De magnalibus urbis Mediolani', ed. F. Novati, *Bullettino dell'Istituto Storico Italiano*, xx (1898), 87, quoted in Frova, *Istruzione*, p. 106; cf. Ricuperati, p. 986.

[56] E. Bertanza and G. Dalla Santa, *Documenti per la storia della cultura in Venezia*, i: *Maestri, scuole e scolari in Venezia fino al 1500* (Venice, 1907), p. xiv.

[57] Petti Balbi, esp. ch. 3. (That not all went smoothly is neatly illustrated by the offer by the college in 1398 of a pension of 250 *lire* per annum for five years to Maestro Oddo

In all these towns communal salaried posts came late, and usually only at the intermediate, pre-university level. It was only here that the need to regulate and support teaching was felt. In Venice there is no sign of communal appointments before the fifteenth century.[58] Then the Venetians set up two schools, the Scuola di Rialto, opened in 1403, for the teaching of philosophy, and the Scuola di San Marco which grew in the mid fifteenth century for the teaching of *studia humanitatis* to those sons of the Venetian patriciate destined for the Chancellery. These were distinguished schools of secondary-to-higher level, but they made no impression on elementary teaching.[59] In Genoa communally-paid teachers and a public school made belated appearances in the late fourteenth century, and in the fifteenth century this communal school gradually took over at the higher level. Fifteenth-century Milan saw ducal patronage of pre-university-level grammar teachers, but no evidence has been found of salaries for elementary teachers.[60] In Florence the university rolls incorporate a few masters of grammar from the early fifteenth century, but they were only a small proportion of the teachers in the town as a whole: there were two from 1452, and four (usually) from 1469 onwards.[61] Again it seems that these were not teaching at the elementary level. Communal intervention was necessary because of the very small proportion of children in these schools.[62]

Mention has been made of grammarians on university rolls. In university towns (where, as has been seen, the communally-salaried schoolteacher first appeared) an administrative body for education already existed – *savi* or *riformatori dello studio* – and it was natural that the organisation, hiring and paying of schoolmasters should be delegated to that body.[63] The practice is first found in Perugia in the fourteenth century.[64] Under these auspices, continuity and regulation were

Mallone if he promised not to teach in Genoa during that period! p. 85.)

[58] Historians are agreed that we must exempt the payment of a pension to Maestro Corbaccino, a grammarian who lost his possessions in a fire in 1322 and who lived largely off the state until his death in old age over 25 years later. This is a caritative rather than an educational subsidy: M. Pastore Stocchi, 'Scuola e cultura umanistica fra due secoli', in *Storia della cultura veneta* (Vicenza, 1980), vol. III, i, 102; cf. Grendler, p. 38.

[59] F. Lepori, 'La scuola di Rialto dalla fondazione alla metà del '500', in *Storia della cultura veneta*, vol. III, ii, 539-605 (esp. p. 548 ff.); F. Gilbert, 'Humanism in Venice', in *Florence and Venice: Comparisons and Relations* (Florence, 1979), i, 13-26 (pp. 15-16 esp.); J.B. Ross, 'Venetian Schools and Teachers Fourteenth to Early Sixteenth Century; a Survey and a Study of Giovanni Battista Egnazio', *Renaissance Quarterly*, xxix (1976), pp. 521-66 has a good historiographical survey. Cf. Grendler, p. 61.

[60] L. Banfi, 'Scuola ed educazione nella Milano dell'ultimo Quattrocento', in *Milano nell'età di Ludovico il Moro* (Milan, 1983), 387-95 (esp. pp. 392-93).

[61] Grendler, p. 25.
[62] Grendler, p. 75.
[63] On this theme, see now Grendler, pp. 23-29.
[64] Grendler, p. 24.

facilitated, and by the fifteenth century grammar teachers were often provided for the different administrative areas of the town. In this respect the two, later four, salaried posts under the Florentine *studio* represent a small-scale and belated gesture; fifteenth-century Bologna had anything from eight to fifteen grammarians on its civic payroll,[65] while Rome, in covering thirteen *rioni*, had from eight to sixteen grammar teachers covering those posts in the late fifteenth century, on a wide band of salaries.[66]

The spread of communal schools was also less universal in the more specialised area of abacus teaching. Here communal appointments were sporadic and tended to lack continuity. Verona, for example, hired an abacist in 1284 (the earliest known appointment), but the next abacist certain to have received a salary there appears only in 1424.[67] The teaching of abacus was a Tuscan, and particularly a Florentine, speciality (many northern Italian towns hired Florentines), and it is not surprising that the practice of offering communally-salaried abacus posts is to be found particularly in Tuscany (though not in Florence itself).[68] Abacus appointments took second place to those in grammar and reading, and were often the first posts to be sacrificed.[69] The exception is Siena, where communal abacus teachers were regularly hired and paid from the late fourteenth century and where, also exceptionally, the organisation of abacus teaching was brought under the control of the *savi dello studio* and eventually even appeared on the university lecture list.[70]

Pre-university education, then, took the form of a 'mixed economy'. Communal schools predominated at the local and small-town level, and appeared in more restricted forms and proportions in the larger cities. Grendler has rightly observed that 'parents and civil governments created the schools of Renaissance Italy'.[71] He is right, too, to place at least the

---

[65] Grendler, pp. 26-29. The extent of this provision, and its increase in the next century, led Grendler to observe (p. 29) that 'Bologna in the first half of the sixteenth century came the closest to establishing a comprehensive state school system in the modern meaning of the term'.

[66] M.C. Dorati da Empoli, 'I lettori dello Studio e maestri di grammatica a Roma', *Rassegna degli Archivi di Stato*, xl (1980), 142-45; E. Lee, 'Humanists and the "Studium Urbis", 1473-1484', in *Umanesimo a Roma nel Quattrocento*, ed. P. Brezzi and M. De Panizza Lorch (Rome, 1984), p. 145.

[67] E. Garibotto, 'Le scuole d'abbaco a Verona', *Atti e Memorie dell'Accademia di Agricoltura, Scienze e Lettere di Verona*, ser. 4, xxiv (1923), pp., 315-16; Grendler, pp. 5, 22, 308.

[68] See esp. Grendler, pp. 22-3 for examples.

[69] For the example of Arezzo, R. Black, 'Humanism and Education in Renaissance Arezzo', *I Tatti Studies. Essays in the Renaissance*, ii (1987), pp. 175-76, 196-97, 232-33.

[70] P. Denley, 'The University of Siena, 1357-1557', unpublished D.Phil. thesis, Oxford, 1981, p. 184; N. Adams, 'The Life and Times of Pietro dell'Abaco, a Renaissance Estimator from Siena (Active 1457-1486)', *Zeitschrift für Kunstgeschichte*, xlviii (1985), 384-95 on an interesting individual example.

[71] Grendler, p. 3.

initial emphasis on parents more than governments. Communal appointments were initially made more out of necessity than out of commitment to education, and in the smaller communes the moving forces behind such decisions were likely to be self-interested parties.[72] But there is more to it than that. Once the pattern of communal schools was established, in all but the largest towns it tended to drive out private teaching, as the town became reliant on the system it had set up. Robert Black has pointed out the rarity of private teachers in late fourteenth- and fifteenth-century Arezzo for this reason; evidence from Siena and other Tuscan towns supports the conclusion.[73] Moreover, the existence of a schoolmaster on the communal payroll naturally prompted the framing of conditions of service and, more generally, legislation about education in the town. The contracts of communal teachers are of special interest. They often reveal much more than their private equivalents. Contracts between parents, or groups of parents, and teachers of necessity confined their stipulations to specific cases and to the relationships between master and pupil, master and parent;[74] but it is in communal, collective contracts that practices could become formalised and codified, and in communal legislation that matters of policy can be traced.

It is in communal contracts and declarations, too, that the motives for intervention were expressed. The communes saw a variety of advantages in hiring a teacher. Foremost of course was the desirability of educating the young in the basics necessary for useful citizenship and perhaps for higher learning. The declarations in the contracts are formulaic and ubiquitous: grammar is described, in echoes or variations of Isidore of Seville's definition, as 'fundamentum et origo omnium liberalium artium' (Siena),[75] or as 'origo et fundamentum omnium virtutum et scientiarum' (Lucca).[76] The benefits to the commune are also frequently stressed, by

[72] Grendler, p. 15: 'Of course, the decision to pay a Latin teacher's salary had personal benefits for the city's leaders; their sons were more likely to attend school than the sons of the laboring classes'.

[73] Black, 'Humanism and Education', p. 175; idem, 'Schools and Teaching in Florentine Tuscany, 1350-1500', paper at the Warburg Institute, June 1988; and see my forthcoming article on Sienese schools.

[74] That is not to say that the terms of such contracts may not be extremely revealing; cf. the Portovenere contract of 1260 (Frova, *Istruzione*, pp. 107-9), or the lengthy and detailed Florentine abacus contract published in R.A. Goldthwaite, 'Schools and Teachers of Commercial Arithmetic in Renaissance Florence', *Journal of European Economic History*, i (1972), n. 17, pp. 421-25.

[75] ASS, *Consiglio Generale*, 193, fo. 85v (10 Jan. 1384); cf. *Consiglio Generale* 176, fo. 40 (26 June 1367), and *Consiglio Generale*, 185, fo. 115v (21 Dec. 1375).

[76] Barsanti, p. 212; cf. also p. 107 (document of 1371). On Isidore and his influence in late medieval Italy, Grendler, pp. 162-63. A good anthology of such formulae is to be found in Black, 'Humanism and Education', pp. 206-11, where the declarations are enriched by the Aretines' affirmation of their own glorious tradition of grammar teaching.

the fifteenth century in terms of the promotion of civic values.[77]

Beside their salaries teachers would often be given privileges, exemptions and subsidies of one kind or another, as described above. But once in communal pay, teachers came firmly under communal legislation, and there was often a clear determination that the paymasters should get their money's worth. Often teachers were forbidden to hold other offices, even communal offices; in Siena in 1469 a priest, Ser Marco, had a clause in his contract forbidding him to leave his teaching in order to bury the dead.[78] On the other hand communes might equally wish to make use of their teachers in the areas in which they had expertise. Abacus teachers were particularly liable to such exploitation, and often had an obligation to do surveying work for the commune as and when required. Nicholas Adams has traced the activities of one such Sienese master, Pietro dell'Abbaco, and it is clear from his work and from the communal records that the teaching of a communal abacus teacher could be very interrupted indeed.[79]

The large number of communal contracts also gives a reasonable idea of how such teaching was organised, and shows, not surprisingly given the equally evident mobility of teachers, that a system of considerable homogeneity soon developed. Contracts were short-term – anything from one to five years – though it should be pointed out that three to five years was a longer contract than would be normal for university lecturers in this period. Salaries could vary considerably and were determined by many factors: the age, experience or eminence of the teacher, the likely number of students, the other terms of the contract, and, above all, 'market forces': what sort of teacher the town would get for what it was prepared to offer.[80] The salary would also take into account the need for assistants: it was often stated that a teacher who had more than a stipulated number of scholars had to hire a *ripetitore* to help with the lower classes,[81] and that this was to be paid for by the teacher (although often the commune demanded control over the appointment). The *ripetitori* are neglected figures. Occupying 'the lowest rung of the pedagogical ladder',[82] they

[77] Grendler, pp. 13-14 has a number of examples.

[78] ASS, *Concistoro*, 614, fo. 22v (1 Feb. 1469).

[79] Adams, *ubi supra*. The presence of *ripetitori* or assistants in the classroom could go some way to mitigate the consequences of this policy, but it would not necessarily do so; Maestro Pietro had his sons in with him as *ripetitori* – one of them eventually succeeded him, and indeed the whole school was something of a 'family business' – but they were equally likely to collaborate on their surveying tasks. ASS, *Concistoro*, 626, fo. 62v (22 Feb. 1471); *Concistoro*, 702, fo. 8v (10 Sept. 1483); *Concistoro*, 704, fo. 42v (24 Feb. 1484), etc.

[80] Grendler, pp. 15-20, esp. on procedures for appointment, salaries and contractual conditions.

[81] In Ivrea the number was eighty: Manacorda, i, 183 n. 4 (and p. 184). In Genoa the limit set by the guild was a hundred (Petti Balbi, p. 84). In Parma it was laid down that a *ripetitore* could not have more than fifty students in his charge: Frova, *Istruzione*, pp. 109-11.

[82] Grendler, p. 40; pp. 40-41 generally on *ripetitori*.

provided badly-paid jobs, sometimes for university students,[83] and at the same time were a form of apprenticeship for aspiring schoolmasters.[84]

The division of classes (if that is not too formal a word) is usually also described, since the fees were scaled according to the level of teaching required by the student. It is interesting to note here a range of categories: in Arezzo, Feltre and Cuorgnè into three (*de tabula, non latinantes, latinantes*),[85] in Chioggia, Cuneo and Pistoia into four,[86] in Recanati and Rieti five (*epistolantes* which included the *ars dictandi, latinantes, primi latinantes, illi de Donato* and *scolares de Donato infra*, the last category including those *de charta* or, as described in the Recanati document, *infimi gradus* or *donatistis cum testu, vesperistis, et abecedaristis*).[87] These scales, and the divisions into notional groups (even if they were taught in the same room), do not seem to have differed greatly from their counterparts in private schools. One important point that they do establish, though, is that, in the public schools of small and medium-sized towns, the teacher was employed to teach the whole range of 'arts' education, from how to read through to the pre-university grammar stage. Further evidence of this is the legislation of 1455 in Palazzolo (in the Bresciano), which demanded evidence of attendance of students over fourteen; this was because a number of them had registered as scholars in order to avoid paying tax, but had then abandoned their 'studies' almost immediately.[88] It was by no means always the case that private schools taught at all these levels; indeed, since the weight of demand lay at the elementary level, it is unlikely that many did.

The authorities often also stipulated the fees that teachers could exact from their pupils, which enables the historian to trace the gradual trend in the fifteenth century towards free provision. This is not a dramatic or extensive development. The cost of education did not vary greatly from town to town. It is characterised rather by its overall cheapness; the master aimed to make money by teaching large numbers rather than by charging high fees. The range within the scale of fees did vary, however. In fifteenth-century Recanati and Cuneo those in the highest class paid two-and-a-half times that paid by those in the lowest;[89] in Cuorgnè it was five

[83] P.F. Grendler, 'The Organization of Primary and Secondary Education in the Italian Renaissance', *The Catholic Historical Review*, lxxi (1985), p. 198. In 1430 Udine actually invited a Paduan student to a communal schoolmastership: Ongaro, p. 14.

[84] Cf. Grendler, p. 36.

[85] On Arezzo, Black, 'Humanism and Education', p. 185; on Feltre, Gargan, pp. 73, 75; on Cuorgnè, Frova, *Istruzione*, p. 115.

[86] On Chioggia, Bellemo, p. 283; on Cuneo, Frova, p. 113; on Pistoia, Zanelli, *Pubblico insegnamento*, pp. 36-37; cf. Manacorda, i, 181.

[87] On Recanati, Borraccini Verducci, p. 129; on Rieti, Manacorda, i, 179.

[88] Chiappa, p. 35.

[89] Borraccini Verducci, *ubi supra*; Frova, *Istruzione*, p. 113.

times;[90] and in Pistoia ten times.[91] In Vigevano the students were charged by height, and therefore according to the bench they occupied.[92] In Feltre in 1364 the scholars *de tabula* were to be taught free of charge, *non latinantes* had to pay 6 *grossi*, *latinantes* 12 *grossi* (15 if they were boarders); in addition, the teacher could levy one *grosso* from each scholar at Christmas, and for students from outside Feltre he could charge exactly what he wished.[93] This discrimination between citizens and non-citizens also featured in Arezzo, where by the mid fifteenth century grammarians were allowed to charge only non-citizens.[94] The concept of the genuinely 'public' school, free to all comers, also emerged in the fifteenth century. Three Piedmontese towns removed fees.[95] In Siena similar terms were stipulated by 1462, when Maestro Nicolo da Camerino was forbidden to take any fees in his grammar school;[96] the principle was later extended to the abacist.[97] But these instances are far from universal.

Communal legislation or activity concerning its own salaried teachers forms the bulk of the documentation on educational policy. It seems clear also that it acted as the main vehicle for such policy. But the authorities could legislate on educational matters in general. The quality of privately-contracted teaching could also be of concern. Communes ranged in their attitudes: from the extreme of granting salaried teachers a monopoly (Bassano, Montagnana, Ivrea),[98] to the opposite extreme of declaring, as did Parma in 1347, that anyone could teach without the need for a licence.[99] The middle way, of communal licensing of all teachers, was taken by Ferrara in 1443 on the occasion of the refoundation of the university:

There exists at this time in this city a seminary of evil learning and ignorance. Our citizens desire to instruct their sons and their adolescents in good letters, and they are sunk in I know not what pit from which they can never extricate themselves. That is, certain barbarous teachers – who, far from knowing, never even saw any good literature – have invaded our city, opened schools, and professed grammar. Citizens ignorant of these men's ignorance entrust their sons to them to be educated. They want them to learn and to graduate learned, but they learn those things which later they must unlearn. Lest this

[90] Ibid., p. 115.

[91] Zanelli, *Pubblico insegnamento*, pp. 36-37.

[92] Manacorda, i, 180.

[93] Gargan, p. 73.

[94] Black, 'Humanism and Education', pp. 185-86.

[95] Grendler, p. 104; pp. 104-5 for a discussion of the various attempts to provide free schooling for (some) poor students. Cf. Manacorda, i, 172.

[96] 'Et non havendo altro salario dalli scolari come per lo passato tempo s'e costumato': ASS, *Consiglio Generale*, 229, fo. 256v (23 Aug. 1462).

[97] ASS, *Concistoro*, 704, fo. 42v (24 Feb. 1484).

[98] See above, at nn. 7, 8.

[99] Frova, *Istruzione*, p. 111.

calamity and pest progress further, they decree that no one take scholars to train, nor hold a school, unless first he shall have demonstrated that he is acquainted with good literature or has been approved by the board of the Twelve *Savi* as suited to open a school. If anyone shall dare to do different, let him be ejected from the city as a pestiferous beast.[100]

With this, the authorities were beginning to match the level of regulation achieved by the guild of masters of Genoa, the most powerful example of its kind in Italy.[101]

There could be other forms of control. In Milan the Sforza, while stopping short of licensing teaching, exercised close vigilance over many aspects of teaching in the city, establishing salaries and legislating on classrooms.[102] A final area of state interest that needs further investigation relates to the problem of access to education. As has been seen, some towns made efforts to provide free schooling for the poor. A parallel problem, more pressing perhaps for the middle classes, was that of access to higher education. Subsidies for individuals embarking on further education were not new; Venice provided subsidies for some ducal notaries to enable them to attend school in 1336,[103] and tax exemptions for scholars were also common. In the fifteenth century some towns began actively to subsidise students who wished to go to university: Lucca regularly voted such subsidies,[104] and many Sicilian students received scholarships to enable them to attend northern Italian universities.[105] From 1473 Pistoia administered a bequest to send twelve poor students to university.[106] By the mid sixteenth century the practice was widespread, but for the fifteenth century this remains a neglected topic.

Some towns went further, hiring teachers of higher subjects, and, in the case of Pistoia, even establishing a *Sapienza* or college for pre-university students.[107] For part of the late fifteenth century, Pistoia nursed hopes of becoming the seat of the Florentine *studio*, and this serves as a reminder of the artificiality of the boundary between school and higher education. University towns exemplify the dangers of treating them as discrete categories. The growth of government control of universities in Italy was contemporaneous with that of the schools, again with salaried appointments being the key development. University administration

[100] F. Borsetti, *Historia almi Ferrariae gymnasii*, i (Ferrara, 1735), p. 50; translation in L. Thorndike, *University Records and Life in the Middle Ages* (New York, 1971), p. 337.

[101] Milan also had such a college from the end of the fourteenth century, though it awaits study: Banfi, p. 392.

[102] Banfi, *ubi supra*.

[103] Grendler, p. 61.

[104] Barsanti, pp. 68-83.

[105] Tramontana, p. 39.

[106] Zanelli, *Pubblico insegnamento*, pp. 59 ff.

[107] Zanelli, *ubi supra*.

involved many of the same issues: the attraction and retention of good teachers; provision of opportunities for study for the poor student; efficient use of financial and physical resources. The fact that they administered their schools as part of the *studio* should also make it clear that their educational policy cannot be fully understood unless all aspects are considered.

A final point relates to the larger educational revolution of the fifteenth century. The role of the communal school system in the spread of the humanistic educational programme needs to be studied too. Grendler has traced it very clearly; the terms of communal contracts often make it clear what style of teaching, sometimes even what texts, were required.[108] What has perhaps not been sufficiently emphasised is the value of these schools for the spread of humanism. From the humanists' point of view, government control of education had become extensive at a highly convenient point in time. The humanists were involved in communal schools from very early on. Guarino himself taught at several centres in northern Italy, as did Gasparino Barzizza; their pupils all gravitated towards public posts. Ognibene Leoniceno, a pupil of Vittorino, began teaching as an independent in 1436; in 1441 Treviso appointed him to a public post, and there followed a teaching career of four decades, of which thirty years were in communal pay.[109] The great mobility of many of these teachers, as well as their number, ensured that many towns had an opportunity to hire a humanist. The communal schools provided much of the infrastructure on which careers could be launched; the system constituted a ready network, the public schools of the smaller towns feeding into the more prestigious ones, such as San Marco in Venice, or into university lectureships. Udine provided the springboard for Marcantonio Sabellico to gain a chair in Venice;[110] Arezzo, by its constant and dedicated emphasis on the teaching of grammar by its public teachers, continued its long tradition of supplying men of letters to the Florentine republic.[111] If there is validity in the currently fashionable view that the success of the humanists had to do with their alliance with power as much as with the intrinsic merits of their approach,[112] then the role of the communal schools, and particularly the educational policy of governments, deserve closer study.

[108] Grendler, pp. 136-41.

[109] Grendler, pp. 133-35.

[110] Ongaro, pp. 40 ff.; M. King, *Venetian Humanism in an Age of Patrician Dominance* (Princeton, 1986), pp. 425-27.

[111] Black, 'Humanism and Education'; idem, *Benedetto Accolti and the Florentine Renaissance* (Cambridge, 1985) are recent studies.

[112] Cf. A. Grafton and L. Jardine, *From Humanism to the Humanities* (London, 1986), esp. chs. 3 and 4.

9

'Una Città Fatticosa': Dominican Preaching and the Defence of the Republic in Late Medieval Siena

Bernadette Paton

The contribution of the orders of preaching friars to the civic spirit of the late medieval Italian communes has long been acknowledged by historians, and particular attention has been paid, over the last thirty years, to the political theology of Florentine Dominicans as it was developed and propounded in sermons and other pastoral expositions. The works of preachers such as Remigio de' Girolami, Giordano da Pisa, and Girolamo Savonarola have been analysed, in the context of the social and political environment of late medieval Florence, to try to ascertain the extent to which their political theories were moulded by contemporary influences and events.[1] Such examinations have drawn attention to the way in which these individuals formulated their moral theology largely in response to local experience and adapted traditional theological *auctores*, such as Augustine and Aquinas, to deal with problems peculiar to their time and place. This method is, perhaps, most clearly seen in the response of preachers like Remigio and Savonarola to specific crises of the Florentine Republic.[2]

The aim of this essay is to extend this discourse by examining, within the context of the Sienese republic of the late fifteenth century, some political imagery in the sermons of two Sienese Dominican preachers.

[1] C.T. Davis, 'Remigio de' Girolami and Dante: A Comparison of their Conceptions of Peace', in *Studi Danteschi*, xxxvi (1959); idem, 'An early Florentine Political Theorist. Fra Remigio de' Girolami', *Proceedings of the American Philosophical Society*, civ (1960); L. Minio-Paluello, 'Remigio Girolami's *De Bono Communi*: Florence at the time of Dante's Banishment and the Philosopher's Answer to the Crisis', *Italian Studies*, ii (1956); C. Delcorno, *Giordano da Pisa e l'antica predicazione volgare* (Rome, 1975); D. Weinstein, *Savonarola and Florence: Prophecy and Patriotism in the Renaissance* (Princeton, 1970). For a general overview of mendicant preaching in the Italian communes, see Delcorno, *La predicazione nell'età comunale* (Florence, 1974) and R. Rusconi, *Predicatori e predicazione in Italia (sec. IX-XVIII)*, in *Storia d'Italia, Annali*, iv. *Intellettuali e potere* (Turin, 1981); for Sienese preaching in particular, B.T. Paton, *Preaching Friars and the Civic Ethos in Late Medieval Siena* (Oxford, D.Phil. thesis, 1986).
[2] Minio-Paluello, p. 59; Weinstein, chapter viii.

109

Such an analysis should help to answer an important question: was the close relationship beween Dominican preaching and political experience, as found in Florence, in fact common to all city-states in which the Dominicans contributed markedly to the development of a civic ethos? Or are the political sermons of the most notable Florentine Dominicans best seen as the isolated reactions of individual preachers of exceptional civic awareness to conditions and events peculiar to that city?

The political environment of Siena in the late fifteenth century was not such as to incite a dramatic response on the part of local preachers, as had been the case in Florence either in the early fourteenth century, when the warring factions of Black and White Guelfs inspired Remigio de' Girolami's denunciations of division, or in 1494, when the expulsion of the Medici and the threat of French invasion drew forth the apocalyptic political theology of Savonarola. In contrast to Florence, the city-state of Siena has received scant attention from historians, and this has, in the past, made the analysis of sermons preached there somewhat problematical.[3] In recent years, however, a number of studies have focussed attention on Florence's unfortunate sister-state in her last century as a republic, and these works have delineated the prevailing political trends clearly enough to enable us to characterise the environment in which such sermons were written and delivered.[4]

Perhaps the most striking feature to emerge from these analyses is the extent to which the Sienese experiences in the period may be seen as negative rather than positive. The period of affluence and peace which the city had enjoyed under the relatively stable rule of the Nine in the late thirteenth and early fourteenth centuries had given way, in the late fourteenth century, to revolution, division and economic recession. The

[3] Historians have, for the most part, been dependent on the Sienese chronicles for the late medieval period, especially those collected in L.A. Muratori, *Rerum Italicarum Scriptores* (new edn., Bologna, 1931), XV, part vi, *Cronache Senesi* (ed. A. Lisini and F. Iacometti). The two sixteenth- and seventeenth-century histories of the city (O. Malavolti, *Historia de' fatti e guerre de' Senesi*, 2 vols. (Venice, 1599) and G. Tommasi, *Dell'historie di Siena* (Venice, 1625)) are based largely on these chronicles, as is F. Schevill's *Siena: The Story of a Medieval Commune* (Siena, 1909, repr. 1964).

[4] Those used in this survey include: M. Ascheri, *Siena nel Rinascimento. Istituzioni e sistema politico* (Siena, 1985); W. Bowsky, *A Medieval Italian Commune: Siena under the Nine* (University of California, 1981); idem, 'The Impact of the Black Death upon Sienese Government and Society', *Speculum*, xxxix (1964); D. Hicks, 'Sienese Society in the Renaissance', *Comparative Studies in Society and History*, ii (1960); idem, 'The Sienese State in the Renaissance', in C.H. Carter, *From the Renaissance to the Counter-Reformation. Essays in Honour of Garrett Mattingly* (London, 1966); J. Hook, *Siena: A City and its History* (London, 1979); eadem, 'Siena and the Renaissance State', *Bollettino senese di storia patria*, lxxvii (1980); A.K. Isaacs, 'Popolo e Monti nella Siena del primo Cinquecento', *Rivista Storica Italiana*, lxxxii (1970); V. Wainwright, 'Conflict and Popular Government in Fourteenth-century Siena: *Il Monte dei Dodici*, 1355-1368' in *I ceti dirigenti nella Toscana tardo comunale* (Florence, 1983).

half-century of political turmoil which followed the fall of the Nine saw the emergence of a number of vying parties which rose to power and fell in rapid succession. By the early fifteenth century, these factions had settled into an uneasy coalition known as the *Monti*, but its unity was tenuous and the insecurity of its member-parties gave rise to the pursuit of self-interest amongst Siena's rulers which, even by contemporary Italian standards, seems to have been exceptional.[5] By the late fifteenth century, the remnants of these groups had formed a new oligarchy, whose income was drawn not from the old mercantile and banking industries, which had been the main source of Siena's wealth under the Nine, but from investments in land or from the holding of government office.[6] It has been argued that these interests, which dominated the ruling classes during Siena's last century as a republic, gave rise to and facilitated governmental injustice greater than had been seen under the more self-confident and less self-interested mercantile rulers of the period of the Nine.[7] Without doubt, however, the rise of this so-called 'new aristocracy' ushered in a period of greater political unity and bureaucratic centralisation than the city had known since the middle of the fourteenth century, especially with the establishment of the *Balìa* as the permanent organ of central administration in the mid fifteenth century.[8]

Broadly speaking it may be said that by the latter part of the fifteenth century the city had come to be governed by a tenuously united if self-interested oligarchy. Externally matters were less settled. The territorial expansion of the period of the Nine was reversed after the fall of that regime, and the next century and a half saw the gradual shrinkage of Sienese territory as the great powers of Italy, particularly Milan, Naples and the Papacy, fought for domination on the Tuscan stage and, more especially, as Siena's old enemy Florence reached new heights of imperial aggression and acquisition.[9] The pride engendered by the victory of Montaperti in 1260 turned to bitter humiliation in the fourteenth and

[5] Bowsky, 'Impact of the Black Death'; Wainwright and Isaacs, *ubi supra*.

[6] This process has been described as the development of the Sienese 'Renaissance State' by Hicks ('Sienese Society' and 'Sienese State'). Philip Jones' challenging of the whole idea of the Italian 'Renaissance State' ('Communes and Despots. The City-state in Late Medieval Italy', *Transactions of the Royal Historical Society*, xv (1965)) has led to reinterpretations of the Sienese situation, especially that of Judith Hook ('Siena and Renaissance State').

[7] Hook, 'Siena and Renaissance State, pp. 118-21.

[8] Hook, *Siena*, p. 161; Ascheri, pp. 40-41.

[9] The most detailed account of Siena's relations with Florence, Milan, Venice, Naples, the Papacy and the foreign powers of Europe in the period are still to be found in Malavolti, iii, *passim*; see also Schevill, ch. xiv; Hook, *Siena*, p. 12; and N. Rubinstein, 'Political Ideas in Sienese Art: The frescoes by Ambrogio Lorenzetti and Taddeo di Bartolo in the Palazzo Pubblico', *Journal of the Warburg and Courtauld Institutes*, xxi (1958), 205.

fifteenth centuries as Florence won back town after town from the Sienese *contado*, and at times actually threatened the city itself.[10] As time went on the Sienese found they only had recourse to two methods of defence against the constant threat of invasion, the first of which was costly, the second humiliating, and both of which contributed substantially to the eventual downfall of the republic in 1559. The first, the hiring of an army, was both expensive and dangerous, for, as the Sienese learned to their cost, mercenary soldiers could and did cause as much damage to their employer's territory as they did to the enemy.[11] By the late fifteenth century a substantial percentage of Siena's public revenue was being spent on the maintenance of such armies, the benefits of which were uncertain.[12] The second method of defence to which Siena resorted throughout the fourteenth, fifteenth and early sixteenth centuries was to appeal for protection to one of the great foreign lords: the duke of Milan in 1399 and 1428, the pope, the king of Naples and the duke of Calabria in 1477-80, and Charles V in 1530.[13] Such treaties did little for local pride, for Siena's position in these contracts was inevitably that of supplicant, and such princes were noted for their fickleness. A great lord who befriended the city could as easily turn against it.

One further threat presented to the commune in its last century as a republic came from the land-hungry magnates of the surrounding territory. During the period of the Nine, the magistracy of Siena, like that of Florence, had exerted considerable influence to keep at bay the barons whose interests were so at odds with those of the mercantile commune, but the weakening of the city's centralised power structure in the fourteenth century allowed magnates such as the great lords of the Maremma to reassert their hold on outlying posts of the *contado*. Many members of the new regime of the fifteenth century, with their heavy investments in land, found collaboration with the warlords more rewarding than confrontation, frequently at great cost to the populace of city and *contado* and in opposition to the interests of civic justice.[14]

The historian Malavolti's description of Siena in 1442 as 'una città fatticosa' – a wearied city – is thus scarcely surprising.[15] However, the

---

[10] Hook, *Siena*, pp. 12-13; D. Webb, 'Cities of God: The Italian Commune at War', *Studies in Church History*, xx (1983), 124; Schevill, p. 389; for details of individual conflicts, see Malavolti, iii, *passim*.

[11] Throughout the late fourteenth and fifteenth centuries the *signoria* paid out large sums of money to mercenaries, both to enlist their aid and to keep them at bay: Malavolti, iii, 1, 2, 12, 13, 30, 31, and *passim*.

[12] Hook, *Siena*, p. 177.

[13] Hook, *Siena*, pp. 160, 182; P. Partner, 'Florence and the Papacy in the Early Fifteenth Century', in *Florentine Studies*, ed. N. Rubinstein (London, 1968), p. 392; Schevill, pp. 391, 396, 397.

[14] Hook, 'Siena and Renaissance State', pp. 118-21.

[15] Malavolti, iii, 32.

century of internal and external disquiet which had drained the city's confidence and its coffers seems only to have reinforced its sense of being the last bastion of republicanism, a free and independent commune fighting for its liberty against the aggression of its tyrannical neighbours.[16] The reassertion of the republican civic spirit in the early fifteenth century, after a half-century of political turmoil, may be seen in publicly financed *opere* such as the Fonte Gaia, the Loggia di Mercanzia, and the paintings by Taddeo di Bartolo in the Palazzo Pubblico. In all of these works, the city is compared to the Roman Republic and represented as its successor with even greater emphasis than in the fourteenth-century frescoes of Ambrogio Lorenzetti, painted during the regime of the Nine.[17] The Roman Republic, however, served as a warning as well as a model, and those responsible for commissioning such works were not slow to point the moral: an independent state could only survive if its citizens were committed to the pursuit of peace, unity and the common good, and were prepared to eschew their own interests in favour of those of the *res publica*.[18]

Both these aspects of the republican message – the emphasis on the virtues of the *res publica* and the warnings of its corruptibility – are, as we shall see, echoed in the themes of Sienese preaching in the fifteenth century. Where the rhetoric of politics enters the sermons of Dominicans in Siena, it may be seen less as a response to a single event in the history of the city than as part of a continuing preoccupation with the welfare of the republic, which the friars of the mendicant houses shared with their compatriots and which, from the early fifteenth century on, acquired a new urgency.[19]

The Dominican convent was one of the city's most important civic institutions and, as the oldest and best-endowed of Siena's three mendicant houses had, since the late twelfth century, exercised the greatest spiritual and moral influence within the city. In its sanctuary were guarded the records of the commune, its chapels housed the city's most important lay confraternities, its doctors of theology dominated the curricula of the *università degli studi*, and, as the *fasti* of its *beati* show, over the centuries its inmates had included the sons of the city's wealthiest and politically most influential families.[20] Its spiritual ascendancy within the

[16] Hook, 'Siena and Renaissance State', p. 116.

[17] Hook, *Siena*, pp. 99-100. For a comparison of the frescoes of the earlier and later periods, see Rubinstein, 'Political Ideas in Sienese Art'.

[18] Rubinstein, 'Political Ideas', p. 197.

[19] A comparison of Sienese mendicant sermons from the late fourteenth, early fifteenth and late fifteenth centuries shows that the theme of the republic was a much more common *topos* in the later than the earlier period, suggesting a correspondence between the homiletic and secular reassertion of republican ideals (Paton, p. 103).

[20] V. Lisini, 'San Domenico in Camporeggi', *Bollettino senese di storia patria*, xiii (1906), 263-95, gives an account of the importance of San Domenico to the city; for its beatified inmates, see Isodoro Ugurgieri, *Fasti Senesi*, B[iblioteca] C[omunale di] S[iena], mss. A.IV.22, vol. I, fos. 207-393 (*beati Domenicani*).

city was confirmed by the fact that it had given Siena its two most important saints: Ambrogio Sansedoni, the great thirteenth-century reformer and scourge of heretics, and Caterina Benincasa, the Dominican tertiary whose mysticism had been encouraged by some of S. Domenico's most influential inmates and whose canonisation was assiduously promoted by her Dominican devotees.[21] S. Ambrogio, S. Domenico's most distinguished *alumnus*, was indeed afforded a special position in relation to the city: he was depicted, alongside the allegorical frescoes in the Palazzo Pubblico, holding a model of the city protectively in his arms.[22] This moral and spiritual authority, which the convent also claimed for itself, appears, for the most part, to have been accorded it by the Sienese.[23] Given this close identification of S. Domenico with the city, it is understandable that members of its congregation, conscious of the role of spiritual guardians that they had inherited from their beatified forebears, took upon themselves the task of formulating and expounding republican ideals.

The two Dominican preachers under discussion here were by no means the most prominent representatives of their order, nor were they lauded outside their city as their Franciscan brother, Bernardino, had earlier been. Their comparative obscurity, however, adds to their interest for our purpose, for it serves to confirm that intense civic consciousness was not the prerogative of isolated, unusually inspired rhetoricians or of great moral reformers but was, rather, a recurring theme in much of the Dominican pastoral literature formulated in the Italian city-states.

Of the preachers themselves we unfortunately know very little. The first of the works is an anonymous set of *sermones quadragesimales* (Lenten sermons), from the latter part of the fifteenth century and, according to its rubrics and internal evidence, written by an inmate of S. Domenico in that period (he will be called, hereafter, the S. Domenico Preacher).[24] The writer's preoccupations place him squarely in both the Thomist tradition of Dominican political philosophy and in that of local republicanism. The second set of sermons is the work of Fra Petrus Paulus Salimbeni, a scion of one of Siena's most important families. Salimbeni, whose sermons were preached in Lent 1478, and recorded in the same year, is of interest not only for his family background but also for his political and cultural

---

[21] The records of their efforts are collected in the *Fontes vitae S. Catherinae senensis historici;* see also Raymond of Capua, *The Life of St. Catherine of Siena* (trs. G. Lamb, London, 1934), and P. Misciatelli, *Mystics of Siena* (trs. M. Peters Roberts, Cambridge, 1929), pp. 103-39.

[22] G. Kaftal, *Saints in Italian Art*, i. *The Iconography of the Saints in Tuscan Painting* (Florence, 1952), pp. 31-32 and fig. 32. On Ambrogio Sansedoni's life and cult, see Misciatelli, p. 14 and Hook, *Siena*, pp. 136, 223.

[23] Hook, *Siena*, p. 121.

[24] Anon. da San Domenico, *Conciones quadragesimales et sermones de sanctis per totum annum,* BCS, cod. F.X. 19. For origin and dating: L. Ilari, *La biblioteca pubblica di Siena: Catalogo disposto secondo le materie* (Siena, 1846), vii (*Scienze sacre*), p. 226.

connections. As a member of the humanist group which flourished under the patronage of Aeneas Sylvius Piccolomini (later Pope Pius II), Salimbeni combines the sophistication of the pontiff's circle with a local loyalty and awareness which result, in his sermons, in an unusual blend of cultural and political consciousness.[25]

The response of these preachers to the social and political milieu in which they wrote and delivered their sermons is reflected in two very distinct ways in their work. The first, which is concerned with the internal condition of the city, is found in sermons on obviously political topics such as justice, civic peace, the *bene commune*, and the ideal nature of the *res publica*. The second, present more by implication yet strikingly pervasive, reflects local preoccupation with the defence of the republic against its external enemies. The sense of the city of Siena as a vulnerable republican island surrounded by an ever-encroaching sea of despotism found expression, as will be seen, in the sermons of its preachers on many subjects other than those concerned ostensibly with the government of the city-state.

The sermons of both these Dominican preachers on topics which may be described as overtly political draw upon three authorial traditions already well-established in the civic rhetoric of the Italian city-states. The first is that which Quentin Skinner has called the 'pre-humanist', classical tradition; the second is the Dominicans' own Aristotelian/Thomist moral theology; and the third, found chiefly in the work of Salimbeni, is that of the fifteenth-century Florentine and Roman humanists.[26] Their amalgamation of these influences is neither methodical nor, one suspects, even conscious, but it may be seen, firstly, in the variety of *auctores* they cite or writers to whom they make reference, from Cicero, Seneca and Sallust, through Aquinas (and via him, Aristotle) to Dante and Petrarch; and, secondly, in the themes which they choose for expansion, which are drawn from all three traditions.

---

[25] Petrus Paulus Salimbeni, *Sermones*, BCS, cod. F.X.18. The rubric above his index page reads 'Hic est tabula hujus libri, quem librum predicationum composuit scripsit et propria fantasia ordinavit Fra Petrus Paulus ordin. predicatorum conventis San Domenici de Camporegio de Senis' (fo. 1). Also, fo. 3, 'In 1478, prima mensis madij incepi sermones quadragesimales ad materias'. Salimbeni also composed an *Oratio habita coram Pio II aliique sermones* (Florence, Bibl. Medicea Laurenziana, Plut. lxxxix, sup. 27 (XV)). See also T. Kaeppeli, *Scriptores ordinis praedicatorum medii aevi* (Rome, 1980), iii, 249, for information on Salimbeni's career and connections.

[26] Q. Skinner, 'Ambrogio Lorenzetti: the Artist as Political Philosopher', *Proceedings of the British Academy*, lxxii (1986). Humanist influences appear to have pervaded the university of Siena from the 1430s on (K.W. Humphries, *The Library of the Franciscans of Siena in the Late Fifteenth Century* (Amsterdam, 1978), p. 40); given the Dominicans' traditional connection with the *Studi*, it seems likely that at least some of these ideas would have reached writers like the San Domenico preacher, as well as self-conscious classicisers like Salimbeni.

Perhaps the most apparent manifestation of this conflation of influences is to be found in these preachers' direct identification of the *res publica* of the classical political philosophers with the Thomist ideal of the *bene commune*, so that the two concepts become almost interchangeable. This is most clearly seen in Salimbeni's sermon entitled *de republica*, in which he sets out the ideal nature of the republic. His exposition blends classical ideas of the state as a *corpus* with the theological metaphor of the mystical body, to produce an image of the republic as a body whose members are bound together by the interests of the common good and who must therefore seek to be at peace with each other. In Salimbeni's allegory, as in tradition, the head consists of the ruler or rulers of the state, whose eyes must seek not only their own interests but that of the whole body; the arms are those who fight to defend the body; and the feet are those who labour to conserve its physical well-being. When reason and good morals govern such a well-ordered society, he declares, numerous benefits ensue, including just laws, equity, peace, and mutual trust between citizens, all of which virtues tend, ultimately, to the conservation of the *bene commune*, without which the republic cannot survive.[27]

For local preachers, then, the well-being of the republic rested largely on the civic virtue of its citizens. As might be expected from the representatives of one of the city's most patriarchal and conservative institutions, the chief emphasis in political sermons is not on the rights and duties of the individual citizen but on the qualifications and responsibilities of the republic's rulers. It is, perhaps, in these discussions of the ideal nature of republican leadership that we find the greatest departure from the Dominican, Thomist *auctores* to accommodate local experience and ideals. For while scholastic political philosophy, nurtured in the Paris schools of the thirteenth century and heavily influenced by French monarchist ideas, had claimed monarchy as the best form of government, republican tradition and, above all, Sienese experience of the tyrannies and greed of foreign princes had bred in local preachers, as in their compatriots, a suspicion of the motives of earthly princes which accorded ill with the Thomist ideal of the just king. This cynicism is reflected in the condemnation, by the S. Domenico Preacher, of corrupt earthly princes and magnates who pervert the law for their own ends and who seek to invade others' territory. Such princes, he concludes, will be judged more heavily by God for their abuse of their power.[28]

Such a view of monarchy, however, inevitably left a hiatus in the traditional Thomist political model upon which Dominican writers drew so heavily, and which depended for the preservation of the *bene commune*

---

[27] Salimbeni, fos. 177-79.
[28] San Domenico sermons, fos. 33v, 36v.

largely on the figure of the just king.[29] The response of the preachers to this problem, while not novel, shows clearly the influence of both republican traditions and Florentine humanist ideas, for, in defiance of Thomist ideals and in accordance with local tradition, the sermons of both Salimbeni and the S. Domenico Preacher replace the rule of the just monarch with that of an oligarchy of 'wise men', a council of philosopher-rulers.[30] This idea is expounded by the S. Domenico Preacher in a number of passages on the nature of both church and state councils. In describing the ideal composition of a republican council, his emphasis is on the need for exclusiveness in such a body, and he debars the ignorant, the unqualified and those with partisan interests. The question of egalitarian representation does not concern him – rather, he maintains that wisdom and reputation should be the chief criteria for the selection of its members.[31] His warnings against the corruptibility of such an oligarchy and his stress on its subjugation to the law (but not, significantly, to popular opinion) may be seen to reflect local experience of governmental corruption in the period, but his promotion of the idea of government through such a body corresponds strongly to traditional Sienese notions of the nature of republican government, an ideology strengthened by popular myths and memories of the stable regime of the Nine and emphasised in the city's political iconography.

The position embraced by Salimbeni, a member of one of Siena's oldest ruling families, further supports the contention that the friars of S. Domenico saw the well-being of the republic as best preserved through the rule of a beneficent, disinterested patriciate. In Salimbeni's sermons on the nature of the republic may be seen a conflation of this conservative patrician attitude with traditional Thomist political theory and, above all, with the classical *auctores* so favoured by the humanists. Drawing on a number of these, including Plato, Cicero and Seneca, Salimbeni declares

[29] For a summary of the Aristotelian/Thomist ideal of kingship, see J. Dunbabin, 'Aristotle in the Schools', in *Trends in Medieval Political Thought*, ed. B. Smalley (London, 1965), pp. 67-70.

[30] The idea of the 'council of the wise' as the form of government most suitable for a republic is a familiar one in Italian medieval political philosophy (Skinner, p. 2). This is not the place to enter the debate on the significance of the central figure of the Ruler in the Lorenzetti frescoes, but it is worth noting the correspondence between the preachers' substitution of council for monarch and the same solution proffered (in the personification of the Nine) by the painter. The prevalence of the ideal of the oligarchic council in the Tuscan republics may be seen in the idealisation of the Venetian council in Florentine political theorising, an ideal also put forward by Bernardino in 1427 as a possible solution to the problem of factionalism in Siena (Bernardino da Siena, *Le prediche volgari*, ed. P. Bargellini (Milan, 1936), p. 339), and by Savonarola when seeking a political model for the new Florentine republic of the 1490s (Weinstein, *Savonarola*, p. 284; see also, in general, F. Gilbert, 'The Venetian Constitution in Florentine Political Thought', in *Florentine Studies*, pp. 463-500; Jones, 'Communes and Despots', p. 73).

[31] San Domenico sermons, fos. 77 and 97.

that the head of the republic is best composed of the state's wisest and most noble citizens, corresponding to Plato's philosopher-rulers, whose duty it is to guide the body politic towards the common good and the ideal state, in which good morals govern all.[32] For Salimbeni, as for his predecessors in the republican tradition, the ideal republic is represented by that of the Romans at its height, while civic virtue is personified in Rome's most eminent citizens, especially Cicero.

Such an analogy inevitably carries with it a warning of the vulnerability of the state to the self-interest of its leaders. Like the city's secular rhetoricians, who had, in the early fifteenth century, decreed that the Roman model should be set on the walls of the Palazzo Pubblico as a reminder of the ideal nature of the republic and of its corruptibility, Salimbeni is not loath to stress this point.[33] While, as a member of the city's ruling class, he supports and promotes the idea of government through a patrician oligarchy, he is by no means blind to the dangers inherent in the limitation of power to a select group; his warnings carry more than a hint of awareness of the failings of the contemporary regime. Yet despite his reservations concerning the virtue of any given ruling group, Salimbeni, like his secular contemporaries, never questions the virtue of the republic as a corporation. His chief concern is to reassert the importance of the republican state, represented historically by Rome and now by Siena, in a period in which its very existence as a political entity was increasingly threatened by the great despotisms of the Italian peninsula.

One of the most profound differences between the Thomist monarchical model and the preachers' ideal of the republican oligarchy lies in their differing attitudes to the law. For the scholastic political philosophers, the formulation of the law was held to be the prerogative of the just monarch; in Sienese Dominican preaching the law is represented as an absolute, unchangeable and unchanging, established by traditions and authorities above and outside the government of the commune. Implicit in the Thomist philosophy is the assumption that the state is as good as its ruler; in Sienese political preaching the republic, given its inherent virtues, transcends its rulers who, like its citizens, are bound by

---

[32] Salimbeni. fos. 177–79. Salimbeni's ideal of an enlightened despotism of philosopher-rulers has much in common with the ideas put forward by the Florentine Neoplatonists when justifying the regime of their Medicean patrons in the 1470s and 1480s. However, it is also compatible with more traditional Ciceronian ideas in which wisdom is held to be the most important virtue in a republican ruler (Skinner, p. 18).

[33] There may, in fact, be a direct link between Salimbeni himself and the man who devised and commissioned the Taddeo di Bartolo frescoes, Pietro de' Pecci; the latter, a distinguished lawyer, was one of Aeneas Sylvius Piccolomini's teachers at the university of Siena (Rubinstein, pp. 204–5). Given Salimbeni's connections with Aeneas Sylvius, it seems likely that he himself may have come into contact with Pecci, or at least with his ideas, at some point during his career.

its laws. In this emphasis on the necessary subordination of the city's rulers to the law, we again find a reflection of the political tradition so graphically illustrated in the Lorenzetti frescoes, where the figure of the ruler is represented as bound to justice and the community.[34]

The importance of the law in Sienese republican ideology, and its subsequent reflection in local preaching, is perhaps most clearly seen in the Dominicans' treatment of the issue of justice in the republic. When dealing with justice as a political virtue both preachers are, superficially at least, heavily indebted to their Thomist forebears. Like them, they establish two aspects of justice: a 'distributive' function, whereby each individual is assured his due place in the social hierarchy, and a 'commutative' function, by which the good are rewarded and the evil punished.[35] In their greater emphasis on the importance of commutative rather than distributive justice in preserving the peace of the commune, they seem to reflect classical rather than theological *auctores*. For them the reward of good and especially the punishment of evil remain the most basic functions of the law, and the Christian quality of mercy occupies very little space in their judicial scheme. Salimbeni declares one of the primary functions of justice to be the removal of wrong-doers for the preservation of the health of the republic, while the S. Domenico Preacher emphasises the importance of punishment as part of the process of social restitution, even going so far as to claim that the greatest injustice is the failure to punish evil.[36] Unlike the Parisian Thomists, who drew heavily on Aristotelian notions of man's innate inclination to maintain *aequitas* and the social order, for the S. Domenico Preacher especially, as for many of the political writers of the pre-humanist republican tradition, man is an innately unruly animal who must be compelled by law to accept the dictates of justice.[37]

To be effective, the law had to be justly administered by carefully-chosen officials; as the moral guardians of the city, Dominican preachers were not averse to offer both recommendations and reprimands to the judges of the commune. The S. Domenico Preacher, who devotes considerable attention throughout his sermons to the question of judicial administration, declares wisdom, old age, experience, and complete knowledge of the law to be necessary qualifications in the city's judges. He adjures them to hear cases impartially, to weigh the evidence carefully, and to punish in accordance with the seriousness of the crime.[38] This

---

[34] Skinner, p. 43. On the importance of law in maintaining the *bene commune*, see Salimbeni, fo. 166v; S. Domenico sermons, fo. 78.

[35] Detailed analyses of these two aspects appear in Salimbeni, fos. 177v-178, and the S. Domenico sermons, fos. 132-33.

[36] Salimbeni, ibid.; S. Domenico sermons, fos. 131-32. Cf. Skinner, p. 16.

[37] S. Domenico sermons, fos. 167-70; Skinner, pp. 17-18.

[38] S. Domenico sermons, fos. 4, 56, 128, 164.

preacher's stress on the value of wisdom above all other virtues reflects the influence of Roman ideas of the *vir sapiens* as the preserver of justice and peace.[39] Yet his very emphasis on the qualifications and duties of judges and civic officials suggests that the issue of judicial corruption was a particularly vexed one in late medieval Siena, a suggestion borne out by accusations against local judges made elsewhere in his sermons. He claims that the city's judges are more often swayed by false rumours, favouritism and bribes than by a desire to do justice;[40] above all, he declares, they are afraid to castigate the great and powerful for fear of retribution.[41] His angry denunciations of the weaknesses of judges, which recur throughout his sermons, go beyond standard homiletic rhetoric, and confirm contemporary reports of judicial corruption as undermining the city's administration in the period.[42] His comparison of the law to a shepherd, set to guard the sheep from the wolves, suggests that for him, as for his contemporaries, the law was seen as the only protection the weak had against the great and powerful, a safeguard weakened in contemporary Siena by the failings of the city's judicial administrators.[43]

The Sienese preachers' emphasis on justice as the most important of civic virtues assumes greater significance in the contemporary context when compared with their treatment of peace, the political virtue traditionally given precedence over all others in the homiletic rhetoric of the Italian city-states. Both Salimbeni and the S. Domenico Preacher, as might be expected, stress the importance of peace in conserving the *bene commune*, and hence the *res publica*.[44] But they are less concerned with the subject of the disruption of peace through factionalism than were Remigio, Giordano, or even Bernardino.[45] It is difficult not to see in this reticence a direct reflection of the comparative stability of the late fifteenth-century regime when compared with the earlier period of the warring *Monti* parties. More importantly, their expositions of the nature of peace and its disruption cast considerable light on contemporary Sienese awareness and experience. Salimbeni, when extolling the virtues of peace, declares it to be of two types, the true and the false. *Pax vera*, he states in Thomist fashion, is brought about through the rational behaviour of citizens who should, according to the dictates of their natural instincts, seek peace and concord rather than disruption and division; *pax falsa*, on the other hand, is founded on the forcing of subjects into obedience by

---

[39] Skinner, p. 18.

[40] S. Domenico sermons, fos. 33v, 56v, 131, 164v.

[41] Ibid., fo. 33v.

[42] Hook, 'Siena and Renaissance State', p. 114.

[43] S. Domenico sermons, fo. 78. Bernardino uses a similar analogy: he tells the city's judges that they must not punish the weak, 'the ass and the sheep', while protecting the strong, 'the wolf and the fox', from the consequences of their crimes (Bargellini, p. 352).

[44] S. Domenico sermons, fos. 42-44, 55; Salimbeni, fos. 166-67.

[45] For Bernardino's famous sermons against division (1427): Bargellini, pp. 215-66.

corrupt and tyrannical rulers. His claim that even such false peace, although contrary to the *bene commune*, could serve a republic better than division and discord may be seen as a comment on the benefits brought by the relatively stable government of the period after the divisions of the earlier regime; however, his emphasis on the duplicity of false peace is clearly intended to convey a warning of the damage done to the common good in a republic united only by fear, bribery and the other forms of governmental coercion which increasingly characterised the Sienese oligarchy of the period.[46]

While these late fifteenth-century Dominicans, then, acknowledge the importance of peace in preserving the republic, their failure to concern themselves to any great extent with the issue of factionalism suggests that the question of political disunity was not one which preoccupied them or their contemporaries as it had their predecessors. Of rather greater significance, however, is the S. Domenico Preacher's bemoaning of the destruction of peace through inter-city warfare.[47] This concern repeatedly manifests itself, in a variety of ways, in the sermons of both preachers, reflecting an awareness of the physical vulnerability of the city which had been increasingly borne upon the Sienese by the military threats and intermittent warfare of the period.

This consciousness is most apparent in innumerable exemplars and allegories in which both the soul of man and the kingdom of God are likened to the besieged republican city-state. The notion of the soul as an entity under continual siege from the devil was not new in pastoral literature, nor was the use of the city as a metaphor.[48] What distinguishes the work of these preachers is its amalgamation of these images into a single, urgent message. They transform the lonely warrior of the Augustinian tradition, fighting his battle against temptation, into an allegory of an entire community under threat. The metaphor is taken to its greatest lengths by the S. Domenico Preacher, whose sermons abound with images of the *civitas de nostra anima*, whose walls are fortified and protected by God against the invading tyrant, for the preservation of its internal peace and the well-being of its citizens.[49] 'The more precious a thing is, the more closely it must be guarded', he concludes in one such passage. 'Our soul is a very precious thing, and so must have walls and

---

[46] Salimbeni, fo. 166.

[47] S. Domenico sermons, fo. 55.

[48] The image of the soul as a lone warrior is particularly characteristic of patristic penitential literature, and is to be found, for example, in contemporary Siena in the writings of the reformed Leccetan Augustinians, such as the *Adiutorio* of Girolamo da Lecceto (L. Ildefonso di San Luigi, *Dell'opere toscane di fra Girolamo dell'ordine romitano* (Florence, 1770)) and the *Libro della spirituale battaglia* (BSC, cod. I.II.26) from Lecceto. The use of the city as a religious metaphor is also common in both the Judaic and patristic traditions, especially, in the latter, following Augustine's *City of God*.

[49] E.g., S. Domenico sermons, fos. 21, 27, 75, 113, 145.

towers, even as such walls guard a city'.[50] Where the traditional imagery of the spiritual battle likens the weapons of the soul to the arms of the foot-soldier, the spirit as a besieged city has need of good commanders and troops; in the sermons of the S. Domenico Preacher, the sword, shield and arrows of the lone combatant have been replaced by the walls, towers, fortresses and fighting companies of the city-state. The extent to which this preacher, albeit unconsciously, reflects local experiences in the imagery he chooses may be seen in his likening of the sin which divides a man from God to inter-city warfare, in which communications between towns are severed and a person from one town may not venture to another until a treaty has renewed peaceful relations.[51]

The emphasis on the vulnerability of the republic to outside forces found in the imagery of the S. Domenico Preacher is reiterated in the sermons of Salimbeni. Perhaps its most interesting manifestation is the appearance, in his sermon *de republica*, of the warrior-emperor Trajan as an exemplary figure.[52] This use of Trajan as a model of civic virtue (alongside Cicero, Brutus and the other republican heroes so beloved of the humanists) shows that Salimbeni, along with his compatriots, was intensely aware of issues more pressing than the internal organisation of the city and the maintenance of civic virtue within it. Rather, it may be seen as a further indication of contemporary Sienese preoccupation with the question of the defence of the city against tyranny and external invasion. In this context the qualities represented by Trajan – courage, patriotism and military expertise – could be seen, even more than the prudence, temperance and wisdom of the earlier Roman heroes, as vital prerequisites for the successful survival and defence of the city.

Salimbeni's preoccupation with the question of the physical security of the republic is not restricted to his lauding of the military virtues. Like the S. Domenico Preacher, he makes effective use of the imagery of civic defence in his sermons on the spiritual battle. Unlike the patristic writers, he too represents the struggle to save man's soul as a collective or communal rather than single-handed affair. He declares that the spiritual aids that God provides work in unison, as each member of a community has some special role, according to his abilities, in the defence of the city. Thus a confessor is likened to the commander of troops, the archers are the doctors of the church, the physicians who care for the wounded are the priests and pastors, healers of spiritual wounds, and the religious orders are the guards who watch for the enemy from the city walls.[53]

In their allegorical emphasis on the externals of civic defence – the walls, towers, and gates – both our preachers reflect the importance of

[50] Ibid., fo. 145.
[51] Ibid., fo. 17.
[52] Salimbeni, fos. 177-79.
[53] Salimbeni, fos. 118-120.

such structures to Italian cities, an importance amply attested in contemporary iconography.[54] A city's walls were, like its *palazzi* and churches, works of art and monuments to civic pride. They were the fortifications upon which the city depended for survival in time of trouble. Within them lay comfort and security; without, the threat of foreign powers, roaming companies of soldiers and the powerful feudal magnates. Such awareness must have been borne even more strongly upon the friars of S. Domenico than upon their compatriots, physically situated as they were atop the western walls of the city and occupying one of its most strategic look-out points.[55] Since they were no strangers to the logistics of civic defence, it is not surprising to find its imagery pervading their message, alongside their reiteration of republican ideals, at a time when the city's sense of physical insecurity was matched only by its vision of itself as the last of the Italian republics, the true heir to Rome.

[54] On the significance of walls in civic iconography, see J. F. Codell, 'Giotto's Peruzzi Chapel Frescoes: Wealth, Patronage and the Earthly City', *Renaissance Quarterly*, xli, 4 (1988), 584, 599, 602. The importance of the walls, as much as the cathedral and palaces, in characterising Siena is to be seen in medieval representations of the city, like those of Lorenzetti, or that of the *Biccherna* cover of 1467 (reproduced in Hook, *Siena*, facing p. 133).

[55] The position of San Domenico in relation to the city's defences is graphically illustrated in a number of contemporary depictions of the convent on the end-leaves of the S. Domenico manuscript.

10

The Crown and the Economy under Ferrante I of Naples
(1458-94)

David Abulafia

Ferrante I of Naples has suffered since his own time from a dual reputation. To Commynes he was one of an evil pair: 'never was any prince more bloody, wicked, inhuman, lascivious or gluttonous' than Ferrante's son Alfonso II, 'yet his father was even more dangerous, because no man knew when he was angry or pleased'. Since Machiavelli never mentions Ferrante in *Il Principe* it may be unfair to characterise him as a Prince before *The Prince*. But it is increasingly clear that the humanists at his court were beginning to articulate ideas of the relationship between political power and morality that have parallels with, even if they were not actually ancestral to, the ideas put forward by Machiavelli.[1] At the same time Ferrante's reign was a remarkable success story. He ruled for thirty-six years over a kingdom that his close neighbour the pope and many of his most powerful subjects wished to hand over to rival claimants whom his father Alfonso the Magnanimous had seen out of Italy once already. His repression of the barons earned him a fine reputation for brutality but also confirmed him in authority for long periods. Marriage alliances and vigorous military or diplomatic activity made him a pivotal figure in the politics of late fifteenth-century Italy. The lack of a modern biographer thus remains embarrassing testimony to the neglect of important southern dimensions to the history of Quattrocento Italy compared to the unweakened magnetism for historians of Venice, Florence and Siena in the selfsame period.[2]

A particular aspect of Ferrante's rule that has attracted some attention is his economic policy. His attempts to revive industry in Campania had a

---

[1] J. Bentley, *Politics and Culture in Renaissance Naples* (Princeton, 1987).

[2] The nearest to a biography is the collection of six studies by E. Pontieri, *Per la storia di Ferrante I d'Aragona Re di Napoli* (Naples, s.d.); there are good brief accounts of the reign in Bentley, pp. 23-34, and (more at second hand) in A. Atlas, *Music at the Aragonese Court of Naples* (Cambridge, 1985). At the other end of the spectrum there is the sensationalism of e.g. O. Prescott, *Princes of the Renaissance* (London, 1970), pp. 65-77, which labels him 'Ferrante, King of Villains'.

natural appeal for Italian political economists of the nineteenth century such as Ricca Salerno.[3] Moreover, alongside the evidence of privileges there exists the contemporary advice offered to the king's daughter Eleonora on how a prince could create wealth for himself by fostering the economic activities of his subjects. Although the princess went to live in Ferrara, it is surely right to see in Diomede Carafa's *De regis et boni principis officio* an assessment of economic conditions and opportunities in southern Italy.[4] Ferrante's liberality to merchants also needs to be considered in the light of the modern debate about the origins of southern 'underdevelopment'. The most recent work has concentrated on Sicily and Sardinia rather than the mainland Mezzogiorno, yet historians of Ferrante's Naples have insisted that the evidence reveals an export trade in raw materials and foodstuffs, and a dependence on foreign imported textiles.[5] What needs to be established in addition is whether by the late fifteenth century Ferrante and his court were aware of this imbalance or considered it a problem. In other words, how far were the privileges for foreign merchants, the efforts to stimulate a silk industry and so on, attempts to alleviate what were seen as economic problems, and how far were they motivated by a short-term desire to create sources of revenue that could pay for grandiose political schemes in the Italian peninsula? This question has added point since no one doubts that Ferrante's father Alfonso the Magnanimous was ruthless in finding new financial resources in Naples, Sicily and Spain, which were exploited in order to pay for his imperial dreams in Lombardy, Corsica, Africa, the Balkans and even Hungary.[6]

It is intended here to analyse four types of information about the economic 'health' of the *Regno* in Ferrante's time. First, there is the fictional world of the *Novellino* of Masuccio Salernitano, which presents a picture of the interaction of native and foreign merchants in the ports of Naples and Salerno, and shows a degree of awareness of the economic fluctuations that were affecting the trade of Naples and Salerno in the fifteenth century.[7] Then there is the idealised view of the role of the prince

[3] G. Ricca Salerno, *Storia delle dottrine finanziarie in Italia*, ed. S. Guccione (Padua, 1960), pp. 38-45.

[4] I have not had access to T. Persico, *Diomede Carafa: uomo di stato e scrittore del secolo XV* (Naples, 1899).

[5] H. Bresc, *Un monde méditerranéen: Économie et société en Sicile, 1300-1450*, 2 vols. (Rome and Palermo, 1986); J. Day, *La Sardegna sotto la dominazione pisano-genovese* (Turin, 1987; originally published as part of the U.T.E.T. *Storia d'Italia*); cf. the forthcoming critique by S.R. Epstein, *Sicily and its Markets, 1300-1500: Regional Development and Social Transformation* (Cambridge, 1991).

[6] On Alfonso's finances, see A. Ryder, *The Kingdom of Naples under Alfonso the Magnanimous: the Making of a Modern State* (Oxford, 1976); idem *Alfonso the Magnanimous, King of Aragon, Naples and Sicily, 1396-1458* (Oxford, 1990).

[7] Masuccio Salernitano, *Il Novellino*, ed. A. Mauro (Bari, 1940).

in the direction of economic life presented by Carafa.[8] Thirdly, the commercial privileges of Ferrante give some clue as to the ruler's aspirations, even if not all fulfilled; for war, with Florence and elsewhere, compromised these grants significantly.[9] Finally, there is the hard evidence of the commercial contracts from Salerno and Naples, particularly the contracts of the notary Petruccio Pisano.[10] The question remains acute how far the native merchants of the Mezzogiorno were really swamped by foreign competitors. The contracts help to answer this at least as far as long distance trade is concerned.

Imagination

Masuccio was a member of the Salernitan nobility. But his eyes were open both to courtly society and to the activities of all types of merchants. While he was clearly indebted to earlier writers of *novelle*, notably Boccaccio (who was also familiar with the commerce of Naples), we do have Masuccio's assurance that he heard his stories from traders of note.[11] Certainly, the society he portrays is one in which the Catalans and the Genoese hold a special place as men of wealth. At the start of the *Novellino* we are presented with a short tale of a greedy and accordingly very wealthy Genoese merchant who picked up a gold ducat that he saw under the nose of an unsuspecting poor tailor; when the tailor protested, Guardo Salusgio of Genoa argued that he alone could place the coin in the good

[8] I have used the Latin edition of 1668: *De regis et boni principis officio opusculum a Diomede Carafa primo Magdalunensium comite compositum* (Naples, 1668). Part of the Italian original was published by Petrucci, pp. 261-96; a new edition by F. Petrucci (author of the biography in *Dizionario biografico italiano*, xix, 524-30) is in preparation: see Bentley, p. 142n.

[9] Some previously unpublished privileges are printed in A. Silvestri, *Il commercio a Salerno nella seconda metà del Quattrocento* (Salerno, 1952), pp. 141-50.

[10] G. Coniglio, 'Mercanti forestieri a Napoli attraverso gli atti del Notaio Petruccio Pisano (1465-66)', *Samnium*, xxviii (1955), 78-85; Silvestri, *Commercio*, docs. i-cii, pp. 59-87; A. Sapori, 'La fiera di Salerno del 1478', *Bollettino dell'Archivio storico del Banco di Napoli*, viii (1954), 51-84, repr. as 'Una fiera in Italia alla fine del Quattrocento: la fiera di Salerno del 1478', in his *Studi di storia economica (secoli XIII-XIV-XV)*, 3rd edn., (Florence, 1967), pp. 443-74 – references in these notes are to the reprint. See also A. Grohmann, *Le fiere del Regno di Napoli in età aragonese* (Naples, 1969), especially pp. 225-34, 464-90. But the acts still need to be placed in a wider economic context, not merely of the *Regno* but of western Mediterranean trade as a whole. This is now possible thanks in part to the existence of good studies of the relations of the Catalan merchants with the Aragonese Kingdom of Naples: M. del Treppo, *I mercanti catalani e l'espansione della Corona d'Aragona nel secolo XV* (Naples, 1972); idem, 'Il re e il banchiere: strumenti e processi di razionalizzazione dello Stato aragonese di Napoli', in *Spazio, società, potere nell'Italia dei Comuni: Europa mediterranea, Quaderni*, i, ed. G. Rossetti (Naples, 1986), pp. 229-304; E. Ashtor, 'Catalan Cloth on the Late Medieval Mediterranean Markets', *Journal of European Economic History*, xvii (1988), 227-57.

[11] Masuccio, *Novella* XLVIII.

company to which it was rightly entitled.[12] In the *Novellino*, the Genoese form part of the fabric of a cosmopolitan Salernitan society in which, for instance, the governor of the city, who has *una certa infermità*, marries a beautiful Genoese damsel but is unable to consummate their marriage, with the predictable result that his wife looks elsewhere for pleasure.[13]

The second important group of merchants is the Catalans. They are treated with even more reserve than the Genoese:

> Nel tempo che tra Napoli e le castelle fieramente se guerriggiava, in Salerno più che in niun'altra parte del reame usavano mercanti d'ogne nazione; ove tra gli altri essendoci recapitato un richissimo catalano chiamato Piero Genefra, vi facia de gran trafichi e per mare e per terra, como de'mercanti è già usanza.[14]

He fell in love with the wife of an Amalfitan silversmith, named Cosmo; 'e ancora che da alcuni nostri salernitani, como a poco ne le loro faccende occupati, Cosmo fusse stato provisto che de prattiche e tratti catalani se guardasse', Cosmo paid no attention whatsoever. He was duped into helping his own wife elope aboard Genefra's ship; Masuccio comments acidly:

> Nondimeno giudico che'l poveretto sia in alcuna parte da escusare, atteso che le prattiche de'catalani in tali tempi non erano si note per lo nostro regno como sono ogge, quali sono in manera cognosciute e vintilate, che non solo chi vuole se ne sa e può guardare, ma offenderli con vergogna e danno, si come ogne dí le esperienze ce ne rendeno testimonio.[15]

The story apparently claims to refer to the period of Alfonso's contest with René of Anjou for the throne of Naples; that is, to a period when the Catalans had not yet established themselves as the leading commercial presence in Campania.

Elsewhere too Masuccio appears to look back on the early fifteenth century as a golden age of Salerno's prosperity. In *Novella* XII he begins:

> Negli anni che la nostra salernitana citá sotto l'imperio del glorioso pontifice Martino quinto si reggeva, in essa de grandissimi trafichi se faceano, e mercanti infiniti de continuo e d'ogni nazione vi concorreano: per la cui cagione venendoce ad abitare con tutte loro brigate de molti artesani forestieri.[16]

[12] Masuccio, *Prologo* to the *Novellino*.
[13] Masuccio, *Novella* XIII.
[14] Masuccio, *Novella* XL.
[15] Ibid.
[16] Masuccio, *Novella*, XII.

This passage refers back to the period when Joanna II had granted Salerno to the Colonna, from whom Alfonso the Magnanimous abstracted it, to hand it instead to their old rivals the Orsini. It is hard to say whether a decline in Salerno's prosperity might have occurred in the fifty or so years between the grant of Queen Joanna and Masuccio's *Novellino*. In 1474-78 Salerno had 856 assessable hearths, while La Cava had 1,000, Amalfi with Atrani 276, Maiori 235, Scala and Ravello 110 each, and Minori a mere 50.[17] Thus it was a notable regional centre, but greatly overshadowed by vast Naples; nor could the towns of what had once been a flourishing centre of international commerce rival in size the ports of northern Italy. This was true despite the marked contraction in population in Genoa and its rivals following the Black Death. It is known too that by 1400 much of the commercial business carried on by natives of the Campanian towns was restricted to the Tyrrhenian Sea: Amalfi briefly played a notable role in the salt trade with Sardinia and Gaeta traded as far east as Egypt, but Salerno itself had become an entrance gateway into the Mezzogiorno for foreign merchants, and its own merchants are rarely encountered outside the region by this period.[18]

Masuccio was aware of current political changes. In *Novella* XLVII he talks of how the 'rich and powerful city of Barcelona' returned to the fidelity it owed King John of Aragon at the time of the Catalan civil wars and the occupation by Louis XI of Perpignan. Masuccio moved in courtly circles, acting for a time as secretary to Roberto di Sanseverino, one of the leading figures in the kingdom, and a close adviser to King Ferrante. The stories themselves were dedicated to members of the royal house and to influential courtiers; thus Masuccio offers unctuous praise of the future King Alfonso II, an able military leader but a man of shameless brutality.[19] The stories are evidence, if not for the preponderance of foreign merchants in the trade of Salerno and Naples, at least for the reputation that the Genoese and Catalans had gained as somewhat unscrupulous merchants, whose hallmark was sophistry and trickery, both in business affairs (which aroused Masuccio's criticism) and in affairs of the heart (which aroused his wry admiration).

Idea

Diomede Carafa had no reason to extol the Angevin period in Naples. Born around 1406, he was always active in defence of Aragonese interests, and had even suffered exile from Naples in 1423. An accomplished soldier, he led or helped the armies of Alfonso I and Ferrante to key victories in the *Regno*, in Tuscany and even in north Africa. He was rewarded with the

---

[17] Silvestri, *Commercio*, pp. 40-47.
[18] M. del Treppo and A. Leone, *Amalfi medioevale* (Naples, 1977).
[19] Masuccio, *Novella* XLIV.

title and lands of the county of Maddaloni. In the 1470s he wrote a work on *I doveri del Principe* that has been described as 'more realistic in many ways than the sensational thought of Machiavelli', and less imbued with the preoccupations of the Italian humanists.[20] It is an intensely practical work, as is shown by the great amount of space it devotes to the management of the economy. Carafa was prepared to face the difficulties that arose when a choice had to be made between two policies, both in some sense evil; but the essence of this short book lies in the attempts to secure good governance not merely in order to obtain peace and freedom for the ruler to pursue his own objectives, but also so that the king's subjects can flourish. The sure result of a sound economic policy will be that the king's subjects are bonded to the ruler, and will contribute also to the greater wealth of the kingdom, which itself will provide the ruler with the funds he needs. The argument thus completes a full circle. Benign economic policies, mainly non-interventionist, bring wealth and peace, and free the ruler from the tiresome obligation to engage directly in trade and industry. Bentley remarks that 'Carafa developed stunning insights into the wealth of principalities', and suggests that he played a significant role in framing Ferrante's distinctive economic policy.[21] Perhaps it would be no exaggeration to describe him as an exponent of a rough-hewn sort of economic liberalism. His view was that when the prince has rich subjects he cannot possibly be poor.

The keynote of Carafa's approach to royal finance was the insistence that the ruler should maintain a sensible division between three types of expenditure: money needed for the defence of the realm; for the maintenance in its accustomed state of the royal family; and for the unpredictable emergency expenses that every ruler knew would arise, but few rulers bothered to anticipate.[22] This practical advice was one reason why the nineteenth-century political economist Ricca Salerno praised him in such resounding terms: 'eccetuati i migliori politici della repubblica fiorentina, non vi era in tutta l'Italia del medio evo uno scrittore, che intendesse al pari del Carafa l'ordine delle cose finanziarie'.[23] Carafa's astuteness is visible when he warns the ruler against heavy taxation and against manipulating the coinage – against, in other words, the sort of financial opportunism that Ferrante's father had ruthlessly practised in Italy, Sicily and Aragon. In a particularly strongly worded passage he states:

[20] Bentley, pp. 141-43; Ricca Salerno, pp. 38-39. For an older account of Carafa, see A. de Reumont, *The Carafas of Maddaloni: Naples under Spanish Dominion* (London, 1854), pp. 112-21.

[21] Bentley, p. 144.

[22] Carafa, pp. 53-54.

[23] Ricca Salerno, pp. 39-40.

Furthermore, we consider that those who steal other people's goods under cover of the word 'loan' deserve the strongest reproof. But similarly we should censure with equal severity those who, starting to feel the pinch, avoid the above method, and choose instead to sink themselves into the shadows of the treasury: from whose recesses they dig up obsolete and antiquated laws, statutes prised out with subtle ingenuity, like the most miserable of usurers . . . And straightaway you will see the Prince, without consulting anybody, dissipate and squander these precious monies – with no idea how much toil and misery on the part of his subjects brought them into his hands.[24]

There was a link between the economic health of the kingdom and the political order:

So it is no casual remark, when they say: Where one just rule flourishes, there the cities flower and the riches of the citizens grow. But where brute force reigns, there all concerns slide to ruin, and vanish forthwith.[25]

And later he expresses his economic theories in less than a dozen words: 'Neque enim Rex inops esse potest, cuius imperio ditissimi homines subjiciuntur.'[26]

Carafa insisted that the ruler should levy taxes on trade, saltworks and other potential assets not directly but by way of tax farmers.[27] The problem was that salaried officials tended to be careless, but those who had to maximise their own income as tax farmers would actually be more assiduous in collecting the king's dues; the king would in the end receive more funds, even allowing for the tax farmer's cut. In general, Carafa wanted royal intervention in the day-to-day operation of the economy to be reduced. It was undignified for the king actually to engage in commerce (an ancient tradition of the Sicilian and Aragonese rulers, of course).[28] But it was also certain that the king would make more profit from fostering the wealth of his subjects than from competing with them in business, since royal wealth was actually built upon the successful commerce of those subjects. For an essential difference still must be recognised to exist between the public and private domain. The ruler was being counselled not to stray into the latter domain. But this did not mean that he should leave mercantile affairs to look entirely after themselves. Carafa counselled government help to trade in two principal ways. The ruler should continue to provide ships for merchants, a practice already in force under Ferrante – as indeed under his predecessors on the throne of Naples and his precursors the kings of Aragon:

[24] Carafa, pp. 62-63.
[25] Ibid., p. 63
[26] Ibid., p. 79.
[27] Ibid., pp. 64-66.
[28] Ibid., p. 66.

And this has been the outstanding work of your most generous father these last years. At enormous expense he built a fleet of vessels – heavy transport ships and light craft – for one purpose, that they should be at the disposal of those who wanted to engage in trade. No other profit is extracted from them, than that the citizens can take to the sea and thereby either make their fortune, or increase it. Nor does he content himself solely with the provision of these ships (fitted, moreover, with all the necessary tackle); in addition, he entrusts to them the alum and wheat, and the other natural resources of his kingdom. The result of his activity is that, while in previous eras none except foreign merchants could be seen in our realms, now on the contrary you can find many native inhabitants devoting themselves to the business of buying and selling, and many ships ideally suited to that purpose; and more are built every day: to the extent that in the farthest reaches of east and west, our countrymen are there, ceaselessly trading.[29]

This insistence on the resurgence of native merchants is a striking claim to make, but Carafa is insisting at this point that he is writing from direct observation of Ferrante's policies. We are thus being presented with a view slightly at variance with Masuccio's image of a kingdom two of whose principal ports are swamped by Genoese and latterly Catalan businessmen. Carafa may not be saying that the foreign merchants have been pushed into second place, but his assertion that native merchants have established themselves as a significant economic force deserves to be tested.

Carafa pointed to Ferrante's role in the creation of native industries. His motive here was not simply to argue that the kingdom was less dependent on foreign merchants for the supply of essential goods, but also to demonstrate that royal patronage of a domestic textile industry would be a source of wealth to the crown and peace to the kingdom:

I hope it will not be long before it is easily apparent to everyone, how much that scheme, devised by your father for no purpose other than the advantage of his subjects, profited this kingdom. He acted likewise, again, in introducing the techniques of working wool. For when he realised the amount of gold being exported from the cities because of the scarcity of clothing, he at one stroke made them an interest-free loan of one hundred thousand gold pieces, so that they might have the means of getting started. Moreover, he never ceases, even at his own expense, exercising these same subjects in various skills, and in the conduct of magistracies or household management, each according to his own particular talent; and in all this it appears he has nothing else in mind, than to keep the vice of idleness from his peoples, and to increase individual inheritances.[30]

[29] Ibid., p. 77-78.
[30] Ibid., pp. 78-79.

Carafa apologises for this illuminating enough discourse on the usefulness of wealthy cities to princes, but in many senses it forms the empirical basis on which the rest of his argument about economic policy is built. Nor does the author confine himself to the urban economy. The prince should ensure that farmers have enough oxen for ploughing, 'ne agricultura deferatur', and similar care should be taken to protect the flocks of sheep which had become an especially important element in the economy under Ferrante's father.[31] All this meant that key economic activities should not have life squeezed from them by over-taxation; export taxes are seen as an obstacle to the maximisation of the kingdom's wealth, and so once again the idea is that the ruler can actually stimulate the production of resources, and thus his own income, by limiting his intervention in the productive cycle. Generosity to one's subjects was in any case a morally desirable act commendable for its own sake.

The vision of a prince who understands the relation between his own and his subjects' interests was taken further by Carafa in his discussion of the money supply. Carafa's main concern was that neither the ruler nor his subjects should play games with the coinage. He was clear on money's function: 'money is struck not for the profit of the prince, but for ease of buying and selling, and for the advantage of the people'.[32]

Carafa presents an interesting combination of practical and moralistic arguments in favour of his policies. On the one hand, the ruler should rule through love rather than fear; on the other hand, he must understand that in helping his subjects he helps himself: 'ubi vi agatur, ibi omnia in deterius ruere, ac celeriter euanescere.'[33] Carafa's prince is genuinely interested in the prosperity of his subjects, both for altruistic and for fiscal reasons. Above all, Carafa's observations were the product of experience. In some of these ideas Carafa was simply following a trend. The contemporary Neapolitan courtier and intellectual Giovanni Pontano, more aware than Carafa of recent debates among the Tuscan humanists, also portrays a liberal prince who will use his honesty and generosity to gain the respect of his subjects, and who will protect them from unjust imposts.[34] It would thus be wrong to assume that Carafa on his own moulded the economic outlook of the Aragonese dynasty at this period. It is now necessary to examine the application of these ideas – whether or not they originated with Carafa – to the government of Aragonese Naples.

Intention

Ferrante certainly adopted approaches to the economy that have much in

---

[31] Ibid., pp. 79-80.
[32] Ibid., pp. 84.
[33] Ibid., p. 63.
[34] Ricca Salerno, pp. 44-45; cf. Bentley, pp. 247-52 and *passim*.

common with those advocated by Carafa. His most famous initiative was the attempt to revive the silk industry.[35] But there were also vigorous efforts to stimulate internal trade by breaking down internal tariff barriers, mainly imposed by the powerful lords of the interior; Ferrante's assaults on the *diritti di passo* were frequent enough to indicate that the work could not be achieved all at once (he issued decrees in 1466, 1468, 1471).[36] By 1471 the king was indeed acting closely in accordance with Carafa's precepts, which were being penned at about the same time; on 20 January he attempted to abolish export taxes on raw materials, on bullion and on finished goods, stating that such taxes were not merely inconvenient to native and foreign merchants but were restraining the prosperity of the kingdom. Ferrante sees the complex export taxes as a disincentive to trade: he states that there would be many more exports if his subjects did not find existing taxation so vexatious.[37] It has to be said that the decree of January 1471 was not particularly effective; nevertheless, these comments come close enough to Carafa's views to suggest that there was, if not a direct influence from one to another, at least a common pool of ideas at court about the best way to stimulate economic life in the *Regno*. Some of these ideas certainly antedated Ferrante. Alfonso the Magnanimous had laid stress on the need to expand pastoral activities in the kingdom of Naples; the *mena delle pecore* is in many ways his creation, though even he was building in part on earlier Norman, Swabian, Angevin and even Spanish models.[38] On the other hand, the economic liberalism evinced by Carafa and Ferrante is generally absent from Alfonso's government of Naples, Sicily or Aragon.

More effective were individual grants of tax exemption to visiting merchants, such as those granted to the inhabitants of the Lipari islands by Alfonso and confirmed by Ferrante, or a privilege of 1461 to the inhabitants of Mazzara and privileges of 1467 and 1487 to the merchants of Dubrovnik.[39] The major foreign communities received privileges from Ferrante, who explained to the Genoese in 1480 that 'si aliter quam sic faceremus esset commercium in nostro regno prohibere et interdicere, quod in dampnum evidens puplicum privatum nostrorum cederet.'[40] The privilege begins with the remark that the ruler has ordained that all merchants of whatever nation who are present in the kingdom must be guaranteed the right to pursue their activities in safety; the motive that is

[35] Silvestri, *Commercio*, pp. 25-27.

[36] Ricca Salerno, p. 43.

[37] L. Bianchini, *Della storia delle finanze del regno di Napoli*, 3 vols. (Naples, 1834-35), ii, 72-73; Ricca Salerno, pp. 43-44n.

[38] Ryder, pp. 359-63; cf. J. Marino, *Pastoral Economies in the Kingdom of Naples* (Baltimore, 1988).

[39] Silvestri, *Commercio*, p. 13. For Dubrovnik, see M. Spremić, *Dubrovnik e gli Aragonesi (1442-1495)* (Palermo, 1986).

[40] Silvestri, *Commercio*, doc. I (iii), pp. 147-50.

cited is not in fact the good of these merchants, but 'pro bono puplico subditorum nostrorum et pro nostra nostreque Curie utilitate et comodo'. It is not perhaps easy to know how much can be made of any medieval *arenga*, but the striking emphasis on the good of Ferrante's subjects in a document in favour of the Genoese cannot be ignored; once again we seem to be in the mental world of Carafa and his peers.[41] Silvestri cites another revealing remark from a safe conduct issued to a Valencian merchant in 1488: the king must protect foreign merchants 'quippe cum ipsorum comitiva et negocia ad nostra vectigalia atque opes augendas plurimum pertinere videantur.'[42] It is in this light that should be understood the continuing generosity of the crown to alien merchants. True, they were encouraged to settle in Naples, being permitted the same tax reductions as Neapolitans if they took a Neapolitan wife or bought a residence in the city.[43] But – whatever Carafa may have implied in his remarks about the *transmarini* – it was privileges in their favour, rather than attempts to remove tariff barriers in the interior, that really produced results, both in fiscal and in political terms.

Thus in 1461 Ferrante was already trying to attract north European merchants to the *Regno*. In a grant of that year to Jean Duramont, consul of the French, Germans and English in the *Regno*, the consul's rights were confirmed over the merchants, artisans and all other 'gallicos seu francigenos, theotonicos seu alamagnos, anglicos etiam et scotos' who attended fairs in the kingdom.[44] This document should be placed alongside attempts to create a Neapolitan-managed trade route to England, though this met with only very limited success. Ferrante's willingness to look after the interest of the major Mediterranean maritime powers was more variable. The Florentines did well at the start of the reign, and saw many of their extensive rights of tax reduction, industrial monopoly and so on confirmed from 1459 onwards.[45] The Florentine banks responded, as they had done to earlier kings of Naples, with financial help in times of need, notably during the Turkish attack on Otranto (1480-81) and during the rebellion of the barons (1486). Even the quarrel between Ferrante and Florence in 1478-80 was no more than a large blip in a financial relationship that was too close to be destroyed by the official (and unfulfilled) sequestration of Florentine goods; it was Lorenzo de' Medici's good personal knowledge of Ferrante that made a rapid reconciliation possible, and that brought the Florentines to new

---

[41] For the Genoese bankers at Ferrante's court, see A. Silvestri, 'Sull'attività bancaria napoletana durante il periodo aragonese', *Bollettino dell'Archivio storico del Banco di Napoli*, ii (1952), 80-120; also del Treppo, 'Re e banchiere'.

[42] Silvestri, *Commercio*, p. 17.

[43] Ibid., p. 15.

[44] Ibid., doc. I (i), pp. 141-45.

[45] Pontieri, pp. 267-70.

strength in the *Regno*.[46] By 1483 Ferrante had decided to elevate Lorenzo to the office of Grand Chamberlain of the Kingdom of Naples, and to extend the rights of the Florentine merchants to such an extent that they came to form a virtual state within a state.[47]

The Florentines in Naples were by no means all Medicean in sympathy: the Strozzi exiles long possessed an important banking house in Naples and flourished undisturbed in 1478-80.[48] However, it was the close link between Naples' political interests in the Italian peninsula and the desire of Lorenzo's Florence to avoid a new pan-Italian conflict that guaranteed the ascendancy of Florentine businessmen at Naples in the last years of Ferrante's reign. Pontieri pointed out how the crown had actually tried to play off one group of foreigners against another, but in the end failed. He says: 'era un'utopia sperare che, imperante tale sistema, potessero fiorire quelle industrie nazionali (seta, lana, ferro, ecc.) che Ferrante, sfidando anzi tutta l'opposizione indigena, aveva pur tentato d'incrementare col palese scopo di sottrarre Napoli al monopolio dei mercati stranieri'; economic dependence on Florence developed into political dependence too.[49] It is thus interesting to see how in 1480 the king, in need of friends, was addressing the Genoese as a specially favoured nation.[50] There were certainly many powerful Genoese bankers in the kingdom alongside the Florentines, but the Florentines had the real pulling power. A letter of 20 March 1477 from Ferrante to Lorenzo de' Medici's bank in Naples stated that, in view of the king's debt of 964 ducats, 3 tari and 4 grana, the bank could export foodstuffs from the kingdom of a quantity sufficient to be liable for an equivalent sum in customs dues, from which the Medici Bank would then be exempt.[51] It was on such deals, linking the financial needs of the crown to the business interests of the Florentine merchants, that Florence had built its influence in the *Regno*.[52]

There is another example of Ferrante's intention of stimulating an

[46] On the Medici in Naples, see Silvestri, 'Attività bancaria', pp. 102-4.

[47] Pontieri, p. 269.

[48] Silvestri, 'Attività bancaria', pp. 99-101: del Treppo, 'Re e banchiere', pp. 233-40; R.A. Goldthwaite, *Private Wealth in Renaissance Florence: A Study of Four Families* (Princeton, 1968), pp. 26, 53-58, 238-39; of particular importance is *Il Giornale del Banco Strozzi a Napoli (1473)*, ed. A. Leone (Fonti e Documenti per la Storia del Mezzogiorno d'Italia, vii, Naples, 1981).

[49] Pontieri, p. 270.

[50] Silvestri, *Commercio*, doc. I (iii), pp. 147-50.

[51] Silvestri, 'Attività bancaria', p. 102.

[52] As was visible as early as the start of the fourteenth century: David Abulafia, 'Southern Italy and the Florentine Economy, 1265-1370', *Economic History Review*, ser. 2, xxxiii (1981), 377-88, repr. in idem, *Italy, Sicily and the Mediterranean, 1100-1400* (London, 1987), cap. VI; G. Yver, *Le commerce et les marchands dans l'Italie méridionale au XIIIe et au XIVe siècle* (Paris, 1903).

economic revival and at the same time of producing good fiscal returns: his policy towards the Jews. There is little reason to doubt that Ferrante's willing toleration of the Jews was prompted as much by financial motives as by dislike for the current fashion for persecuting Jews.[53] His encouragement of the Jews in fact aroused the ire of several Apulian towns, such as Bari and Trani. But by welcoming refugees from Spain, he and his father hoped to stimulate capital investment and to benefit from the know-how of exiles who were often highly experienced in the textile or metal industries. The large contingent of Syracusan Jews who arrived in Calabria at the end of Ferrante's reign were especially welcome because of their expertise in the indigo-dyeing industry.[54] Yet the monarchy was less happy about moneylending. It saw the Jews primarily as a specialist artisan force, and permitted at one stage a moratorium on debts to be proclaimed.[55] When a large influx of Spanish, Sicilian and Sardinian Jews arrived in 1492-93 (and of Portuguese in 1497) they were not turned away, but Ferrante and his successors were particularly keen to secure the services of the wealthy and cultured Isaac Abravanel: it was the elite of financiers and bankers who naturally appealed to them most. King Federigo, the last Aragonese ruler of Naples, even permitted the Jews to resume collection of debts, so long as he received half the proceeds.[56] Financial motives were never far from the surface. On the other hand, the obligation for Jews to wear a distinguishing mark was relaxed by Ferrante and by Federigo, and Jews (including new immigrants) were given the right to form communities, with synagogues, in the south Italian towns.[57] What appeared to Cecil Roth a good example of royal tolerance was in fact a deliberate attempt to ensure that the Jews of each city had a formal organisation which could compound legally for the payment of taxes to the crown.

The economic policies of Ferrante must in fact be placed in the context of a long history of similar initiatives. The abolition of tariff barriers on the passage of goods within the kingdom can be traced back to 1187, when King William II admitted that the problem of tax pirates in southern Italy had become so acute that the taxes due to the crown were not reaching him; he therefore abolished all such taxes.[58] Equally, attempts to revive

[53] But C. Roth, *The History of the Jews of Italy* (Philadelphia, 5706/1946), pp. 275-9, was as ever more optimistic.

[54] Roth, p. 278.

[55] Ibid., p. 277; Silvestri, *Commercio*, pp. 30-36, assembles some data on Jewish lending around 1490; but his vicious remarks on p. 34 are an unusual departure from the Italian norm.

[56] Roth, p. 281.

[57] Ibid, p. 276.

[58] David Abulafia, 'The Crown and the Economy under Roger II and his Successors', *Dumbarton Oaks Papers*, xxxvii (1983), 9, repr. in idem, *Italy, Sicily and the Mediterranean*, cap. I.

the cloth industry were far from new. These attempts should be divided into two classes: the creation of a specialist textile industry aiming to satisfy the needs of the royal court, such as the Norman silk workshops, and a genuine export oriented industry, which it does seem Ferrante aimed to create. The Jews had long been known in southern Italy as skilled dyers, and in some towns – notably Salerno – they exercised a dyeing monopoly as far back as the twelfth century;[59] and Frederick II had already looked abroad in the thirteenth century for Jewish cultivators of indigo.[60] Attempts to create a luxury woollen industry under Charles II and Robert the Wise may fall into the second category, but were unsuccessful, apparently among other reasons because the textile workers were suspected of heresy.[61] Moreover, in northern Italy the visible success of new or expanding silk industries would have suggested to any thoughtful Mediterranean ruler where industrial success might be sought; Genoa, previously lacking in any major industry other than shipbuilding, developed a successful silk industry in this period, by copying Byzantine secrets; and Florence tried to do the same now that the international market in fine woollens had contracted. The problem for Ferrante was that others had conquered the market first. Southern Italy's advantages would presumably lie in a combination of the ability to produce silkworms on a large scale and (it was hoped) a skilled labour force able to create the finished product. The conclusion must be that Ferrante's innovations were not entirely remarkable given the long history of government intervention in the south Italian economy; what may have been relatively new was a more sophisticated understanding of the operation of the economy, which was not simply seen as a fiscal tool.

Reality

The central question must be whether these intentions were translated into action. Ferrante's inheritance was not especially auspicious: Alfonso I had placed his political interests first, and saw the reformed government of the *Regno* as a source of supply for funds to be spent largely outside the region. He also left Ferrante the task of securing recognition for his royal title, potentially an expensive business if (as happened) the Angevins reappeared in southern Italy. On the other hand, Alfonso had scored a striking fiscal success with his pastoral reforms. In 1444/5 the income from the *mena delle pecore* was 38,516 ducats; in 1448/9 it was 92,973 ducats; but by 1449/50 it was 103,012 ducats, the proceeds of over a million

[59] E.M. Jamison, *Admiral Eugenius of Sicily: His Life and Work* (London, 1957), doc. IV, pp. 323-32.

[60] David Abulafia, *Frederick II: A Medieval Emperor* (London, 1988), pp. 335-36.

[61] R. Caggese, *Roberto I d'Angiò e i suoi tempi*, 2 vols. (Florence, 1922-30), i, 530-31.

sheep.[62] The monarchy was able to take advantage of the rural depopulation that followed the arrival of plague, while demand for wool (particularly the fine wools of the Abruzzi) remained healthy. The gains were short-lived since the wool of Castile captured the Italian market by the end of the fifteenth century. However, Ferrante clearly had a solid base on which to build. A second legacy was the favouritism that had always dominated Alfonso the Magnanimous' approach to government. According to John Marino, Ferrante made few substantial changes in the management of the Apulian pastures. Foggia grew in importance as the setting for a Spring fair specialising in pastoral products. Yet corrupt management of the flocks culminated in 1474 in the death of 700,000 sheep (41 per cent of the total) when inadequate grazing facilities were provided during a severe winter. Ferrante's approach remained that of his father; the *mena* was a valuable source of revenue, and if that meant taking sides with the great pastoralists against agricultural interests he was prepared to do so. There were frequent worries about whether the fisc was receiving all its dues from the *mena*. Even so the number of sheep had reached about 1,700,000 by 1496/7, and control of its revenues became a French ambition during the wars for control of Naples.[63]

Seen from Naples, the *mena* appeared to be a qualified success story. Revenues increased significantly over the years, and the main difficulty remained that of placating a wide variety of competing interests: owners of flocks and of land, powerful nobles with a stake in the pastoral economy, and petty pastoralists who had little clout at court. However, there was little success in creating an export-oriented woollen textile industry, and much of the best wool was sent outside the kingdom by foreign merchants; the very repetitiveness of attempts to stimulate the woollen industry into life suggests how far the king was from achieving his objectives.[64] The next question has therefore to be whether the monarch explored other ways to gain an important stake in the management of exports. The most ambitious attempt to do so was surely the creation of a trade route linking Naples to England. Once again the origins of this enterprise have to be sought in Alfonso's reign, when the first Neapolitan galleys ventured to Flanders and England (1451-52).[65]

[62] Marino, pp. 24-28, Ryder, pp. 361-62.

[63] Marino, p. 27.

[64] For relatively positive views, however, see G. Coniglio, 'L'arte della lana a Napoli', *Samnium*, xxi (1948), 62-79; and Silvestri, *Commercio*, p. 9n, mentioning an attempt in 1473 to clear an area of Naples so that industrial plants could be set up for wool production. In 1480 Ferrante invited Spanish, Genoese, Ragusan, Milanese, Bolognese, Florentine and other skilled workers to come and establish textile workshops in the *Regno*: Silvestri, *Commercio*, p. 10n; Bianchini, p. 166.

[65] C. Marinescu, 'Les affaires commerciales en Flandres d'Alphonse V d'Aragon, roi de Naples (1416-58)', *Revue historique*, ccxxi (1959), 35-36; M. Mallett, *The Florentine Galleys in the Fifteenth Century* (Oxford, 1967), p. 92n.

Under Ferrante there were further stimuli to this trade. In 1468 King Edward IV of England entered into a treaty with Ferrante; this seems to have had concrete results, since it is known that in 1473 or 1474 two of Ferrante's galleys, captained by Agnello Pirocco, were attacked on their way from England back to Italy by a notorious French pirate named Coulon, who also served as vice-admiral of Louis XI. Pirocco demanded compensation from the French king.[66] The same Neapolitan captain was in Southampton in 1478, and it is reasonable to assume that for much of the decade a couple of galleys, apparently owned by Ferrante himself, were travelling each year to the Atlantic.[67] Ruddock asks whether Ferrante was attempting to imitate the regular sailings of the Florentine and Venetian state galleys to England and Flanders.[68] This is likely enough: the state galleys regularly visited the ports of the *Regno*, and unloaded cloths, sugar, hides and other goods there, taking on board not merely food supplies but raw wool and the raw silk of Calabria.[69] The Neapolitan galleys continued to play a major role in the defence of the kingdom, which suggests that in times of peace several galley-based trade routes may have operated. One route that was probably not dependent so much on galleys as on round ships was the trading link to Tunis, along which the Neapolitans were promised freedom of navigation by a treaty with the Tunisian ruler in 1477. The Neapolitans were to receive privileges identical to those of the Genoese and the Venetians, and these rights were extended not merely to *regnicoli* but to others, in Ferrara, Urbino, Piombino and Faenza, who had political ties to King Ferrante.[70] It is possible that many of the galleys were rented out to foreigners: the galley *Ferrandina* is documented in the 1460s and 1470s, manned by Florentines and probably hired by the Medici from the king of Naples. It was active on the Florentine account not merely in Flanders but in the Levant – both Alexandria and Constantinople.[71] Such activities may have brought Ferrante some profit, but they did little to stimulate a renaissance of long-distance trade among the *regnicoli*.

The most extensive evidence for the role of Ferrante's subjects in international trade comes from the commercial contracts of the fair of Salerno in 1478, published by Silvestri. The role of the *meridionali* was in fact respectable: 211 merchants mentioned in Silvestri's collection were

[66] A. Ruddock, *Italian Merchants and Shipping at Southampton, 1270-1600* (Southampton, 1951), pp. 67-68.

[67] *Calendar of Patent Rolls, 1476-85* (London, 1901), p. 88.

[68] Ruddock, p. 68.

[69] Mallett, pp. 125-26.

[70] Pontieri, p. 179; J. Ribera, 'Tratado de paz ò tregua entre Fernando I el Bastardo, rey de Napoles, y Abuamer Otman, rey de Tunez', *Centenario della nascita di Michele Amari* (Palermo, 1910), ii, 373.

[71] Mallett, pp. 102-3.

southerners, as against forty-three north Italians, twenty-three Catalans, eight French and a single German.[72] These figures must themselves be modified in favour of the south Italians since several so-called foreigners had taken up permanent residence in the *Regno*. Removing the names of those who only appear as witnesses, we have twenty-three north Italians whose trading activities are recorded, seven Catalans, five Frenchmen and the single German, plus 104 south Italians. But the most important group of foreigners was not the Florentines, who were most numerous overall (ten *operatori* and fourteen witnesses); it was the slightly smaller group of the Genoese (thirteen *operatori* and five witnesses).[73] The Genoese bought goods to the tune of 6,704 ducats and sold goods for the slightly higher sum of 7,563. Florentine purchases totalled a mere 700 ducats, though sales totalled 4,525. The Catalans have a more modest profile: purchases at 1,128 and sales at 1,244. The French, primarily from Languedoc, come low down the scale, with 47 ducats in purchases, but 563 in sales.[74] Their real importance lay in the goods their home towns produced, rather than in their visible presence.

These figures must be qualified, since there is no guarantee that the source, the Neapolitan notary Petruccio Pisano, recorded a typical cross-section of the business of the Salerno fairs. It is not even clear what a notary from Naples was doing at Salerno. However, his records are strikingly consistent, whether he was working at home or in Salerno. In a group of his acts from Naples, dating to 1465-66, we find eight Florentines, seven Frenchmen, five Catalans, three Genoese, two Sienese and one Pisan.[75] We also find the same concentration among the foreign merchants on the sale of foreign cloths. Thus in July 1466 a merchant of Montpellier sold Languedoc cloth to a Neapolitan purchaser;[76] it was the revived strength of the cloths of Languedoc and Roussillon that brought southern French and some Catalan merchants to Naples and Salerno at this period.[77] In the Salerno acts of 1478 Languedoc has first place in the number and value of woollen cloths sold: 451 woollen cloths were traded, worth a little over 4,149 ducats; but the average price of these cloths was rather low: 9.1.0.[78] (In the Naples contracts of 1465-66 the cloths of Languedoc also hold first place, with 164 cloths worth a total of just over

---

[72] Sapori, p. 448.

[73] Sapori, pp. 452-53; Grohmann, pp. 229-31.

[74] Sapori, p. 448.

[75] Coniglio, 'Mercanti forestieri', p. 79.

[76] Ibid, p. 80.

[77] Ashtor, pp. 253-54.

[78] A good example of a sale of Languedoc cloth is Silvestri, *Commercio*, doc. xcix, p. 86, where Taddeo de Alborea, a Gaetan merchant resident in Naples, declares that he owes Geronimo de Scozio 267 ducats for the purchase price of 'pannorum viginti octo de Linguadoca de lana novorum diversorum colorum et racionum'. Scozio was a Neapolitan: Silvestri, ibid., pp. 132-33.

1,327 ducats, making an average of 8.3.0 per cloth.) By comparison, Florentine woollen cloths averaged a price of 45.4.3 a piece, and fifty-six of them were traded at a total of 2,566.[79] Florentine silks worth 318 ducats were also exchanged. English woollen cloths, apparently absent in the acts of 1465-66, were in 1478 worth only a little less on average than Florentine ones (43.0.18), and 78½ of them were exchanged, making a total of 3,390 ducats, that is to say much more than the value of Florentine cloths.[80]

It was Catalonia that made a rather poor showing, probably in the wake of the destructive civil wars of the 1460s. Ten Catalan and 33½ Barcelona cloths were traded, for 517 ducats; the cloths of Barcelona were of nearly twice the value per piece of the other Catalan cloths.[81] In addition there were cloths from the major Catalan industrial centres of Perpignan (a city now at issue between France and Aragon) and Majorca. Perpignan cloths were on average worth 31.4.17, and seventeen of them were sold, making a total of 543;[82] Majorcan cloths were on average worth 11.0.6 and a good 74 were sold, adding up to 819 ducats.[83] In 1465-66 one sale of a Majorcan cloth in Naples is recorded, worth 24 ducats.[84] Some cloth of Verona and Piedmont was sold at Salerno, but the major north Italian supplier other than Florence was Genoa, with 239 cloths at an average of 6.2.15 per piece and a total of 1,566 ducats.[85] These were evidently much more modest cloths than those of Florence, Perpignan or even Barcelona.[86] However, the contracts serve as a reminder that labels attached to cloths may indicate type rather than provenance: there is a reference to Genoese cloth in the style of Majorca, whose average price is closer to the Genoese than the Majorcan norm.[87] But the most modest

[79]   See for example Silvestri, *Commercio*, doc. liii, pp. 72-73, an interesting contract for the purchase both of Florentine woollen cloth and of fine silks.

[80]   Silvestri, *Commercio*, doc. xxix, p. 66, shows a Catalan merchant resident in Naples buying London cloth (as it is described) from some prominent Genoese traders, Manuele de Almano, Giuliano de Mari and Francesco Lomellino. See also Sapori, pp. 454-55; Ashtor, pp. 254-55.

[81]   Silvestri, *Commercio*, doc. xxxi, p. 67, reveals a sale of various types of Barcelona cloth by the prominent Catalan merchant Bartolomeo Camporodone, on whom see also Silvestri, *Commercio*, pp. 99-100. He handled skins and grain as well, and made loans to the king.

[82]   See e.g. Silvestri, *Commercio*, docs. xi-xii, p. 62, for sales of Perpignan cloth involving merchants of Roussillon, Catalonia and the south Italian towns.

[83]   Thus Silvestri, *Commercio*, doc. lxv, p. 77, indicates a sale of one Majorcan cloth for twelve ducats.

[84]   Coniglio, 'Mercanti forestieri', p. 79.

[85]   Genoa was also a source of canvas, not surprisingly: Silvestri, *Commercio*, doc. xlii, p. 69.

[86]   Sapori, p. 455; Ashtor, p. 255.

[87]   'Pannorum decem et novem de Janua legatorum a la maiorchina de lana novorum': Silvestri, *Commercio*, doc. lxxxiv, p. 82, and doc. lv, p. 73; also ibid., p. 54.

cloths were those known as *arbasio* or *orbace*, which sold for about 2.0.19 a piece, and of which 73 were traded; these would be relatively rough and heavy cloths, not all (as Sapori assumed) of Tuscan origin, but in most cases south Italian or Sicilian.[88] In fact, Ferrante had tried in 1465 to ban the import of cheap woollen cloths in the hope of eliminating competition for south Italian cloths in domestic markets. Not merely do the acts of 1478 suggest how unsuccessful he was; in 1477 the city of Barcelona requested the king of Aragon to intercede with his kinsman of Naples to lift the ban on cheap Catalan cloths.[89] It is therefore hard to say whether in the early 1460s cheap Catalan cloths would have been more visible in the market-places of the *Regno*. The acts of Petruccio Pisano drawn up at Naples in 1465-66 refer to twelve pieces of Catalan cloth, worth 156.0.5, so these appear not to be especially cheap textiles.[90]

The acts also reveal heavy imports of leather and of untreated skins, notably from North Africa and England.[91] The provenance of the 3,074 skins traded at Salerno in 1478 is not easy to judge; many were certainly south Italian and there is also a reference to 'coirorum centum quadraginta pilusorum de Sardinia' in a contract that links members of the Strozzi bank and south Italian businessmen.[92] Grain is not greatly in evidence among exports, but there are references to wine from Somma and Tropea;[93] there is a particularly important mention of unworked silk from Calabria, worth 769½ ducats, purchased on credit by a Genoese merchant;[94] and in particular there is a mention of silk to be worked at Taverna and Cosenza worth 716.1.10.[95] Thus southern Italy continued to supply silk, but not solely for domestic producers.

The *regnicoli* present at the Salerno fair were not by any means all from the immediate region. Giovanni Campani of Tropea in Calabria bought five pieces of French woollen cloth, already dyed, for 72 ducats; he promised to repay either in specie or in kind or in a combination of the two. The offer in kind consisted of red or white wine to be received either in Naples or in Tropea, according to his partner's choice.[96] It is thus clear

---

[88] Sapori, p. 456n; Ashtor, p. 255. See Silvestri, *Commercio*, doc. xl-xli, p. 69, for examples. For its presence in Sicilian internal trade, see S.R. Epstein, 'The Textile Industry and the Foreign Cloth Trade in Late Medieval Sicily (1300-1500): a "Colonial" Relationship?', *Journal of Medieval History*, xv (1989), 162-63.

[89] Silvestri, *Commercio*, p. 54n; Bianchini, p. 166.

[90] Coniglio, 'Mercanti forestieri', p. 79; Ashtor, p. 255.

[91] Coniglio, 'Mercanti forestieri', pp. 82-84.

[92] Silvestri, *Commercio*, doc. lxxxi, p. 82.

[93] Silvestri, *Commercio*, doc. i, p. 59; doc. xlix, p. 71. The one transaction involving grain is Silvestri, *Commercio*, doc. lvi, pp. 73-75, a deal between the Coppolas and Bartolomeo Donato of Genoa.

[94] Ibid., doc. xcvii, pp. 83-84.

[95] Ibid., doc. xcviii, p. 86; cf. doc. lii, p. 72.

[96] Ibid., doc. xlix, p. 71.

that he was active in trade from Tropea to Salerno and Naples, and was not simply a displaced Calabrian.[97] Among other towns whose merchants were present at the fair in 1478 were Amantea (with about twenty-nine merchants), Castellamare di Stabia (about fifteen), Aversa (about eight) and in pride of place Naples (at least 88).[98] The emphasis of the Salerno fair thus appears to have been on the supply of Campania and particularly Naples, but additional internal trade routes radiated outwards as far south as Calabria.

The five richest merchants or merchant partnerships of south Italian origin had a turnover that was over half of the entire turnover recorded for south Italian merchants; they were Raimondo and Fabiano Cassavergara of Naples, Luigi and Francesco Coppola of Naples, Giovanni di Paolo of Cosenza, Pietro Oliva of Naples and Geronimo Scozio of Naples. The total turnover for all south Italian merchants was 14,071 ducats in purchases and 8,827 in sales, as against 8,635 and 13,897 ducats for the foreign merchants.[99] In other words, the turnover of native merchants was 366 ducats higher, but the balance between purchases and sales was approximately reversed.

The impression therefore is that south Italian businessmen trading at Salerno could not in general command the resources of their north Italian, Catalan or southern French partners; there were only one or two exceptionally wealthy figures, such as the two Coppolas who possessed ties to the royal court.[100] In general the entry of foreign goods into the *Regno* was handled by foreign businessmen, and often (though not always) they handled goods originating in their home region. It is striking too that the Florentines, whose government had at just this point broken with Ferrante, still maintained a high profile in the trade of the Mezzogiorno. The strong Genoese presence may have been enhanced, however, by the friendly approaches of Ferrante to Genoa, and the greater importance of the Florentines in Petruccio's Neapolitan acts of a dozen years earlier may reflect the normal state of business in the major ports of the kingdom. Equally the Catalan presence was certainly stronger in the 1440s and 1450s, when Alfonso I was at war with Florence and gave massive encouragement to Catalan traders in southern Italy, so much so that they rapidly surpassed the Florentines in numbers and scale of investment. The stunning lead gained by Catalan cloths is visible in a register of the royal customs from Naples probably dating from 1457. In October and November of that year 665 Catalan cloths are said to have been sold in

[97] Three other Tropeans are recorded at the fair of 1478 according to Sapori, p. 450, echoed by Coniglio, 'Mercanti forestieri', p. 81; Grohmann, p. 227, identifies only the one Tropean, and is correct.

[98] Sapori, p. 450.

[99] Ibid., pp. 448, 451.

[100] Silvestri, *Commercio*, pp. 104-5.

Naples, rather more than half of the total cloth traded; French cloth came a strong second with 374 cloths (nearly a third), but Florentine sales at 68 pieces were down to about a tenth of Catalan sales.[101] This was not to last. The internal crisis of Catalonia, and the favours Ferrante found it necessary to heap on Florence, deprived the Catalans of a secure lead, even if their presence remained significant. As Manuel Peláez has pointed out, the Salerno acts of 1478 are certainly not evidence for a cataclysmic collapse in Catalan trade after the civil wars.[102] Equally they date from a period when Catalan trade had passed its fifteenth-century peak.

Conclusion

The debate over economic dualism in medieval Italy has suffered from a tendency for its participants to talk at cross purposes. Terms such as 'under-development', 'exploitation', 'colonialism' have been used with abandon.[103] The argument that penetration of south Italian, Sicilian and Sardinian markets helped to generate growth in the north Italian towns and in Catalonia is not necessarily the same as the argument that the northerners took over and ruthlessly manipulated the economy of those regions. Equally it would be wrong not to lay considerable stress on the failure of the south Italian maritime cities to maintain an active international trade in the face of north Italian and Catalan competition. Amalfi did decline. The question is when and why, not whether, it did so.[104] Yet there were important internal markets that Amalfitans, Neapolitans and others continued actively to supply; and the Salerno fair was one of the major regular opportunities they had to gain access to finished products that were simply not available from domestic suppliers. And attempts to stimulate internal production met with only a limited success. Ferrante's initiatives were frustrated by the growing complexity of international trade. The *Regno* was a valued source of raw materials, not least silk, but by the early fifteenth century concentrated investment in silk and other good-quality textiles had enabled several north Italian cities, and the towns of Languedoc-Roussillon, to gain or strengthen their grip on the international trade in textiles. This trade was itself dominated by famous names: Majorca, Florence, Barcelona, among many Mediterranean examples. Naples failed to add itself to the list, and

---

[101] Del Treppo, *Mercanti catalani*, p. 244; Ashtor, p. 254.

[102] M. Peláez, *Catalunya després de la guerra civil del segle XV* (Barcelona, 1981), especially 166-69, where he remarks of the 1470s that 'la vinculació entre el commerç de Nàpols i el de Barcelona fou, sens dubte, una realitat'.

[103] See the work of Bresc and Day for fairly extensive use of these terms; compare the stern strictures of Epstein in his forthcoming book: note 5 *supra*.

[104] See del Treppo and Leone, *Amalfi medioevale*, for the best discussion of the contraction of its trade to a mainly Tyrrhenian orbit by 1400.

investment in the production of raw silk or wool resulted in an increase in the sale abroad of unworked fibres, rather than creating a domestic industry on a large scale.

It has to be remembered that Ferrante and Carafa were not hostile to the foreign commercial presence. Ferrante did see the commercial and financial links to Florence, Genoa and Catalonia as a means to win wealth for the kingdom. Carafa's recommendations were imaginative and closely reasoned. He and his king observed precisely enough the desirability of providing a sound industrial and agrarian base in the *Regno*. What they were not actually able to do was to conjure the image into life.

11

Crossing the Romagnol Appennines in the Renaissance

John Larner

It is a commonplace that medieval and Renaissance roads, particularly over mountains, were rarely constructed or engineered in the Roman fashion but rather created by use. A route which was much frequented became a physical track, which might, occasionally and in certain sections, be maintained. Even then, it was not, over any period of time, to be easily traced on a map with any permanency, but rather something which fluctuated, seasonally or over years, through landslides, floods, collapse of bridges, infestations of bandits, or new imposition of tolls.[1] It is as much a commonplace to remark upon the resulting insufficiency of these routes for individuals, trade, or armies.

I. Soldiering in the Appennines

Such complaints were not uncommon at the time. There is a well-known passage in the *Relazione*, presented to the Venetian Senate in 1527 by Marco Foscari, which dwells upon the theme in respect of Florentine territories with some emphasis.[2] The city, Foscari claims, is 'most strong and by nature most fortified' by reason of the very great difficulty with which it could be approached across the Appennines: 'through the harshest mountains and the narrowest and most difficult vales and passes for at least fifty miles, so that any army with artillery must take at least eight days in their transit'.

Foscari produces an impressionistic sketch of eight routes in all. Four passed from Lombardy (in which he included northern Emilia), 'all difficult and harsh'. These were:

---

[1] For general observations see J. Day, 'Strade e vie di comunicazione' in *Storia d'Italia*, v.1 (Turin, 1973), pp. 90-102; M.R.P. Pedrino and P. Bonora, 'Le vie di comunicazione' in *Storia della Emilia Romagna*, ed. A. Borselli, ii (Bologna, 1977), pp. 107-115. I omit reference to pre-Roman, Roman, Byzantine, and Langobard roads on which there is a growing literature.

[2] Marco Foscari, 'Relazioni . . . de Fiorenza, 1527' in *Relazioni degli ambasciadori veneti al Senato* ed. A. Segarizzi, iii.1 (Bari, 1916), 9-13.

1. From the Via Emilia, just north of Parma (via the Cisa pass), to Pontremoli, and into what he calls 'the plain of Lucca'[3]

2. From Modena into 'the plain of Lucca'[4]

3. From Bologna, along what he calls 'the Valle del Sasso' into the plain of Prato[5]

4. From Bologna via Firenzuola and Scarperia to Florence. This is 'worse than the aforesaid three roads' and could not, as they could, take artillery.

The other four roads reached Florentine territories from the Romagna, and were 'much more harsh and difficult than those that come from Lombardy'. They were:

5. From Faenza along the Val di Lamone. Foscari dwells upon this route in vivid terms: 'as most harsh and difficult as one can say, and I can give your Serenity a true account of it, having gone by that road when I went to Florence, for in truth I did not think to reach that city alive, the roads being then particularly broken, through the heavy rains there had been'. He goes on to tell of the defeat of the Great Company of Count Landau there in 1358, of how Piccinino's army had been overwhelmed by the peasants of the mountains in 1425, and of the failure of the Venetians themselves to make progress in the valley during the War of Pisa in 1498.[6]

6. From Forlì, along 'the valley of Castrocaro', 'little less difficult than the first'.

7. From Cesena, via the Val di Bagno, into the Casentino, 'which is more difficult and harsh than any of the others', with very narrow and difficult passes, and incapable of taking artillery.

8. From Rimini, along the Marecchia valley, via Sansepolcro to Arezzo. This route is 'wider and more convenient than the others and one can take artillery by it', though it is also much longer.

These eight roads whose deficiencies served as a natural defence of Florence were to be remembered for a long time by the Venetians. Over sixty years later, Tomaso Contarini (almost certainly because he had read of them in Foscari's report) was informing the Senate about them in his

[3] See Pedrino and Bonora, pp 109-111; A.C. Quintavalle, *La Strada Romea* (Milan, 1976).

[4] Pedrino and Bonora, pp. 111-12.

[5] This passed from Bologna up the R. Setta, down the R. Stura, with routes via Barberino (the Val di Marina) to Prato, and via S. Piero a Sieve to Florence. On Bologna-Florence routes, D. Sterpos, *Comunicazioni stradali attraverso i tempi: Bologna-Firenze* (Novara, 1961); idem, 'Evoluzione delle comunicazioni transappenniniche attraverso tre passi di Mugello', in *Percorsi e valichi dell'Appennino fra storia e leggenda: Futa, Osteria Bruciata, Giogo* (Florence, 1985); G.C. Romby, *Una 'Terra Nuova' nel Mugello: Scarperia: popolazione, insediamenti, ambiente. XIV-XVI secolo* (Scarperia, 1985).

[6] Foscari, in fact, must have passed from the Val di Lamone by the Casaglia pass rather than that of the Scalelle where Landau's defeat actually occurred. On this and other military fortunes of the route, see p. 159.

own *Relazione*.[7] Yet it would be over-hasty to treat what Foscari tells us here, as has perhaps been done,[8] as the whole story of even military communications. His impassioned description of his own crossing to Florence has about it, perhaps, something of the same emotion a Florentine might feel on finding himself for the first time on a galley when the Bora blew down the Adriatic. Recalling those 'monti asperissimi, valli e passi angustissimi' on which he dwells, it is quite surprising to come across Francesco Guicciardini's notes on crossing the Cisa pass. On 2 February 1511 he was at Pontremoli. On the 3rd: 'we went through the mountains of the Appennine, which last for around twelve miles, but it's an easy mountain', and reached Cassio. On the 4th he descended to Fornovo, joined the Via Emilia, and reached Borgo San Donnino (today's Fidenza).[9]

Guicciardini, of course, was not one to make a fuss. Foscari, in this context, was speaking specifically of armies. Yet even here, some among his audience, from the very illustrations which he added, may have regarded his remarks with a certain scepticism. He tells, for instance, of the sudden crossing of 6,000 Spanish soldiers from Bologna to Prato in the decisive days of August 1512. He mentions the passage of Charles VIII's army by the Cisa pass in October 1494, and his return across the same road (this time with heavy artillery) in July 1495. He refers to the passing of the Garfagnana, by John Stuart, Duke of Albany, and his troops in 1524. And in the year of the Sack he could do no less than refer to the movement of the mutinous imperial army upon Rome via the Val di Bagno. Yet all these things, he seems to imply, were mistakes, things which should not, being accompanied by so many difficulties, have happened. Anyone who had been impressed by what he had heard may, two years later, have been surprised to learn that Clement VII had caused thirty-four pieces of artillery to be sent from Bologna to the siege of Florence.[10]

Foscari's description, of course, contains a kernel of truth, namely that to move armies and guns over mountains was not easy. The transfer in 1495 of Charles VIII's army – 7,000 men, 3,000 followers, 14 heavy guns, 23 smaller pieces – across the Cisa pass (1,041 m.) was spoken of by contemporaries as an extraordinary achievement. The Sieur de Commynes, never one to diminish the difficulties which he had

---

[7] 'Relazione delle cose di Toscana di Tomaso Contarini . . . 1588', in *Relazioni*, ed. Segarizzi, iii, 2, 49.

[8] Cf. F. Braudel, *The Mediterranean and the Mediterranean World in the Age of Philip II* (London, 1972), i, 280-81. In the map, illustrating the roads, on p. 280, among some other errors, the creation of the Futa pass is anticipated by over 200 years.

[9] 'Ma è montagna facile', F. Guicciardini, *Diario del Viaggio in Spagna*, ed. P. Guicciardini (Florence, 1932), p. 37.

[10] Sterpos, *Comunicazioni*, pp. 107-8.

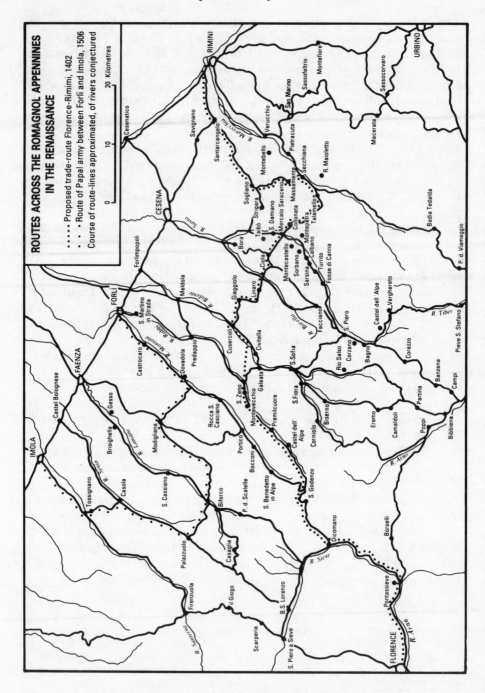

ROUTES ACROSS THE ROMAGNOL APPENNINES
IN THE RENAISSANCE

····· Proposed trade-route Florence-Rimini, 1402
· · · Route of Papal army between Forli and Imola, 1506
Course of route-lines approximated, of rivers conjectured

encountered en route, claimed (untruthfully) that he had seen all the mountains of Italy and Spain, but that it would have been easier to move artillery over any of them than across this pass. It was carried out by Charles' Swiss infantry who, having against orders massacred the inhabitants and fired the town of Pontremoli, volunteered to redeem themselves by taking on the task. Urged on by the French commander, La Trémouille (who adopted a jacket-off, sleeves-rolled-up, joking-with-the-lads manner, not normally associated with the Renaissance officer-class), they succeeded in drawing the guns up, and then, with still more difficulty, taking them down to Fornovo in four days.[11] The only conclusion to be drawn is that, here at least, the transport of artillery was difficult, yes, but possible, given good weather, leadership, morale. And, as in so much concerned with military action, the will counts for a great deal.

It is interesting, in this respect, to examine another well-known, though less dramatic, example of armies in the Appennines, this time in their foothills.[12] In October 1506, amidst difficult weather ('so that, because of the constant rains in many places, the roads were almost non-roads'),[13], Julius II passed along the Via Emilia on his first expedition against Bologna. His footsoldiers were ferried over the River Ronco, where at that time there was no bridge; he himself forded it on his mule, and so reached Forlì. Before him stood Faenza, to the south-east the Val di Lamone, to the north-west Ravenna and its *contado*, all territories held by Venice. Although the Venetians were willing to concede him passage, he did not wish to be obliged to them, and so decided to reach Imola by plunging into the Appennines controlled by Florence. On 16 October, Niccolò Machiavelli, who was at that time Florentine legate to his Holiness, rode ahead along the route, 'in order', as he whimsically put it in his letter to the Ten, 'that I may prepare the way of the Lord'.[14] On the 17th, Julius and his army, consisting of 600 horse, 1900 foot, two bombards, four culverins, and four *passavolanti* (long-range culverins), followed. They left Forlì for Castrocaro and then climbed the ridge to Modigliana. Behind Modigliana the road was crossed 'ten times' by a mountain stream,[15] and

[11] Philippe de Commynes, *Mémoires*, ed. J. Calmette, iii (Paris, 1925), pp. 160-62; H-F. Delaborde, *L'expédition de Charles VIII en Italie* (Paris, 1888), p. 630.

[12] See Paride Grassi, *Le due spedizioni militari di Guilio II*, ed. L. Frati (Bologna, Documenti e Studi della R. Dep. di Storia Patria per le prov. di Romagna, i, 1886), pp. 59-66; N. Machiavelli, *Legazioni e commissioni*, ed. S. Bertelli, ii (Milan, 1964), pp. 1018, 1020, 1024-5, 1028; M. Sanudo, *I Diarii* (Venice, 1879-1902), vi, 444, 446-47, 450-55, Sigismondo dei Conti da Foligno, *Le storie de' suoi tempi dal 1475 al 1510* (Rome, 1893), ii, 351-53; L. Pastor, *The History of the Popes*, vi (London, 1901), 276-80.

[13] Grassi, p. 59.

[14] 'Ut parem viam domino', *Legazioni*, ii, 1025.

[15] Sigismondo de' Conti calls it the 'Marziano'. Today, it is known as the Accereta (which merges with today's T. Marzeno).

proved difficult; at one point the pope was forced to dismount and go up a steep rise on foot. Then he descended into the Lamone valley and halted for the night at Marradi, having, that day, traversed perhaps 55 km. On the 18 October he climbed the next ridge to gain Palazzuolo, where he ate. He continued down the Senio valley and climbed again to reach Tossignano, where he spent the night (for that day, say 38 km.). The following morning he passed down the Santerno to Imola (16 km.).

This route along narrow hill paths, up and down three parallel ridges, represented what in anyone else would have been taken as an effort of exceptional, though in Julius' case, characteristic stubbornness. It is true that, though here the gradients are sometimes steep, the heights to be gained by the army were not particularly daunting (never, probably, more than 600 m.). Nonetheless, the 55 km. covered on the first day represent a very respectable achievement. The pope's panegyricists, of course, made the most of the occasion. His followers are represented as being almost in despair at the difficulty of the route but as being inspired by an apt Virgilian quotation which Julius offered them. Certainly for a man in his sixties, with an unhealthy life-style and an over-high alcohol intake, the route may have been uncomfortable. On the other hand, neither the Ten nor Machiavelli comment upon its difficulty. It was simply something which soldiers (and Florentine officials) were expected to take in their stride.

II. *Florence to Rimini (1402)*

In turning from armies to other groups and individuals, and in narrowing our focus from the Tusco-Emilian Appennines to those of Romagna, we can begin by jettisoning that pattern of exclusive roads which Foscari offered his auditors. Within the mountains, then, as now, there was a network of tracks leading from one valley to another, from the hill pastures to the valley bottoms, and over the high watersheds.[16] From, at least, the second half of the fourteenth century, contemporaries would be well-accustomed to the passage along them of transhumant sheep and cattle: from the Romagnol slopes of the Appennines down to pasture in the Sienese Maremma in September, thence returning in May to the mountains.[17] Again, wherever there was a castle, village, church, or monastery, there was a track leading somewhere else, and wherever a

[16] See, for instance, the mule-tracks leading from the abbey of S. Maria *in Trivio*, as traced by G. Cherubini, *Una comunità dell'Appennino dal XIII al XV secolo* (Florence, 1972), pp. 29-31, 107.

[17] G. Cherubini, 'La società dell'Appennino settentrionale' in his *Signori, contadini, borghesi* (Florence, 1974), p. 133; idem, 'Paesaggio agrario, insediamenti e attività silvo-pastorali sulla montagna tosco-romagnola alla fine del medioevo' in *La montagna tra Toscana e Marche*, ed. S. Anselmi (Milan, 1985), pp. 69-74; *Statuti di San Godenzo (1413-1613)*, ed. F. Zerboni Zoli, introduced by G. Cherubini (San Godenzo, 1985), p. 49; P.J. Jones, 'A

commune or local lord extracted tolls, smugglers would seek out obscure paths across the highest passes in order to avoid paying them.

The capacity to make one's way through the *montagna* and *collina* is illustrated by the Florence-Rimini trade-route planned in Spring 1402, at the height and near the culmination of the war between Florence and Gian Galeazzo Visconti of Milan. By March 1402, Bologna was besieged by Milanese forces, and most other customary Florentine routes were cut. The only outlet for Florentine commerce lay through the Romagna. Yet here the commune's seizure of Castrocaro, only 12 km. from Forlì, in 1394-95, had aroused deep suspicions, and the rulers of the little ports of Ravenna and Cesenatico had accordingly denied Florentine access.[18]

In these circumstances Florence turned to Carlo Malatesta, lord of Rimini, who followed an ambiguous but skilfully conducted policy of alliance with both sides. In April the *Sei della Mercanzia* conceived of a plan for trade through Rimini, whose port in that very month was being reconstructed under, curiously enough, the direction of one Domenico, engineer to Gian Galeazzo Visconti.[19] This route they imparted to Rinaldo degli Albizzi, whom they sent as legate to the lord Carlo in order to negotiate his approval, together with a calculation of how much would be paid in tolls (*pedaggia*) per *soma* (mule-pack load).[20] We can enumerate this as follows:

Florence to Castel dell'Alpe ('which is ours', i.e. a Florentine possession) [89 km.]	1 *bolognino*
Castel dell'Alpe to Premilcuore ('which is ours') [11 km.]	1 *bolognino*
Premilcuore to Montevecchio ('is of the Count of Dovadola') [5 km]	1 *bolognino*
Montevecchio to San Zeno ('is ours') [11 km.]	1 ½ *bolognini*

So far the road would have been familiar to many Florentines, who, it can be seen, had already absorbed many territories in this region. After San Godenzo the mule-trains would strike sharply up the ridge, diverging from today's S.S. 67, thorugh the Orticai pass (1093 m.) and down to San Zeno.

From there the road continued, crossing the ridges between the Ronco and Savio and the Savio and Marecchia rivers:

Tuscan Monastic Lordship in the Later Middle Ages: Camaldoli', *Journal of Ecclesiastical History*, v (1954), 181.

[18] For the circumstances, R. Piattoli, 'Il problema portuale di Firenze dall'ultima lotta con Gian Galeazzo Visconti alle prime trattative per l'acquisto di Pisa', *Rivista storica degli archivi toscani*, ii (1930), 157-190; P.J. Jones, *The Malatesta of Rimini and the Papal State* (London, 1974), pp. 111-21.

[19] Jones, p. 117.

[20] *Commissioni [di Rinaldo degli Albizzi per il comune di Firenze (1399-1433)*, ed. C. Guasti (Florence, 1867-73)], i, 13-14.

San Zeno to Cusercoli ('where the Count is our *accomandato*') [21]
   [16 km.]   *3 bolognini*
Cusercoli to Giaggiolo ('whose count is the brother of him of
   Cusercoli') [22] [15 km.]   *3 bolognini*
Giaggiolo to Ciola ('which is of Forlì') [23] [18 km.]   *3 bolognini*
Ciola to Mercato Saraceno ('which is of the treasurers of the
   Church') [8 km.]   *3 bolognini*
Mercato Saraceno to Talamello ('of the treasurers of the
   Church') [13 km.]   *2 bolognini*

The route then passed for a brief distance down the Marecchia, to mount the ridge again and from there descend to the Romagnol plain:

Talamello to Sogliano (whose count [24] was '*accomandato* of
   signor Carlo [Malatesta]') [20 km.]   *2 bolognini*
Sogliano to Santarcangelo (ruled by Carlo Malatesta)
   [17 km.]   *2 bolognini*

From Santarcangelo it was only another 11 km. along the Via Emilia to Rimini.

Such was the plan. The *Sei della Mercanzia* instructed Rinaldo to enquire whether there might be a cheaper or shorter way compatible with safety, and then to beat down the terms (15 *bolognini* per *soma*) which Carlo was asking for transit through the port of Rimini.[25] At Bologna and at Ravenna, when the Florentines had used them, they had been charged only 12 *bolognini*. The distance for the mules was some 214 km. The

---

[21] I am uncertain of the route here. But since there is no reference to exaction of tolls at Galeata and Civitella, I have marked on my map a direct track from San Zeno across the M. Fusa.

[22] On Galeotto Malatesta of Cusercoli and Malatesta Malatesta of Giaggiolo, see L. Tonini, *Storia civile e sacra riminese* (Rimini, 1848-88), iv. 1, 294.

[23] 'Civola'. There is some confusion here. The logic of the route implies that this must be Ciola on the ridge route (see p. 165 below) between the Borello and the Savio. The Sei seem to have mistaken it for another Ciola, on M. Poggiolo, some 10 km. S.W. of Forlì.

[24] This is Giovanni Malatesta from another cadet-branch of the Riminese house; see Tonini, iv, 1, pp. 356-7.

[25] The Sei specified 'ogni soma di libbre D o circa'. The *libbra fiorentina* (see A. Martini, *Manuale di Metrologia*, Turin, 1883), is the equivalent of 0.339542 kg., which would imply a total weight of circa 170 kg. According to F. Melis, *I trasporti e le comunicazioni nel medioevo*, ed. L. Frangioni (Florence, 1985), p. 165, the medieval mule could carry 200-250 kg. For L. Frangioni, *Milano e le sue strade: Costi di trasporto e vie di commercio dei prodotti milanesi alla fine del Trecento* (Bologna, 1983), pp. 97-99, 141-42, mules carried weights of *c*. 98-196 kg. over the Alps. By modern standards these are heavy loads. Even the famous nineteenth-century Kentucky breed carried only 80-91 kg. in rough terrain. See 'Mules' in *The Standard Encyclopaedia of Modern Agricultural and Rural Economy* (n.p., n.d., but *c*. 1910); and the following note.

journey, it might be, would take nine days.[26]

Rinaldo, in fact, was able to secure an agreement with the Malatesta for Florentine passage along this route, though in the light of subsequent events (the fall of Bologna, and then the death of Gian Galeazzo Visconti at the end of the year), it may never have been used. Nonetheless, it should be emphasised that its course would not have been seen as particularly rigorous. The Datini archives of the second half of the fourteenth and beginning of the fifteenth century reveal a large scale transit of Spanish wool from Porto Pisano on the Tyrrhenian, thence overland to Florence, and across the Appennines to the Adriatic.[27] Federigo Melis has written a few authoritative (though, for our purpose, extremely succint and generalised) remarks on the role of Romagna in this. He shows that though the normal outlet for Florentine merchandise to the Adriatic was via Bologna, Ferrara, and the Po waterways to Venice, there was also some traffic through Romagna. In this period goods were despatched from Florence across the Appennines to the ports of Ravenna, Cervia, Cesenatico, and Rimini. From here they were loaded on small vessels, sailing to Venice, where their cargo was then transferred to larger ships, bound for more distant destinations, sometimes, even, in the western Mediterranean.[28] In some measure, that is, the tracks of the Romagna were linked at that time to a much wider commercial world.

III. Routes across the Romagnol Appennines

In seeking to discover customary routes – and here we are looking for 'route-lines' rather than any precise Renaissance tracks which can only be established (when they can be established) by field archeology – there are, in addition to a variety of miscellaneous references, two principal sources.

[26] According to G. Fleming, 'Mules', in *The Encyclopaedia Britannica*, 9th ed. (Edinburgh, 1884), xvii, it is suggested, from experience in the Peninsular War, that (though the pace is obviously dictated by the terrain and individual stamina), carrying a weight of 200 British Imperial pounds (91 kg.), a mule could travel in mountainous country at about 3 km. an hour for some 25 km. a day.

[27] F. Melis, 'La lana della Spagna mediterranea e della Barberia occidentale nei secoli XIV-XV', in *La Lana come materia prima* (Florence, 1974), p. 247 (and see there his map).

[28] F. Melis, *I trasporti*, pp. 138, 144, 151 (Florentine commercial agents in Cesenatico and Rimini), 163-64, 168, 170. For plans to import grain through Rimini in 1411-12, G. Pinto, 'Commercio del grano e politica annonaria nella Toscana del Quattrocento', *Studi di storia economica nel medioevo e nel Rinascimento in memoria di F. Melis* (Florence, 1987), pp. 264-65. On analogous transpeninsular trade between Florence and Ancona, much more (no doubt because it was more important) has been written. H. Hoshino, *L'arte della lana in Firenze nel basso medioevo* (Florence, 1980), pp. 65-66, 78, 173-74, 183-84, 224, 248, 269-71, 284-5; P. Earle, 'The Commercial Development of Ancona, 1479-1551', *Economic History Review*, ser. 2, xxii (1969), 34-35. Both these works refer, too, to export through Pesaro. For further references see M.E. Mallett, *The Florentine Galleys in the Fifteenth Century* (Oxford, 1967), p. 7, n. 5.

The first of these is the *Descriptio Romandiole*, drawn up upon the instructions of Cardinal Anglic Grimoard in 1371.[29] This does not, in fact, offer any systematic discussion of Romagnol route-systems. On the other hand, on many occasions it describes villages and castles as being 'above' a road ('supra stratam' or 'supra stratam magistram'). This does not necessarily mean 'on' a road, for sometimes 3 or 4 km. and a river separates the castle from where the road ran. In these cases *supra* means 'able to dominate'. Not all castles on roads are indicated as being on them and some roads known to exist are ignored. Again, though less helpfully, the *Descriptio* refers to the exaction of *pedagium* or *passagium*, words normally taken to mean 'toll', at certain points. This occurs very occasionally; none, for instance, of the places referred to as taking tolls in the *Sei della Mercanzia*'s plan of 1402, are recorded as doing so in the *Descriptio* of 1371, and it is difficult to imagine that they have suddenly sprung up in the thirty years between them. Further, on those rare occasions in the *Descriptio* when the annual yield of these tolls is given, they are surprisingly low and frequently compounded with other dues (on mills, judicial exactions and so on). One cannot, indeed, be always certain that *pedagium* is used to mean 'road-toll' rather than 'impost' in general.[30] Nonetheless, by collating these references on a map,[31] some pattern, not of course of the precise tracks, but of the lines of route of the time emerge.

Our second principal source are the accounts of the embassies undertaken by Rinaldo degli Albizzi (1370-1442), whom we have already seen negotiating with Carlo Malatesta in 1402. These contain terse notes on the route he travelled, drawn up primarily, no doubt, for the purpose of claiming expenses, but also – for he often jots down the number of miles beween one village and the next – designed perhaps to imprint the line of the road upon his memory. Rinaldo records eleven crossings in all between Tuscany and the Romagna.

From such information there emerges evidence for nine routes or route systems.

[29] L. Mascanzoni, *La 'Descriptio Romandiole' del Card. Anglic: Introduzione e Testo* (Bologna, n.d.). I cite this, henceforth, as *Descriptio*. Together with its map and patient identification of place-names this edition is invaluable, though I remain unconvinced by Dr. Mascanzoni's interpretation of *focularia*. On this issue, see the cogent discussion of N. Galassi, *Figure e vicende di una città*, i, *Imola dall'età antica al tardo medioevo* (Imola, 1984), pp. 488-89, 560-66.

[30] Cf. *Descriptio*, pp. 229-30: 'Pedagium seu gabella que exigitur in burgo Galliate de rebus que venduntur . . . '

[31] Neither of the two earliest surviving maps of Romagna: the 'Flaminia' of Egnazio Danti in the Galleria of the Belvedere in the Vatican Palace (reproduced in R. Almagià, *Le pitture murali della Galleria delle carte geografiche*, Vatican, 1952, pl. XII) or the 'Romagna' of G.A. Magini (1st edition, 1597; reproduced in his *Italia*, Bologna, 1620, no. 36) show any roads apart from the Via Emilia. I have used the 1:100,000 maps (nos. 87, 88, 98, 99, 100, 101, 106, 107, 108, 109) of the Istituto Geografico Militare.

1. Florence to Imola

This is not revealed by the *Descriptio* but appears in Albizzi's notes. In travelling to northern Italy, it was normal for him to pass directly from Florence to Bologna and back (never by any more northerly pass). He records seventeen occasions (of which on thirteen he passed by the Giogo della Scarperia [882 m.]) when he did this.[32] On an embassy in 1412, however, because of the presence in the city of 'certain exiles and rebels to this commune', he avoided Bologna. The route was:

26 May	Florence to Scarperia. [29 km.]
27 May	Scarperia, down the line of the R. Santerno to Imola.[33] [69 km.]
28 May	He sent back four horses from Imola to Florence. He then passed to Conselice where he boarded a *burchio* (or a flat-bottomed canal-boat) and, passing through the marshes, reached the Po di Primaro, to spend the night at Argenta.
29 May	He went by water to Ferrara where he put up at another inn.
30 May	He went from Ferrara to Francolino, where he embarked on a *burchio* on the Po Grande;[34] and reached Venice on 1 June.[35]

[32] *Commissioni, passim.*

[33] Documents of 1418, 1420, and 1435 refer to the 'strata montanaria' from Imola: N. Galassi, *Dieci secoli di storia ospitaliera a Imola* (Imola, 1966-70), i, 97.

[34] *Commissioni*, i, 218-9. On the Po navigation see, among a large literature, G. Soranzo, *L'antico navigabile Po di Primaro* (Milan, 1964); M. di Gianfrancesio, 'Per una storia della navigazione padana dal medioevo alla vigilia del Risorgimento', *Quaderni storici*, xxviii (1975), 199-206.

[35] As with Albornoz, who in December 1358 passed from Florence to Imola via the Scarperia: S. Claramunt and J. Trenchs, 'Itinerario del cardenal Albornoz en sus legaciones italianas (1353-1367), in *El Cardenal Albornoz y el Colegio de España*, ed. E. Verdera y Tuells (Bologna, 1972), p. 392. For export from Imola to Florence in 1238 and 1279, see A.I. Pini, 'I trattati commerciali di una città agricola medioevale: Imola (1099-1279)', *S[tudi] R[omagnoli]*, xxvi (1975), 78-80, 82-83, 95-96. For export of corn to Florence from Romagna in general (principally, it would seem, from Imola, Faenza, and Ravenna) in the thirteenth and fourteenth centuries, *Statuti della Repubblica Fiorentina*, ed. R. Caggese, i, *Statuto del Capitano del Popolo degli anni 1322-25* (Florence, 1910), p. 180 (construction of road to Or San Michele to help 'mercatores et homines reducentes et deferentes granum et bladum de partibus Mucelli et Romandiole'); G. Pinto, *Il libro del Biadaiolo* (Florence, 1978), pp. 40, 79, 80, 82, 83 (with salt from Ravenna), 93-94, 107 (importance of maintaining roads to Romagna from Florence), 121, 496; J. Glénisson, 'Une administration médiévale aux prises avec la disette', *Le Moyen Age*, lvii (1951), 305; L. Mirot, 'La question des blés dans la rupture entre Florence et le S.-Siège en 1375', *Mélanges d'archéologie et d'histoire*, xvi (1896), 181-205; and note 37 below. On the fifteenth century: G. Pampaloni, 'La crisi annonaria degli grani dalla Romagna', *Atti e memorie della Dep. S.P. di Romagna*, n.s., xv-xvi (1963-65), 277-309.

2. Florence to Faenza

(a) In the *Descriptio* the places mentioned as being 'supra stratam magistram qua itur a Faventia Florentiam' (enumerating them here, and subsequently in this article in the order in which they are traversed passing from the plain to the Appennine watershed) are Gesso, San Cassiano, Marradi, and Rocca Biforco.[36] At the appropriately named Biforco, two routes presented themselves.

(i) Through the Colle di Casaglia (913 m.) to Pulicciano, and down to Borgo San Lorenzo. This route is that envisaged by a trade agreement of 16 May 1390 between Florence and the lords of Faenza and Ravenna. The Florentines agreed with Faenza to pay 2 *solidi bolognesi* per *salma* (or mule-pack load) of Faenza and 1 *solido* for horsemen, animals, carts, and carriages (which shows that some of the road at least was accessible to wheeled traffic) at the 'toll of S. Cassiano and Brisighella'. In the fifteenth-century statutes of the Val di Lamone, again, the '*datium seu pedagium* which *antiquitus* is wont to be exacted in San Cassiano . . . or in Brisighella' is given as 1 *solido* for a horse, 2 *solidi* for each *salma* of a loaded mule, and 6 *denarii* for each *salma* of an ass.[37]

As Foscari observed in his *Relazione*, the road through the Val di Lamone was notoriously difficult from a military point of view. In January-February 1425 Niccolò and Francesco Piccinino were defeated and captured, and Oddo Fortebraccio killed, when, in the service of Florence, they led forces along it from the Mugello against Faenza.[38] Again, in September 1498, the Venetians,

---

[36] *Descriptio*, pp. 152 (bis), 155, 253. See, for this area, L. Mascanzoni, 'Marradi e l'alta valle del Lamone nel *Descriptio Romandiole*', *SR*, xxxii (1981), 53-75. This seems to be the route taken by the Imperial Prince, Henry of Bavaria, in 1173, passing 'a Cassan . . . veniens in planicie Muselle'; see K. Schrod, *Reichsstrassen und Reichsverwaltung im Königreich Italiens 754-1197*, (Stuttgart, 1931), which (p. 163) identifies 'Cassan' incorrectly with S. Casciano (*sic*) of Imola, but (p. 26) with S. Cassiano in the Lamone valley.

[37] G.F. Pagnini del Ventura, *Della Decima e di varie altre gravezze imposte dal comune di Firenze* (Lisbon and Lucca, 1765), ii. pt. iii, 21. The transcription of the document reads 'et ad rationem cujuslibet salmae ponderis quinque librarum in dicta civitate Faventiae'. The *libbra* of Faenza was 0.361851 kg. (Martini, pp. 205, 292). Should this be *L librarum*? (See note 25.) This treaty also agreed that the Florentines should pay 12 *solidi bolognesi* 'pro salina' (*sic*, for 'pro staria'?) of salt at Ravenna and for transit to Russo 6 *denarii bon.* per man, beast, or 'salina'. The Faenza-Russo-Ravenna road is not mentioned in the *Descriptio*. For the Val di Lamone statutes, M.G. Tavoni, 'Le comunità della valle del Lamone', in *Studi in memoria di Federigo Melis*, i (Naples, 1978), p. 565 n. 39. According to P.M. Cavina's *Commercio de' due mari Adriatico e Mediterraneo* (Faenza, 1682) the road in the mountains was in his time well-maintained from Florence to Marradi, and though in poor condition from there to Faenza, was capable of repair with little expense. Mule-trains crossed once a week in summer and winter. See C. Braggioni and G. Tocci, 'Vie di comunicazione e traffici nella Romagna settecentesca: il canal naviglio Zanelli', *SR*, xxiii (1972), 380.

[38] Giovanni Cavalcanti, *Istorie fiorentine* (Florence, 1838-39), i, 104-16 [III, 11-12]; Matteo de Griffonibus, *Memoriale Historicum de Rebus Bononiensium*, ed. L. Frati and A. Sorbelli (*R[erum] I[talicarum] S[criptores]* xviii, pt. ii), p. 108 (emphasising the role of the

seeking to invade the Mugello were – partly because outflanked by Florentine troops at Modigliana – unable to pass Marradi.[39] Yet in April 1440, this time from Romagna against Florence, Piccinino had succeeded in seizing Marradi and taking the pass, through, so Poggio claimed, the cowardice of the defenders.[40]

(ii) From Biforco, too, what is today a mule-track passed up the Fosso di Compigno and across the Alpe di San Benedetto through the Scalelle pass to the Sieve valley. Matteo Villani tells of how in 1358 the Great Company of Count Landau, then in the neighbourhood of Faenza, had been hired by Siena to attack Perugia.[41] In an attempt to limit as far as possible its intrusion on their own territories, the Florentines prevailed upon the company to pass along this route in order to reach Perugia via Bibbiena. On 25 July, however, the men of the Val di Lamone, and particularly those of Biforco and Castiglione, who had suffered severely from its depredations, securing the heights above the Scalelle pass, gained an impressive victory over the Company and the capture of Count Landau. Foscari, in his *Relazione* of 1527, refers to this incident, even citing the ballad, still then current, celebrating the triumph of the peasantry.[42]

(b) North of Ronta, on the Tuscan side of the Casaglia, Johan Plesner detected what he took to be a medieval road, with several one-arched bridges beside today's S.S. 302.[43] Its main section joined the Casaglia. But before this another metre-wide road ascended to gain the Senio Valley. This track can still be seen today leading to Palazzuolo, Casola Valsenio (this section of the route, followed by Julius II in 1506), and down to Castel Bolognese.

(c) In the *Descriptio*,[44] Modigliana is described as 'supra quandam stratam qua itur in Tusciam et Florentiam'. By it one could reach the Faenza-Florence road at Marradi (the route taken by Julius II and his army in 1506) and, it is to be assumed, the Forlì-Florence route at Portico.

'rustici de Marradi' in the defeat); S. Ammirato, *Istorie fiorentine*, pt. i, t. ii (Florence, 1647), pp. 1018-19.

[39] Sanudo, i, 1094; ii, 42; but see *passim* for the strategic and tactical ineptitude of the invasion plans.

[40] Poggio Bracciolini, *Historia Florentina* (*RIS*, xx), pp. 406-7; Cavalcanti, ii, 64-67 [xiii. 2, 3].

[41] *Cronica* ed. F.G. Dragomanni (Florence, 1846), ii. 147-53 (book VIII, c. 73-76).

[42] Published by I. del Lungo, 'Lamento del Conte Lando dopo la sconfitta della Gran Compagnia in Val di Lamone (25 luglio 1358)', *Archivio storico italiano*, ser. 4, xiii (1884), 3-19.

[43] 'Una rivoluzione stradale del Dugento', *Acta Jutlandica*, x (1935), 29, 37.

[44] *Descriptio*, p. 212.

3. Forlì to Florence

(a) In the *Descriptio* the following places are mentioned as being on the 'strata magistra qua itur in Tusciam et Florentiam': Castrocaro (where the *passagium* is said to yield 100 *libri bolognesi* a year), Portico, Bocconi (said to be 'near the road'), and S. Benedetto in Alpe.[45] The road continued via the Muraglione pass (907 m.) down to the Mugello.

Rinaldo degli Albizzi took this route on five occasions in 1404 when travelling from Florence to the Malatesta court at Savignano or Cesena and back. On none of them is the size of his party indicated, and so I omit, what would be otherwise of interest, details of payments. His three journeys from Florence (in May, June, and September) always followed the same routine, for example:

8 May	Florence to Dicomano, where he slept. [35.5 km.]
9 May	Dicomano to S. Benedetto in Alpe, where he ate, and on to Rocca San Casciano, where he slept. [45.5 km.]
10 May	Rocca San Casciano to Forlì, where he ate, and to Cesena, where he slept. [46 km.]
11 May	From Cesena to Savignano. [14 km.][46]

On return, he followed, on one occasion (in August), the same route: Cesena to Rocca San Casciano (slept, 47 km.); Rocca San Casciano to San Benedetto in Alpe (ate and fed his horses), sleeping at Dicomano (45.5 km.). The next day he left Dicomano (payment for horses), ate at Pontassieve, and reached Florence (other payments to smiths and forage-merchants, 35.5 km.); in all three days or parts of days.[47] In April he went from Savignano to Dovadola (53.5 km.), where he slept, and on the following morning negotiated with the Count Malatesta de' Conti Guidi (payments for horseshoes). He passed on to Rocca San Casciano, where he ate and fed his horses, and spent the night at Dicomano (52.5 km.). On the third day he reached Florence (payments for oats, straw, more horseshoes, and the repair of a saddle).[48]

(b) Another route between Forlì and Florence is indicated by a reference in the *Descriptio* to Castel dell'Alpe 'on the River Rabbi and the *strata* by which one goes to Tuscany'.[49] This is the road from Florence which after reaching San Godenzo, climbed up a track through the Orticai pass (1093 m.) to gain Castel dell'Alpe, and which then followed

---

45 Ibid, pp. 190, 192-93, 229, 228 (bis).
46 *Commissioni*, i, 37-38 (8-11 May 1404); i, 43 (3-5 June 1404); i, 50 (2-4 Sept. 1404).
47 Ibid., i, 50 (13-15 Aug. 1404).
48 Ibid., i, 38 (26-28 Apr.).
49 *Descriptio*, p. 228.

on to Premilcuore, Montevecchio, and San Zeno. It constituted, as we have seen, the first part of the projected Florentine trade-route to Rimini in 1402. In order to negotiate the terms for this route with Carlo Malatesta in that same year, Rinaldo degli Albizzi traversed part of it:

24 June	He left Florence in the afternoon and reached San Godenzo. [58 km.]
25 June	He passed 'with a guide' from San Godenzo to Castel dell'Alpe and then on to Premilcuore. [34 km.]
26 June	'With a guide' he went from Premilcuore to Cesena and to Carlo's court at Savignano[50]

His route between Premilcuore and Cesena is not clear. Perhaps he went by what seems the shortest route: via Predappio, Meldola, Forlimpopoli. In which case the distance covered that day was 60 km. He himself estimated it at 28 (Florentine?) miles, which would be about 55 km.

Commenting on the Florentine acquisition of Premilcuore in 1376, Francesco Guicciardini observed that this was 'most opportune for the security of Tuscany and for holding open the *via de' grani* of Romagna, something most important for the city'.[51]

4. Forlì to Tuscany via Galeata

This route, which forks after Bagno, is the only highway in the Tusco-Romagnol section of the Appennines which had any claim to importance in the wider route-system of central Italy.

In the *Descriptio* are mentioned as 'supra stratam magistram qua itur a Forolivio in Galleatum et Tusciam et maxime Aretium', Meldola,[52] Cusercoli,[53] Civitella, S. Benedetto di Galeata ('a mile from the road'), Pondo (a third of a mile from the road), S. Piero in Bagno, Corzano, Bagno ('through which runs the *strata magistra* which goes from Romagna to Tuscany, coming or going from Cesena, and [that coming from] Bobbio [i.e. Sarsina]').[54]

After Bagno the road divided:

(a) The south-westward branch continued, as Antonio Bracci has

---

[50] *Commissioni*, i, 14-15.

[51] *Le cose fiorentine* (Florence, 1954), p. 58 ('molto opportune alla sicurtà di Thoscana et per havere aperta la via de' grani di Romagna, cosa importantissima alla città').

[52] Where *pedagium*, together with dues on butchers, wines, etc. was valued at 200 *lib. bon.*, p. 185.

[53] Recorded in 1503, as 'castello de importantia' because on the route from Galeata to Tuscany, Sanudo, v, 494.

[54] *Descriptio*, pp. 232, 230, 227, 233, 222-23, 221, 217, 216.

shown,[55] not along the line of today's S.S. 71 and through the Mandrioli pass (which was constructed only in the latter years of the nineteenth century) but through the Passo di Serra (884 m.) and the Corsalone valley to Campi and Arezzo.

Rinaldo traversed this road on three occasions. In June 1412 he passed from Rimini to Florence in five days, staying a night at Corzano in the Val di Bagno and another at Nipozzano in the Val di Sieve. That apart, however, his route is not clear.[56] Eleven years later, however, in 1423, he travelled along it, together with Francesco Tornabuoni and eleven horses. At that time Forlì had fallen to Filippo Maria Visconti, and so the customary route from Florence to Cesena was no longer accessible:

1 September	Florence to Pontassieve [18 km.]
2 September	Pontassieve, via Borselli and Poppi to Bibbiena. [40 km.]
3 September	Bibbiena to Bagno di S. Maria [31 km.]

On the return journey, two months later, Rinaldo's notes allow us to confirm Bacci's discovery of the use of the Serra-pass route:

| 28 November | From Corzano, past Bagno, to reach Poppi, noting on the way Corezzo and Banzena. [38 km.][57] |

In his advice to pilgrims seeking Rome, written some time after 1235 (and so before the construction of the Giogo della Scarperia road between Florence and Bologna), Albert of Stade had recommended this route as preferable to the Bologna crossing. His suggested itinerary ran along the Via Emilia to Forlì, then San Martino in Strada,[58] Meldola, Civitella, Bagno di Santa Maria, 'the Alps', 'Champ' (i.e. Campi), Subbiano, Arezzo, and so by Orvieto and Sutri to Rome. As one possible return route Albert suggested the same path to Meldola, then 'avoiding Forlì' to Ravenna. (From Ravenna, Albert offers two routes, either by sea to Venice, or up the Ravenna-Sant'Alberto canal to the Po di Primaro and Ferrara.)[59]

---

[55] A. Bacci, *Strade romane e medioevali nel territorio aretino* (Cortona, 1986), pp. 292-315; C. Dolcini, 'Linee di storia monastica nell' Appennino tosco-romagnolo (sec. IX-XII)', *SR*, xxvii (1976), 84, n. 27.

[56] *Commissioni*, i, 219.

[57] Ibid., i, 464, 582.

[58] Recorded with that name from 962 (Tolosano, *Chronicon Faventinum*, ed. G. Rossini, *RIS*, vii, pt. v, p. 62, n. 2). Frederick I stayed there on his fourth expedition to Rome in Jan. 1167 (Tolosano, pp. 61-62). Frederick II, coming from Forlì, rested there on 25 Oct. 1220, but is next recorded, not on the Bagno route, but at S. Lorenzo in Strada, on the Via Flaminia, 8 km. S.E. of Rimini, *Acta Imperii Inedita Seculi XIII*, ed. E. Winkelmann (Innsbruck, 1880), nos. 189, 190.

[59] Albert of Stade, *Annales Stadenses*, ed. J.M. Lappenberg, *MGH. SS.* xvi, 338-39.

(*b*) The south-eastward fork after Bagno continued across the Valico di Montecoronaro (853 m.) to the Upper Tiber valley, Sansepolcro, and Perugia. On this stretch the *Descriptio* mentions Castel dell'Alpe and Verghereto ('a ballista-shot from the *strata* which goes from Val di Bagno to Pieve S. Stefano . . . and which holds the crossing from Massa [Trabaria] to Tuscany').[60]

This seems to have been followed by Gerald of Wales in 1203. He had intended to cross the Appennines by the Cisa pass, but in order to avoid enemies, continued instead down the Via Emilia. Setting out from Faenza on 28 December, he traversed the Val di Bagno, and is next heard of in the Val di Spoleto, reaching Rome on 4 January 1204.[61] It seems to be indicated, too, on Matthew Paris's strip-map of 1253 ('Faence', 'Furlius', 'Bain Notre Dame', 'Rieta') though the Italian sections of this are very confused.[62] In the fifteenth century it was one of several recommended routes in English pilgrim books. The Anonymous *Waye fro Yngolonde to Rome by Flanders and Ducheland* counsels crossing the Appennines at Bologna on the outward journey, but on return offers an opportunity to visit Assisi. Thereafter, the stages recorded are Perugia, Città di Castello, Sansepolcro, Pieve S. Stefano, 'Sanpiere' (in Bagno), 'Galyad', 'Furse' (Forlì), Ravenna, and thence by water to Venice. It was the route followed by William Wey, prebendary of Eton, in his pilgrimage of 1458.[63] From the 1490s, however, the pull of Loreto, with its Holy House, in the first days of its immense popularity, seems to have diverted pilgrims to roads reaching the Adriatic further south.

In 1527 the mutinous imperial army marching on Rome from the Romagnol plain by-passed Forlì, burnt Meldola (14 April), reached S. Sofia (16 April), S. Pietro in Bagno (17 April), and Pieve S. Stefano (20 April).[64]

---

[60] *Descriptio*, pp. 215-16.

[61] Giraldus Cambrensis, *Opera*, ed. J. Brewer (Rolls Series, London, 1863), iii, 240-41.

[62] See G.B. Parks, *The English Traveler to Italy* (Rome, 1954), plate 8b. In the late thirteenth-century Franco-Italian epic, *Berta e Milione*, Roland is said to have been born at Imola and brought up at Sutri. J. Bedier, in his 'Les chansons de Geste et les routes d'Italie', *Romania*, xxvii (1908), 47-48, taking this, together with a misreading of the Matthew Paris map, concluded that there was a well-known road through Bagno, via Arezzo, to Rome. The argument is as wild (Sutri, on the Via Cassia, could have been gained by many other roads) as it is unnecessary.

[63] William Wey, *The Itineraries* (Roxburghe Club, 1857), pp. xxii-iii, 80.

[64] G. Rossini, 'Il passaggio per le Romagne delle truppe condotte da Carlo di Borbone al "Sacco di Roma" (1527)', *SR*, viii (1957), 269-77. In the mid eighteenth century, the road between Bagno and S. Sofia, then called 'la Frontina', was so muddy between November and April as to be impassable and was not used by the *vetturali da condotta* from Bologna to Rome in those months: L. Dal Pane, 'I rapporti commerciali fra la Romagna pontificia e il Granducato di Toscana nella seconda metà del secolo XVIII', *SR*, viii (1957), 386. Yet the accessibility of Bagno in, at least, some months of the year in our period is revealed by its revival, from at least the thirteenth century, as a hydrotherapeutic

5. Santa Sofia to the Casentino

From Santa Sofia, on the Forlì-Bagno highway, the *Descriptio* gives indications of three local routes across the Appennines:

(a) To the Upper Arno, west of the T. Bidente di Corniolo. On this route are mentioned Santafiore, Piano, S. Benedetto in Galeata, and Corniolo ('where the *strata magistra* which goes from Galeata to Tuscany' is said to run between the village and the tower of La Rovere).[65] The road continued, perhaps, via the La Calla pass (1296 m.) to Romena.

(b) To the Upper Arno via the T. Bidente Ridracoli. On the route is mentioned Biserno ('a mile from a *strata* going to Tuscany').[66] According to Antonio Bacci the road continued via Eremo, Camaldoli and Partina, to Bibbiena.

(c) To the Upper Arno via the T. Bidente di Pietropazzo. The only indication of this route is a reference to Rio Salso as being 'a mile from a *strata* going to Tuscany'.[67]

6. From Cesena to S. Pietro in Bagno

Three roads can be identified or partly identified here:

(a) From Cesena to the west of the Savio, following up the T. Borello, where in the *Descriptio* Linaro is said to stand on a *strata magistra* to Tuscany.[68] This, perhaps, continued to Facciano (see b, below), or/and Santa Sofia.

(b) Along the ridge between the Borello and Savio rivers. The *Descriptio* here mentions only Facciano (the ruins of whose castle are to be seen on Monte Facciano): 'on a certain *strata* by which one goes from Cesena to Bagno and Tuscany'.[69]

This was the road taken by Rinaldo degli Albizzi in his journey of 1423

---

centre; see Cherubini, 'Paesaggio agrario', pp. 79-80; R. Davidsohn, *Storia di Firenze* (Florence, 1956-68), i, 1149. Caterina Sforza's second husband, Giovanni de'Medici, was advised by his doctors to seek relief from the gout at Bagno in 1498, and died there in the same year: P. Pasolini, *Caterina Sforza* (Rome, 1893), ii, 27-28; iii, 305-6. (For this last reference I must thank David Chambers.)

[65] *Descriptio*, pp. 221 (bis), 222, 219.
[66] Ibid., p. 220. See Bacci, p. 296.
[67] *Descriptio*, p. 220.
[68] Ibid., p. 235.
[69] Ibid., p. 235

to Cesena and back. As we have seen, he reached Bagno di S. Maria on 3 September. On the 4th his party climbed the slopes of Monte Facciano from where it followed down the ridge to Cesena [about 49 km.]. On his return he left Cesena ('where I left Il Treccia, my big horse, because he was sick, and I left him with Antonio di Brunello of Pratovecchio, my groom [*maliscalco*]' on 26 November, passed Bora and 'Cevola' (Ciola), to sleep at Facciano [37 km.]. The following day he went to Corzano in the Val di Bagno where he stayed two nights.[70]

(c) Along the west bank of the Savio. The *Descriptio* mentions as being 'supra *stratam* qua itur in Tusciam super flumen Sapis', Taibò, S. Damiano, Montecastello, Sorbano, Calbano, Turrito, and 'Fosse di Canna' (which Dr. Mascanzoni identifies as today's Quarto).[71] On the east bank of the Savio, to the south of Mercato Saraceno, are mentioned as being *supra* (which I take to mean here 'dominating') the Savio and the road, Monte Petra and Collonata.[72]

In 1527 Marco Foscari believed (though incorrectly) that this was the route taken by the Imperial army in that year.[73]

7. Rimini to Tuscany via the Marecchia Valley

On this route the *Descriptio* identifies Montebello (near the river and *strata*), Pietracuta (where *pedagium* of unspecified value was taken), Castello di Secchiano, and Talamello.[74] In addition the now ruined castle of Maioletto on the east bank of the river is described as 'above the R. Marecchia near the road by which one goes to Tuscany'.[75] In December 1503 the Venetians stressed the importance of Verucchio ('one of the principal gates of Rimini') on this road.[76] It continued to Badia Tedalda and, through the Viamaggio pass (983 m.) to Sansepolcro.

In 1527 Marco Foscari believed (though, by now, we have learnt to treat his observations with some reserve) that this was the easiest route from Romagna to Tuscany and that it was capable of taking artillery. When, at the beginning of the nineteenth century, Napoleon decreed the construction of a road between Florence and Rimini, one Don Bindi, parish priest of Petrella Guidi, seized the occasion to write a learned historical account, dedicated to the Emperor, on the Marecchia route. He

---

[70] *Commissioni*, i. 582.

[71] *Descriptio*, pp. 207, 208, 207, 200, 204 (bis), 205, 207.

[72] Ibid., pp. 208, 205.

[73] In the eighteenth century it was described as impassable in winter and in summer to be passed only when the Savio was low: L. Dal Pane, p. 385.

[74] *Descriptio*, pp. 198, 196, 200, 198.

[75] Ibid., p. 197.

[76] 'Una di le porte de Rimano principal et loco importantissimo per quelli di Cesena e obstaculo a quelli di Montefeltro', Sanudo, v, 682-83.

argued that the new road should follow this course and praised it in extravagant terms.[77] I have not found any records of its use as more than a local link. It is perhaps significant that the projected Florence-Rimini trade-route of 1402, having reached Talamello, avoids the direct link to Rimini along the Marecchia and strikes up, instead, to Sogliano.

8. From the Savio to the Marecchia

The *Descriptio* describes Strigara and 'Massa' (which Leardo Mascanzoni identifies as Massamente) as being above the *strata* from the Montefeltro to the Romagna.[78] There are tracks today from the Cesena-Tuscany road which link these two places and join the Marecchia road near Secchiano. Part of this route was that which in 1402 the *Sei della Mercanzia* envisaged for the passage of Florentine trade between Talamello and Sogliano.

9. Leaving Romagna to the South

We have here evidence for a variety of routes taken, some eccentric (which is to say, conditioned by the particular needs of the traveller at the time) and some more normal:

(a) An 'eccentric' and minor route is revealed by a lengthy journey, with very long daily rides, from Rimini to Florence, undertaken by Rinaldo degli Albizzi in May 1404:

25 May	Rimini to Sassocorvaro (via Montefiore? in which case 57 km.).
26 May	Sassocorvaro to Mercatello (in the Metauro valley) where he ate, paid for smithing, and hired a guide to cross the 'Alpe'. Presumaby crossing the Bocca Trabaria (1044 m.), he reached Anghiari. (74 km.)
27 May	From Anghiari to Arezzo, where he lunched with its bishop, and then on to Montevarchi. (60 km.)
28 May	From Montevarchi to Incisa, where he ate, and on to Florence where he paid for more provender and smithing. (44 km.)[79]

At this time, Florence was at war with the counts of Bagno, which probably explains Rinaldo's avoidance of the Savio and Marecchia routes.

---

[77] His manuscript is reproduced in M.A. Bertini and A. Potito, *La viabilità in val Marecchia* (Rimini, 1984), pp. 37-89.

[78] *Descriptio*, p. 199.

[79] *Commissioni*, i, 43.

(b) Rimini to the Scheggia pass: down the coast, via Pesaro, to Fano; then south-west, to Fossombrone, Galleria del Furlo, Aqualunga, Cagli, through La Scheggia (572 m., the easiest of all the Appennine passes). Then either:

(i) by the Via Flaminia: Nocera, Foligno, Spoleto, Terni, Civita Castellana, Rome.[80]

(ii) or, south-east, to Gubbio, Perugia, Todi, Rome. This was the route taken by Eudes, archbishop of Rouen in 1254, and, in reverse as far as La Scheggia by Julius II in his first expedition against Bologna in August 1506.[81]

Variant routes from Romagna to the Flaminia were:

(c) Santarcangelo or Rimini via San Marino (said in the *Descriptio*[82] to stand on a *strata* which went from the Montefeltro to Rimini) and Sassofeltrio (mentioned in the *Descriptio* as a place where the Malatesta exacted *pedagium*),[83] to Urbino, and thence to the Flaminia. In 1506 Julius II, having crossed La Scheggia, reached Urbino. In order to avoid Rimini and its *contado*, then held by the Venetians, he passed on 29 September to Macerata (mentioned as a place where *pedagium* was exacted in the *Descriptio*[84] [29 km.]). He left Macerata after mid-day on 30 September amidst rain, by narrow mountain-trails, arrived at San Marino (30 km.).[85] On his return from Bologna in March 1507 he followed the route in reverse from Savignano to Urbino. On this occasion the Pope's chronicler remarked: 'In my judgment if the road had been rainy and muddy, all or many of us would have remained upon it'. But the weather was warm and the paths dusty.[86] It is at Urbino, following the departure of the Pope on this occasion, that Castiglione places the imagined setting of the dialogues of *The Courtier*.

---

[80] T. Ashby and R.A.L. Fell, 'The Via Flaminia', *Journal of Roman Studies*, xi (1921), 125-90. See *The Pilgrimage of Arnold von Harff*, ed. M. Letts (London, Hakluyt, 1946), pp. 46-50, for a journey in 1497 from Cologne to Rome, via Scarperia and Florence, returning Spoleto, Foligno, Scheggia, Urbino, Fano, Rimini, Ravenna, coast-road to Chioggia, and so to Venice.

[81] See Y. Renouard, 'Routes, étapes et vitesse de marche de France à Rome au XIIIe et au XIVe siècles', in *Studi in onore di Amintore Fanfani* (Milan, 1962), iii, 405-28; Grassi, pp. 50-53.

[82] *Descriptio*, p. 195.

[83] Ibid., p. 200.

[84] Ibid., p. 202.

[85] Grassi, p. 53; Machiavelli, *Legazioni*, ii. 1004-5; Pastor, vi, 274-75.

[86] Grassi, p. 159, who here mistakenly refers to San Marino as 'Castrum Montis Florum'. It is obvious from the route and Grassi's description ('so high that in truth we seemed to pass in the clouds above all mountains') that he means San Marino. Montefiore (385 m.), then in Venetian hands, would have been accessible only from Savignano, via Rimini.

(d) Rimini, via Montefiore, to Urbino, and so via the Flaminia to Gubbio etc. *The Informacion for pylgrymes unto the holy londe*, printed by Wynkin de Worde in *c.* 1498, 1515, and 1524, suggests this as a possible return route from Rome. The stages are 'Cantyane' (Cantiano), 'Fyrmynyane' (Fermignano), 'Urban', 'Mountfloure', 'Remell' (Rimini), and thence by sea to Venice.[87] In 1503 the Venetians noted Montefiore as a place crossed 'by all couriers that go and come from Rome', and it was still on the courier-routes of the seventeenth and eighteenth centuries.[88]

(e) Other options for the traveller to or from Rome were to pass via Rimini along the coast road to:

> *(i)* Rocca Priore, then south-east to Iesi and Macerata (an alternative return-route north suggested by the *Informacion for pylgrymes unto the holy londe*)
> or
> *(ii)* to Ancona, then via Loreto, to Macerata.[89]

From the second half of the sixteenth century, certainly (but, most probably, also from some two centuries before), the route from Bologna to Rome by the 'via di Romagna' was considered inferior to the 'via di Toscana' by the Giogo di Scarperia and Florence. Important considerations here were distance (233 miles and, for those who could afford them, 29 changes of post-horses, as against 196 miles, with 24 posts, on the Tuscan route), provision of inns, and dangers from bandits.[90] Yet pilgrims, seeking the shrines of Loreto and Assisi, or simply, like later

---

[87] *Information for Pilgrims unto the Holy Land*, ed. E.G. Duff (London, 1893), p. 3. For other travellers on this route: Bertranden de La Brocquière, *Le Voyage d'outremer* (*Recueil des Voyages*, xii, Paris, 1892), p. 6 (having gone to Rome via Bologna-Florence, he returned via Urbino-Rimini in Mar. 1432, and then along the coast to Chioggia); and Pero Tafur, *Travels and Adventures, 1435-39*, trans. M. Letts (London, 1926), pp. 44-45 (Rome, Viterbo, Perugia, Assisi, Gubbio, Urbino, Rimini, then taking ship to Venice). On the Venetian cross-peninsular trade-route of the late fourteenth and early fifteenth centuries, passing from Rimini (or Fano) via Urbino, Città di Castello, Perugia, Marsciano, Orvieto, Pitigliano, to the Tyrrhenian port of Talamone, see Melis, *I trasporti*, p. 126.

[88] 'E questo è passo dove tutti corrieri vanno o vengono di Roma passa de lì in el castello over terra', Sanudo, v, 510-11; Francesco Scotto, *Itinerario d'Italia* (1610, and reprint of 1747 edition, Bologna, 1977), p. 294; J. Delumeau, *Vie économique et sociale de Rome dans la seconde moitié du XVIe siècle* (Paris, 1957-59), i, 43. See too Ariosto, *Orlando Furioso*, xliii, 147-49; and for the 'ostaria di Montefiore', B. Castiglione, *Il libro del Cortegiano*, ed. V. Cian (Florence, 1947), p. 272, n. 3 (II. 84).

[89] Schrod, pp. 38-39 (twelfth century); Wey, p. 53 (fifteenth); Delumeau, i, 45-47 (sixteenth). The *Itinerario overo Viaggio da Venetia a Roma* (Venice, Agostino Bindoni, 1550), 4r-7v, 14r, tells of a pilgrimage via Ferrara, Faenza, Rimini (with here an alternative route via Montefeltro, Urbino, Perugia), Ancona, Loreto, Assisi, Perugia; returning from Rome via Florence and Scarperia.

[90] M. Romani, *Pellegrini e viaggiatori nell'economia di Roma dal XIV al XVII secolo* (Milan, 1948), pp. 29-30.

followers of the Grand Tour,[91] wishing to vary their itineraries, would often take different routes on their outward and return journeys. At the same time, of course, those with particular business in the Marche or Umbria would use the Romagnol roads, while men from the south would find advantage in gaining Venice by means of the little Romagnol ports.

IV. Conclusions

There is much here that has not been discussed: smiths, horses, footwear, inns,[92] commercial carriers,[93] and, particularly, road maintenance. Many of the statutes of the Appennine communities and of the towns of the plains provided for the continuous upkeep of roads; yet how far did these edicts remain dead letters?[94] In looking over a wide arc of time, questions about seasonal fluctuations in frequency of traffic have not been answered. The profound contrast in Romagna between the dried-up river beds of August and the overflowing streams of November and, more particularly, March, must have had serious effects on road-use. Road-security has not been touched upon. Safety of passage and the likelihood of highway-robbery must have been contingent upon the circumstances of war and, in peace, the depredations of disbanded soldiers. It would seem likely that the long process by which from the thirteenth century Florentine power established itself in place of the feudatories of the Tosco-Romagnol Appennines would by the mid fifteenth century have brought fewer risks for travellers. Though the men of the mountains were all too likely to exercise considerable violence against each other, they would be less inclined to assaults on others, at least when travelling in company.

At the beginning of the thirteenth century, Gerald of Wales had told his readers of the terror he had felt of snow peaks and robbers in his crossing from Forlì to Val di Bagno and had even portrayed the inhabitants of the

---

[91] See *Viaggi e viaggiatori del Settecento in Emilia e Romagna* ed. G. Cusatelli (Bologna, 1986).

[92] In the Florentine *contado* there is evidence for a large number of inns during the second half of the fourteenth century on the roads between Florence, Firenzuola, and beyond; between Borgo S. Lorenzo and Casaglia; and on the Pontassieve road; *Statuti dell'arte degli albergatori della città e contado di Firenze (1324-1342)*, ed. F. Sartini (Florence, 1953), pp. 317-19.

[93] For 'uno Donato vetturale' at Forlì, see Pampaloni, p. 306.

[94] See, e.g. *Statuta Faventiae*, ed. G. Rossini (*RIS*, xxviii, pt. v, i), 238-40, 243-64; Tavoni, 'Le comunità della valle del Lamone', p. 564; G.L. Masetti Zannini, *Verucchio nel Cinquecento* (Verucchio, 1985), p. 39; *Statuti di San Godenzo*, pp. 29-30; *Statuti della Repubblica Fiorentina*, i, 175-80; statutes of Montefeltro in 1384 in *Statuti di Gradara, Peglio e Montefeltro*, ed. G. Vanzolini (Ancona, 1874), pp. 323-24, 329-31. For a discussion of the effectiveness of such regulations in one part of Tuscany, T. Szabò, 'Strassenbau und Strassensicherheit in Territorium von Pistoia (12-14 Jh.)', *Quellen und Forschungen aus italienischen Archiven und Bibliotheken*, lix (1977), 88-137.

Val di Spoleto as being amazed at his good fortune in surviving them.[95]
Over two centuries later, as we have seen, Marco Foscari was portraying
the difficulties of the Appennines in almost equally disturbing terms. Yet
the testimony of strangers, very likely to dramatise their experiences, can
attract too much attention. Though most of our evidence comes from the
months of April to August, it seems to have been quite easy for Rinaldo
degli Albizzi, in his forties, to have travelled on horse from Florence via
the Mugello to Imola in two days or parts of days and to Forlì, Cesena,
and Savignano in three days or parts of days, pausing for meals, forage,
shoeing of horses, finding inns in which to sleep and guides where
necessary. Travelling to Cesena, by the Val di Bagno, in his fifties, he was
able to pass from Florence in September in four days or parts of days, and
to return by the same route in November.[96] It is obvious that from the
thirteenth century, at least, large quantities of Romagnol grain and salt
were passing on mule-back to Florence, and that from the second half of
the fourteenth century trans-Appennine trade to and from the ports of
Ravenna, Cesenatico, and Rimini was seen as normal. Finally, even
English pilgrim-books of the fifteenth century were recommending the
Val di Bagno and Rimini routes to their readers. For those who dwelt in
the mountains or who lived at their feet, it may be concluded, for
herdsmen, shepherds, couriers, officials, soldiers, merchants, they were
places which it was routine and customary to cross.

[95] Giraldus Cambrensis, iii, 241.

[96] Rinaldo's couriers (*cavallari, fanti del proccaccio*) from Florence to Cesena in 1425
normally took three days or parts of days. On 7 Sept. 1425 the *Dieci di Balia* wrote to him at
Cesena: 'This morning we received your letter of the 5th'; on the 8th they acknowledged
letters of the 6th; on the 11th of the 9th; on the 15th of the 13th; Rinaldo acknowledges on
the 15th receipt of letters dated the 13th (*Commissioni*, i, 475-77; 484-85). On 9 Oct.
Rinaldo's letter from Cesena was received at Florence on the 13th (ibid., 533-34). A letter
of Machiavelli from Cesena of 1 Oct. 1506 reached the *Dieci* – it seems 'by the Castrocaro
road' – on the 3rd (*Legazioni* ii, 1006, 1009). His letters from Forlì to Florence of 9 Oct.
arrived on the night of the 11th, on the 12th, and on the 14th (ibid., 1018, 1024).

12

City, Court and Contado in Camerino, c. 1500

John Easton Law

In the latter half of the fifteenth century, Giulio Cesare Varano, lord of
Camerino in the Marches, acquired many of the attributes of a successful
signore.* He had ruled the Varano inheritance since 1443, first jointly and
then singly after the death of his cousin Rodolfo in 1464. His *signoria* had
been largely unchallenged by internal unrest and foreign intervention. In
1468 his overlord, Paul II, invested him with a hereditary vicariate, and
although that grant embraced his cousin's children, his rule was little
disturbed by dynastic rivalry. Ercole Varano, Rodolfo's eldest son, lived
in exile in Ferrara from 1464, and challenged Giulio Cesare's sole right to
the lordship in 1493; but then surrendered his claim for 1,000 ducats. A
younger brother, Fabrizio, was sufficiently acceptable to Giulio Cesare to
become bishop of Camerino in 1482. Dynastic marriages were not
necessarily guarantees of political alliance, but Giovanna, the daughter of
Sigismondo Pandolfo Malatesta, married Giulio Cesare in 1451 and
helped to secure the succession by providing him with two legitimate
sons.[1]

Like the other *signori* of the Papal States, Giulio Cesare served as a
condottiere, eventually securing high commands from Paul II and Sixtus
IV, as well as from Venice and Naples; his sons embarked on similar
careers. With such a supplement to their income the Varano were able to
follow the example of their neighbours in other respects. Their palace was
embellished and expanded in the years 1465-75 and 1489-99; its designs
and decoration reflected both traditional and fashionable tastes: portraits

* An early version of this paper was delivered to a seminar at Vassar College. I am
grateful for the comments of Professor Benjamin Kohl, Alison Smith and their students. I
would also like to acknowledge the support of the British School at Rome, the Cotton
Foundation and the British Academy.

[1] P. Litta, *Famiglie celebri italiani*, vii (Milan, 1819), tav. 4 (his legitimate children were
Venanzio, Giovanni Maria and Camilla; of illegitimate birth were Pirro and Annibale); T.
Zampetti, *Giulio Cesare Varano, signore di Camerino* (Rome, 1900); G. Boccanera, 'Memorie
dei da Varano di Ferrara a Camerino', S[*tudi*] M[*aceratesi*], iii (1968), 51-52; S. Corradini,
'Il palazzo di Giulio Cesare Varano e l'architetto Baccio Pontelli', *SM*, iv (1969), 186-88.

of Giulio Cesare's immediate ancestors, *intarsia* panelling, a courtyard with the *stemme* of the Varano and Malatesta and mythological subjects, tapestries, a *studiolo*, a portrait bust of Giulio Cesare over the principal entrance. He commissioned a medal bearing a flattering likeness, and attracted – and sometimes also rewarded – the praise of humanists and poets. Nor did he neglect good works, though his piety often carried a family imprint. He paid for work on the façade of the cathedral, as well as for the marbling of the Varano burial chapel. He secured papal support to found a central hospital in 1474 and to endow a convent for his devout daughter Camilla in 1483. It is hardly surprising that some local historians have succumbed to the resonance of his name, hailing him as the greatest of the Varano, the 'Augustus' of the dynasty.[2]

But such achievements did not remove the weaknesses from the Varano *signoria*. As a young child, Giulio Cesare had barely escaped with his life in a revolt provoked by dynastic dissension, foreign intervention and internal unrest; and from 1434 to 1443 the Varano, one of the longest established of Italy's signorial houses, had experienced exile. The city they returned to, with outside assistance, was of some economic importance as a regional centre of commerce and a producer of paper and textiles, but its population was relatively small; at the end of the fifteenth century the urban population perhaps reached 6,000 and that of the *territorio* 28,000. The activity of the Varano as *condottieri*, often hailed by older historians in terms of military virtue, was rather the product of necessity, and the need to secure powerful protectors and additional revenue. The correspondence of Giulio Cesare reveals his constant search for the patronage of governments more powerful than his own, for his subjects and himself. And the hereditary vicariate secured in 1468 expressed a jurisdictional subservience which a more aggressive and ambitious pope was to exploit.[3]

Grounds to deprive Giulio Cesare of his lordship were found by Alexander VI in August 1497 when the papal vicar was adjudged to be heavily in debt to the *Camera Apostolica*. The imposition of a fine and excommunication failed to induce either contrition or payment; by August 1498 the arrears had grown and Giulio Cesare was deprived of his

[2] A. Conti, *Camerino e i suoi dintorni* (Camerino, 1872-74), pp. 24, 61-62 and *passim*; B. Feliciangeli, 'Cenni storici sul Palazzo dei Varano a Camerino', *A[tti e] M[emorie della R. Deputazione di Storia Patria per le] Marche*, n.s., viii (1912), 21-50; Corradini, *ubi supra*; L. Allevi, 'Umanisti Camerinesi: Il Cantalicio e la corte dei Varani', *AMMarche*, 4 ser., iii (1926), 167-95; A.A. Bittarelli, *Camerino: Viaggio dentro la città* (Macerata, 1978), pp. 5-8; A. Armand, *Les Médailleurs Italiens*, iii (Paris, 1883), pp. 230-31; I. de Foville, 'La Médaille de Jules-César Varano', *Révue Numismatique*, 4 ser., vi (1912), 268-72.

[3] B. Feliciangeli, 'Sulle condizioni economiche e demografiche di Camerino e sulla ricchezza della Famiglia Varano', *AMMarche*, n.s., viii (1912), 51-61, 82-83; Bittarelli, pp. 84-89; A. Massari, 'Regesto delle lettere di Giulio Cesare da Varano', *SM*, x (1976), 288-318.

governorship, as well as being faced with a further fine and renewed excommunication. However these punishments were withdrawn in a bull of 28 June 1499 in which the Holy See's readiness to forgive the contrite was rehearsed.[4] Certainly Giulio Cesare took steps to reduce his debts; he may also have had allies and protectors. The Perugian chronicler Francesco Matarazzo records that the willingness of Astorre Baglioni to support a kinsman by marriage dissuaded the pope from punitive action; Lili hints at the good offices of Venice; a papal letter of 14 October 1499 reveals that Alexander had been persuaded by a number of unnamed members of the College.[5]

An explanation may also be found in Cesare Borgia's campaigns in the Romagna, but if that was the case in 1498/9, it no longer applied in 1501 when the Montefeltro and Varano emerged as allied threats to papal authority and Borgia dynasticism. On 1 March a bull was issued denouncing Giulio Cesare as a 'perditionis alumnus' and 'iniquitatis filius'.[6] His failures to pay the census and tallages were rehearsed, as were the pope's hopes for his reform. But Giulio Cesare had displayed the obduracy of Pharoah, and had incited and protected rebels, robbers and coiners of bad money. The pope went further, accusing him of despoiling the church and murdering his cousin Rodolfo.[7] Such excesses could be countenanced no longer, and after discussing the matter in Consistory, Alexander excommunicated Giulio Cesare and found him guilty of perjury, sacrilege, rebellion and *lèse-majesté*. He was deprived in perpetuity of all rights and property, and his subjects were freed from their obedience. While admitting that it would be difficult to publish the bull in some places, the pope ordered it to be placed outside the basilicas of Rome, and denied its target the excuse of ignorance.

Although the campaign against him was delayed, Giulio Cesare was aware of the threat. According to Matarazzo he appealed to the king of France for protection in 1501;[8] on 27 May 1502 he sent an envoy to intercept the Venetian ambassador, Antonio Giustinian, as he travelled to Rome, inviting him to Camerino and admitting that he feared the impending papal attack. Giulio Cesare was anxious for Venetian help and wanted to send a formal embassy to the Republic. Giustinian claimed to have been cautious in his reply: it was not convenient for him to break his journey; he could assure Giulio Cesare of Venetian good will; he could not

---

[4] A[rchivio] S[egreto]V[aticano], *Instrumenta Cameralia*, reg. 13, fos. 292v-95v; reg. 15, fo. 5r-v.

[5] F. Matarazzo, *Chronicles of the City of Perugia*, trans. E.S. Morgan (London, 1905), p. 87; C. Lili, *Dell'Historie di Camerino* (Macerata, 1649-52), p. 245; ASV, *Instrumenta Cameralia*, reg. 13, fos. 294v-95r.

[6] ASV, *Diversa Cameralia*, reg. 115, fos. 112r-116v (a copy of 1539).

[7] This charge is generally dismissed: Zampetti, pp. 27, 72-73.

[8] Matarazzo, p. 207.

comment on the question of a Varano embassy to the Republic.[9]

On 5 June 1502 the excommunication was reissued and the campaign against the Varano and their Montefeltro allies begun. Venetian dispatches from Rome confirmed the isolation of the Varano, but suggested that operations against them would still be difficult.[10] Indeed the Borgia army did experience reverses, but its size (about 4,000 men), as well as the presence of Spanish professionals and eager levies from Spoleto and other adjoining territories, made it difficult to resist.[11] The siege of Camerino began on 17 July, and dispatches to Rome of 19 July reported that Annibale Varano had opened negotiations, possibly prompting reports in Venice on 22 July that the city had fallen 'per trattato'.[12] Burchard recorded that the pope announced on 23 July the capture of Camerino 'per concordiam', and on the following day Giustinian confirmed that the *popoli* had surrendered the city unconditionally; both presumably referred to the ousting of the Varano by Giovanni Antonio Ferraccioli and other leading citizens to save the city from sack and to place themselves on the winning side.[13] Virtually all the Varano and a number of other opponents of the Borgia were seized. Giustinian expressed his doubts that the lavish celebrations held to celebrate the capture of Urbino and Camerino were deserved; both places had fallen through *tradimento*. However his reports fully confirm the observation of Burchard: that Alexander was delighted, especially with the capture of his enemies. On 27 July he wrote that the pope had hailed the event as a miracle, and had stressed that when Giulio Cesare had tried to negotiate, the city had risen for the Borgia.[14]

The pope set about cementing his triumph. The 'Infante di Roma', the five-year-old Giovanni Borgia, already duke of Nepi, was made duke of Camerino on 2 September, and on 13 September the city was entered by its newly-appointed governor, Giovanni Olivieri, bishop of Isernia, and by Giovanni's guardian, cardinal Francesco Borgia.[15] The new regime was formally proclaimed, and the cardinal accepted the obedience of Camerino and the communes of its *territorio*. This was quickly tested. In October, an alliance of *signori* and *condottieri* threatened to dismantle

[9] *Dispacci di Antonio Giustinian*, ed. P. Villari, i (Florence, 1876), pp. 9-10.

[10] Ibid., pp. 17, 27, 29-30.

[11] For the narrative of events, *Cronica di Diatrico*, Biblioteca Apostolica Vaticana, *Codici Borgiani Latini*, 282, fos. 18v-19v; Lili, pp. 251-71; R. Sabatini, *The Life of Cesare Borgia* (London, 1911), pp. 325-34, 363; W.H. Woodward, *Cesare Borgia* (London, 1913), pp. 232-48; G. Sacerdote, *La vita di Cesare Borgia* (Milan, 1950), pp. 509-12, 596.

[12] *Dispacci*, pp. 62-63; M. Sanudo, *I Diarii*, ed. N. Barozzi, iv (Venice, 1880), col. 287.

[13] J. Burchard, *Liber Notarum*, ed. E. Celani, *Rerum Italicarum Scriptores*, 2nd edn., xxxiii. 2 (Città di Castello, 1907), p. 336; *Dispacci*, pp. 68-69.

[14] *Dispacci*, p. 72.

[15] A. Ronchini, 'Documenti borgiani dell'Archivio di Stato di Parma', *Atti e Memorie delle RR. Deputazioni per le Provincie dell'Emilia*, n.s., i (1877), 37-73; *Dispacci*, pp. 108-9.

Borgia power in the Papal States. One of its consequences was the execution of Giulio Cesare on 9 October, but he had had the foresight to send his younger legitimate son, Giovanni Maria, to Venice before the Borgia invasion.[16] On 26 October news reached Rome that Oliverotto da Fermo had entered Camerino with the support of the inhabitants. The Spanish garrison was massacred, Giovanni Maria installed as *signore* and reprisals taken against those who had favoured the Borgia.[17] Under 11 November, Marino Sanudo recorded the text of a letter sent by Giovanni Maria on 25 October telling the *Signoria* of his acclaimed return and asking for the Republic's protection.[18] By melting down church plate and a silver statue of Camerino's patron saint, S. Venanzio, Giovanni Maria risked alienating more powerful protectors, and he was allowed to do little more than taste the fruits of victory before Cesare Borgia struck back. Giustinian's dispatches kept Venice apprised of developments; on 24 December, he reported that Giovanni Maria had fled Camerino that morning.[19]

But the Varano coup had registered a shock; on 27 December Giustinian told his government that the pope was looking for suitable governors who would insure 'che la terra se abi a contentar di lui'.[20] At that stage no suitable candidate had emerged, but the pope's search almost certainly elicited a *relazione* directed 'alla conservatione di Casa Borgia' in Camerino. Its author, Lodovico Clodio, was a churchman, military engineer and papal servant. His qualifications as an expert on Camerino derived in part from the fact that he came from the subject commune of Caldarola of which he was archpriest. He had possibly been instrumental in winning that commune to the Borgia cause, as well as being involved in the siege of Camerino. Then he had been in the city planning the construction of a fortress, and had suffered in the Varano coup. Though never fully edited, his *relazione* has long been recognised by local historians, and it deserves wider appreciation.[21]

---

[16] Most authorities claim that Giulio Cesare was strangled, but see A. Leonotti, *Papa Alessandro VI* (Bologna, 1880), iii, 12-15.

[17] *Dispacci*, pp. 174-75.

[18] Sanudo, coll. 466-67.

[19] *Dispacci*, pp. 224-25, 273, 283-85.

[20] Ibid., pp. 290-91.

[21] The *relazione* was first published in full by A. Conti as 'Un documento inedito per servire alla storia di Alessandro VI e della città di Camerino', *Archivio Storico Marchigiano*, i (1879), 211-34. It has been published with a fuller introduction and commentary by A.A. Bittarelli as 'Ludovico Clodio: Scrittore e politico premachiavellico', *SM*, v (1971), 129-60; my page references relate to Bittarelli's text. To his biographical notes on Clodio can be added: (i) his appointment in Aug. 1494 by Alexander VI to organise the coastal defences of Corneto-Tarquinia, L. Dasti, *Notizie Storiche-archeologiche di Tarquinia e Corneto* (Rome, 1878), pp. 259-60; (ii) on 21 May 1501, the pope granted him *in comendam* the Benedictine monastery of SS. Vincenzo and Anastasia outside Amandole in the diocese of Fermo, ASV, *Diversa Cameralia*, reg. 54, fo. 40v. Confirmation that work was begun on a fortress in

Some of the advice Clodio offers is directed at the immediate situation. The rather unconvincing account offered by Camerino – that Giovanni Maria had found the gates unguarded, and had entered without the involvement of the citizenry – he accepted: 'io credo che fussi bene a simulare di crederlo' (p. 159). His argument is not entirely one of expediency. Clodio believed that the revolt was launched by a few before collecting more general support: 'fu invenzione di tre, participazione di otto e poi la terra seguitò'. Elsewhere he claimed that only four or five 'case' had caused 'tutta questa ribellione' (p. 154). However pragmatism is the main consideration. If many citizens fear arrest 'per ribelli e traditori' they are unlikely to become 'fedeli sudditi'. If all those that have fled are prevented from returning, they are likely to become a source of discontent and support for the Varano; the government of Duke Giovanni will be faced with the impossible task of ridding Camerino of their many *parenti*. The city is already in a sufficient state of terror without taking reprisals and making the streets run with blood as some other – unnamed – advisors want. Skilful government will be worth more than ten or twenty fortresses (pp. 155, 157, 160).

The *relazione* has been described as 'singularly humane and wise',[22] but Clodio's advice is not entirely conciliatory. Exile is not ruled out as a weapon (pp. 150, 159-60). Encouraging the duke's subjects to stay at home increases the chance of them being treated as hostages, especially valuable in the case of those with a record of political agitation: 'massime con quelli che sono travagliosi'. He counsels that the construction of the *Rocca* should go ahead. The number of gates should be reduced; those remaining should be fortified and guarded by foreign troops (p. 160). The citizens of Camerino should be excluded from favours at Rome. The communal council should be reduced in size and should meet rarely, 'per conferire in cento anni una volta qualche cosa' (pp. 157-58).

These points are mostly raised towards the end, and Clodio is more concerned with the long-term survival of the Borgia duchy. Government, *governo*, rather than police and military measures, is the principal theme (p. 149 and *passim*). Although all letters and grants should be in the young duke's name (p. 158), central to the author's strategy is the governor, the *vice-duca*. He must be intelligent, alert, informed of local conditions and able to read the hidden natures and aspirations of men, the 'nature e voluntadi di uomini tante occulte'. He must be energetic and loyal (pp. 152-53). He and his entourage must not lose their heads over local women: not for moral reasons, but because of the jealousy and anger provoked (p.

Camerino before the Varano coup, 'per sospetto di quei popoli', can be found in a report from Giustinian of 22 Sept. 1502, *Dispacci*, p. 129; Clodio's involvement is mentioned in a letter of Galeazzo Sforza of 4 Nov. 1502, B. Feliciangeli, 'Di alcune rocche dell' antico stato di Camerino', *AMMarche*, n.s. i (1904), 147-48.

[22] Woodward, p. 318.

158). Certainly the governor should know when to be an angel and when a devil (p. 153).

What separates these observations from the obvious, the traditional and the ideal is Clodio's almost explicit criticism of the previous regime as supervised by the aging Cardinal Francesco Borgia. The future governor must be sure of his authority, and not afraid of complaints presented behind his back in Rome. Embassies from Camerino should be cautiously received, and answered so as to benefit the whole community (p. 160). The papal treasurer, Angelo di Melchiore, though well-intentioned, threatens the governor's position; his wealth and influence make him an alternative source of patronage (p. 159). The governor should be a layman and even married, so that he is better able to establish a court.

For Clodio, the governor's importance is increased, owing to the difficulties likely to be encountered. Camerino, he claims, is different from other Italian states, and the governor will be without the help of the inhabitants because 'i terrieri non diranno mai il vero' (pp. 148, 153). This leads him to analyse the two principal aspirations, *voluntadi*, identifiable among the inhabitants. The first he associates with those whose power rests on wealth, kin, ambition and skill, 'li quali hanno facultadi, parentado, animo e ingegno' (p. 149). For them, a distinct minority, the abiding goal is liberty, but not in the sense of a republican constitution or even political independence. Rather, 'questa voluntà libertesca' seeks disorder and revolution which destroy public authority; in such circumstances, they hope to gain a following and power, 'seguiti e grandezza', to live like lords and to appropriate public revenues: 'essere Signori, mangiar con pifferi e trombe . . . e godersi fra loro l'entrate dello stato'. Such families – sadly unidentified by name – cloak their ambitions behind sham allegiances, *affezioni*, to the Borgia and the Varano cause, the latter being divided between Giovanni Maria and the Ferrara branch (p. 150).

The author then makes further distinctions within the 'voluntà libertesca'. Some are content to obey the government in power, 'da starsi a obedientia del Palazzo', and to receive benefits from the regime. Others, whatever their pretended allegiance, are trouble-makers intent on change and looking to dominate, 'di nature travagliose che tendono a mutazione e superiorità'. None are seen as constituting parties or factions; each family is out for itself and ready to do down its rivals (p. 149).

The second *voluntà* also challenges the Borgia regime; although sustained by the 'plebei, poveri e contadini', those who 'non tendono a governo', almost all its adherents – a majority of the city and *contado*? – support the 'Casa di Varano' (p. 150). Their *signoria* had been a generous distributor of alms. Giulio Cesare had followed family precedent in providing daily doles of bread. The *contadini* had received unspecified favours worth 1,000 ducats a year; by acts of kindness and friendship, 'le carezza e domestichezze', by preferring them over citizens in the audience hall and in every way, 'in audienza et in ogni cosa', the Varano could count on their support. As Clodio vividly expressed it, thanks to the loyalty of these sections of the population, the Varano had been able to keep the 'liberteschi' cooped up like hens, 'oppressi come galline', and it would now take the appearance of only a fly from the exiled house, 'una mosca di Casa Varano', to make them rebel.

In the light of such observations, Alexander might have concluded that the task of ruling Camerino was impossible, and Clodio does stress the unique problems that the city presented its would-be governors (pp. 148, 150). But perhaps this is only to underline the value of his own advice, and the author claims that the 'voluntà libertesca' can be controlled, while those loyal to the Varano can be won over. To show how this can be achieved, the causes of the recent uprising are analysed under five headings, and appropriate lines of action are suggested.

The first principal cause of the revolt was the excessive favour shown to the members and followers of two families that had helped oust the Varano, 'li quali per il favore che aveano avuto . . . parendoli aver dato Camerino' (p. 151). Jealousy had enhanced the appeal of the Varano. The advice offered appears qualified by the observation that those who seek 'liberty' will never be won over (p. 153); indeed the more they are given, the more they will want. Clodio's advice also appears flawed by contradictions. Only Borgia supporters, 'ducheschi', should be rewarded, but the governor should be above party and favourites, 'senza parti' and 'senza idoli'. Equity should be followed in both secular and ecclesiastical affairs, 'che nessuno cresca più dell'altro un capello' (pp. 154-55); the benefices accumulated by one Francesco – Francesco Borgia? – should be redistributed (pp. 158-59). Of course, equity is urged to remove sources of discontent and intrigue, the 'imprese secrete di libertà', and not as an abstract political ideal. The duke's 'stato' would be kept 'fermo' and 'quieto', and his subjects would return to work, 'a suoi esercizi di lana et altri industrie'. Clodio's aim is also to enhance the authority of the duke, as the source of all patronage, making his subjects know their place as they are reduced to 'bassezza egualita e vilta, et ignoranza come galline', grateful for small favours and low-paid office (pp. 156, 158).

Further contradictions emerge when Clodio tackles the second, closely related, cause of the revolt (pp. 155-56). There has been no method, *ragione*, to the distribution of offices and favours in Rome and Camerino. Some needy families of good birth, *buon sangue*, and those who had suffered during the Varano coup by having their houses burned down, had received nothing, while others had been advanced for no good reason. This had caused disillusionment, and Clodio recommends greater care in the distribution of office in city and *contado*, especially so that the *buone Case* and those that had suffered reprisals should benefit. But no office should be given for more than six months, partly to prevent jealousy and partly to prevent office being used as a stepping-stone to power – as had been the case with the Varano.

The third cause of unrest was the loss of the Varano court (pp. 150, 151-57). All had felt this, but 'massime di giovanni'. The court had been the sole source of recreation for the inhabitants, 'di tutta la ricreazione sua che avevano in Camerino', and had been a twenty-four-hour source of warmth and news, a place to play games, cards and chess. At night people had been able to talk to their lord; during the day they had been able to play football and hunt with him. Women now missed the company of Giovanna Malatesta, so that when the news of Giovanni Maria's return had spread, all had shouted eagerly that good times had returned, 'tutti con desiderio gridando, "Varano con ogni ricreazione sua venuto"'. Hence Clodio argues that the governor should preserve the style of the Varano court, 'tenga in corte quelli stili che facevano Varani', making himself familiar and accessible. Should he be married, his wife should treat the women of the city in a similar way (p. 156).

Clodio then returns to more formal aspects of lordship. The departure of the Varano had deprived between 250 and 300 individuals of a livelihood, and had ended the gift of alms to the poor; for these reasons Giovanni Maria had been seen as a 'Messiah' (pp. 150, 152). Accordingly he recommends that the Borgia spend 1,000 ducats a year – at least for a transitional period – on poor relief, and that the governor should recreate the Varano household, at least in part, as a source of employment. The grant of such trifles, 'coselle', the employment of young men at court, and the daily distribution of alms would build up the Borgia cause (p. 156).

Lastly Clodio criticises a new tax which falls most heavily on the *contado* (p. 152). Because the Varano had chosen to pay their secretaries and magistrates from central funds they had levied low charges, or none at all, when letters and sealed documents were issued from the chancery. Presumably the costs of such administrative services as hearing appeals and answering petitions were now passed on, to burden most heavily those groups previously favoured by the accessibility and paternalism of the Varano, the poor and the *contadini*. Clodio advises the abandonment of such charges, otherwise the passing of the Varano will continue to be lamented in both city and *contado*, and the *contadini* will be quick to rally in support of their erstwhile, 'natural', lords – 'naturalmente a contadini pareva strana star senza Varani' (p. 157).

Clodio's appraisal of the popularity of the Varano might have led to the execution of those male members held in captivity,[23] while his contempt for Camerino's communal constitution might have been behind the

---

[23] Most sources suggest that Venanzio, Annibale and Pirro were executed in Oct. 1502. However, in Feb. 1503 Sanudo records a report from merchants in the area of Pesaro that Venanzio and Octaviano (*sic*) had been hanged near Rimini, Sanudo, col. 734.

introduction of a reduced council of sixty members. The recommendation that 1,000 ducats be invested in good works might explain why in June 1503 the *Camera Apostolica* was instructed to transfer to the Borgia account the 1,000 ducats received from Duke Giovanni as his census payment from Camerino.[24] Clodio's advice might have contributed to the appointment of a Spanish lay governor, Pietro Perez, one of whose more ceremonial acts was to lay the foundation stone of the *Rocca* on 1 May. That project was probably the clearest consequence of the *relazione*; work begun before the coup was pressed ahead under Clodio's direction. However, the regime that benefitted was not that of the Borgia; the death of Alexander VI on 18 August 1503, and Cesare's illness, allowed the triumphant return of Giovanni Maria.[25]

The failure of Clodio's efforts in stone and on paper do not remove the interest of his *relazione* as a treatise and historical source. As a political theorist, Clodio has understandably been compared to his more famous contemporary, Machiavelli. Although the Florentine secretary's dispatches are virtually silent on Camerino, he observed Cesare Borgia at close quarters in the Marches in June 1502 and again between October 1502 and January 1503.[26] Moreover, the problem of how states are acquired and retained was central to his historical and political writings, and surfaces in 1503 in the *Del modo di trattare i popoli della Valdichiana ribellati*.[27]

Though the authors' paths may have crossed and the circumstances and aims of their *relazioni* were similar, differences emerge in the method and focus of their argument. Machiavelli places the revolt in the Valdichiana in an Italian context. He also draws heavily on Roman history to lend authority to his argument; though he had visited Arezzo after its rebellion his treatment of the situation facing Florence is cursory and contains little political or social analysis. By contrast, Clodio's longer *relazione* is more detailed, investigative and focussed almost entirely on contemporary Camerino; the author eschews such drastic and anachronistic ideas as mass exile or colonisation, solutions to rebellion that occurred to Machiavelli from a reading of Livy. Clodio's *relazione* is also characterised by uncertainties and contradictions on such matters as the extent and depth of loyalty to the Varano, the use of exile and the distribution of favours; in tone it veers between conciliation and contempt. Such lack of precision and detachment, but wealth of detail and

[24] ASV, *Diversa Cameralia*, reg. 55, fo. 70r-v.
[25] M. Santoni, *La Rocca di Camerino* (Camerino, 1867); Conti, pp. 24-26; B. Feliciangeli, 'Le Memorie del convento di S. Pietro in Muralto', *Picenum Seraphicum* (25 Mar. 1917), pp. 12-15. Santoni and Conti attribute the design to Leonardo da Vinci.
[26] N. Machiavelli, *Legazioni, commissarie, scritti di governo*, ed. F. Chiappelli, ii (Bari-Rome, 1973), pp. 113-26, 192-401.
[27] N. Machiavelli, *Opere*, ed. M. Bonfantini (Milan-Naples, 1954), pp. 428-32.

opinion, are perhaps to be expected of a man who had been centrally involved in dramatic events, who had had to compose his thoughts in a hurry and who came from a subject commune and now found himself in a position of influence.

Clodio's closeness to events also explains one of the principal points of interest of his *relazione*: the author's attempt to describe the various sections of the population and to analyse their political aspirations. The picture that emerges confirms aspects of society suggested by research on other Renaissance cities: despite the long, virtually unbroken *signoria* of the Varano, there survived a small number of politically restless and ambitious families who measured their strength in the extent of their kin and clients, and the offices held in church and state. Their actions, more especially in periods of considerable political change, could rouse the rest of the population, and as Philip Jones has observed in the context of the Romagna and the Marches: 'In no city probably could the lord count on equal loyalty from all classes'.[28] Clodio's observations also help us to make sense of the apparent contradictions that emerge in other well-informed contemporary accounts. On 27 May 1502 Giustinian reported that Giulio Cesare was 'confidentissimo' of the loyalty of his subjects, yet fearful of the power of the papacy and anxious for Venetian protection.[29] Sanudo noted that in 1502 Giovanni Maria had entered Camerino 'chiamato dal populo e con gran jubilio', and on 25 October the *signore* wrote to the doge of the 'singular devutione et amor' of all his people. Yet a dispatch from Giustinian of 24 December told the Republic that Giovanni Maria had fled on hearing of negotiations between the citizens and the returning papal army.[30]

Clodio's prescriptions tried to take account of such calculating or shallow loyalties. The small number of poorly supported Borgia adherents could be increased, but total loyalty could never be achieved. The Varano had successfully attracted the loyalty of the poor and the *contadini*; their support, too, could be won over, but could not be guaranteed. Although aware of the military factors that had toppled Giulio Cesare (p. 155), and which would be necessary to support the Borgia duchy, for Clodio the long-term answer was essentially political, and the formula he recommends to Alexander is traditional and modelled on the achievements of the Varano. It is also traditional in the sense of being localised. *Stato* is used by Clodio to mean the regime in Camerino and the extent of its jurisdiction. It is not used to describe a new, greater 'territorial' or 'Renaissance' state, and Clodio urges the pope to keep his subjects away from the temptations of the 'capital', Rome. Hence central are: the presence and accessibility of the ruler; the constant and skilful use

[28] P.J. Jones, *The Malatesta of Rimini and the Papal State* (Cambridge, 1974), p. 259.
[29] *Dispacci*, pp. 9-10.
[30] Sanudo, coll. 411, 466-67; *Dispacci*, p. 285.

of patronage in forms ranging from office to alms; and the role of the court as a social centre.

In Clodio's judgement, under Giulio Cesare, Camerino may have been 'ridotto molto quieto e sicuro' (p. 148). He may not have ruled 'per amor' (p. 155), and the favour he showed the poor and *contadini* had been designed to keep the greater citizens in check rather than to improve their lot.[31] But now everyone felt his absence, and that of his court, and lamented by their firesides, 'Ove sta Casa Varana?' (p. 152). The modern visitor to Camerino, watching the *passeggiata* that nostalgically still takes in the damaged *cortile* of the ex-Varano palace, may well feel the same.

[31] A contemporary records that Giulio Cesare obtained labour services and materials for his palace 'a uso di servitio di Corte', without payment, Corradini, p. 196.

13

Commune and Despot: The Commune of Ferrara under Este Rule, 1300-1450

Trevor Dean

'Despotic government was not totalitarian';[1] rather, as Philip Jones went on to argue, the political structure of the Italian city-lordships, and of the regional states which grew out of them, was highly complex. Far from creating 'Renaissance states', 'unitary, absolute and secular', the *signori* not only took over the communal legacy of laws and institutions, but also tolerated large areas of immunity and privilege. They made little effort to unify or centralise their states, and their legislative and fiscal achievement was unremarkable. Born of faction, their rule proved fragile when tested and often ended in bloodshed.[2] But if total power eluded them, how far did such lords' personal authority and control extend? How was power distributed in a society with many layers or centres of influence? How was power structured and exercised in areas where the lord's touch was light, distant or indirect?

Examination of the relations between *signori* and the communes over which they ruled can supply some further answers to such questions. It is unnecessary here to rehearse the old debates over the origins and early legitimation of the *signorie*, which focussed on the growth of lordship within the former communal institutions;[3] suffice it to remark that Ercole's view, that the resulting partnership between lord and commune gave way in the fifteenth century to the 'unitary and centralising system' of the principalities, seems still to lie behind those continuing studies of signorial government which locate in the fifteenth century a transition to new princely institutions, such as councils, chanceries, ceremonies and courts.[4] These, it is assumed, were the points of growth, while the

---

[1] P.J. Jones, 'Communes and Despots. The City State in Late Medieval Italy', *Transactions of the Royal Historical Society*, ser. 5, xv (1965), 74.

[2] Ibid., pp. 87-94.

[3] F. Diaz, 'Di alcuni aspetti istituzionali dell'affermarsi delle signorie', *Nuova rivista storica*, 1 (1966), 122-24.

[4] F. Ercole, 'Comuni e signori nel Veneto', in idem, *Dal comune al principato* (Florence, 1929), pp. 108-18.

communal institutions, having first been exploited by the *signori*, were then stifled and dismantled when they had no further use for them: they were an embarrassing relic, a reminder of better days, to be suppressed and forgotten as quickly as possible or otherwise kept on only as a transparent façade, with no real political significance. Wherever possible, large assemblies of citizens (the *maggior consiglio, parlamenti* etc.) were avoided and the oligarchic tendencies of small committees were encouraged.[5]

Such an interpretation has supported a tendency to examine the communes under signorial rule in the nostalgic light of what they had been, rather than to investigate and assess whatever positive functions they might have had in mobilising and organising consent and participation in signorial rule.[6] Thus Ventura described Alberto della Scala, lord of Verona, as turning 'the principal municipal organs . . . into sure instruments of power in his service' and then 'condemning them to progressive atrophy'.[7] Vasina saw the creation of the Este *signoria* as the 'final liquidation of the communal experience at Ferrara . . . Thus on a now stagnant society fell the curtain of court conformism'.[8] And Mozzarelli, describing the transition from *signoria* to principality in Mantua, saw the 'forms of communal government, still alive in the signorial structure' as 'now reduced to mere formality'; while Nicolini, writing of a strange consultative exercise on the state of the city carried out by the Gonzaga lords in 1430, makes much of the fact that it was *not* conducted via the commune: the prince conversed directly with his people.[9]

This rejection of the commune as having any role in the government of lordships and principalities possibly reflects the tendency of historians to view government from the top and from the centre, but there is a growing recognition of the limits of central government and of the value of other points of view: central government was often confused and inefficient, and it left large space for local autonomy and collective action. In the first place, historians have discovered 'community', 'collectivity' and 'neighbourhood' as features of a new, non-hierarchical analysis of society.

---

[5] A. Ventura, *Nobiltà e popolo nella società veneta del '400 e '500* (Bari, 1964), pp. 17-37; L. Green, 'Lucca under Castruccio Castracani', *I Tatti Studies*, i (1985), 141.

[6] C. Mozzarelli, 'Il senato di Mantova: origine e funzioni', in *Mantova e i Gonzaga nella civiltà del Rinascimento* (Mantua, 1977), pp. 68-69.

[7] Ventura, pp. 28, 64.

[8] A. Vasina, 'Un' autonoma patria cittadina', in *Ferrara*, ed. R. Renzi (2 vols., Bologna, 1969), i, 68.

[9] C. Mozzarelli, 'Lo stato gonzaghesco: Mantova dal 1382 al 1707', in UTET *Storia d'Italia*, xvii (Turin, 1979), pp. 358-59; U. Nicolini, 'Principe e cittadini: una consultazione popolare del 1430 nella Mantova dei Gonzaga', in *Mantova e i Gonzaga*, pp. 44-46; and cf. Federigo da Montefeltro: Vespasiano da Bisticci, *Le vite*, ed. A. Greco (2 vols., Florence, 1970), i, 403.

Susan Reynolds, in the most powerful exposition of this trend, has argued that 'lay society and government depended in a mass of different ways on the collective activities of a wide range of people' and that society's values 'combined acceptance of inequality and subordination with a high degree of voluntary cooperation'.[10] The clear message here is that institutional and social hierarchies form only one part of medieval history: another part is filled by collectivities. Secondly, studies of Italian territorial government in the fifteenth century, especially in the Milanese state and the Venetian *Terraferma*, have stressed how much was left to local autonomy and how little the local political structure was changed by the regional states: the Venetian government was disinclined to touch the political organisation of its newly subject cities; restraining *capitoli*, by which the cities tried to define and limit the authority of their new lords, were ubiquitous; and rural lordship, particularism and 'separate' status were not just accepted, but promoted by the Dukes of Milan.[11] Finally, it is perhaps useful to note that large and sometimes permanent assemblies of citizens were not absent from principalities in other parts of Europe, even though they have seemed to be in Italy (despite the possibility that princely institutions in northern Italy and in other parts of Europe developed along broadly similar lines).[12] Elsewhere, representative assemblies gave consent not only to taxes and military levies, but also to legislation and dynastic changes; they expressed the complaints and grievances of the 'governed'; and they allowed a certain amount of interchange between the prince and (some of) the people. Is their absence in princely Italy explained by the persistence of local autonomy and privilege? And does it in turn explain the fragility of territorial states? What room was there in Renaissance principalities for collective action, for councils and assemblies? Some answer to these questions is provided by examining relations between the marquises of Este, lords of Ferrara from 1264, and the surviving communal institutions in that city.[13]

[10] S. Reynolds, *Kingdoms and Communities in Western Europe, 900-1300* (Oxford, 1984), p. 332.

[11] J.E. Law, 'Venice and the "Closing" of the Veronese Constitution in 1405', *Studi veneziani*, n.s., i (1977); G.M. Varanini, 'Note sui consigli civici veronesi', *Archivio veneto*, ser. 5, cxii (1979); G. Chittolini, 'Il particolarismo signorile e feudale in Emilia fra Quattro e Cinquecento', in *Il Rinascimento nelle corti padane: società e cultura*, ed. P. Rossi (Bari, 1977); idem, 'Le "terre separate" nel ducato di Milano in età sforzesca', in *Milano nell'età di Ludovico il Moro* (Milan, 1983); R. Mistura, 'Dei privilegi più speciosi concessi dalla Serenissima repubblica di Venezia alla città di Brescia', in *Studi in onore di Ugo Gualazzini* (2 vols., Milan, 1981).

[12] T. Dean, *Land and Power in Late Medieval Ferrara: The Rule of the Este, 1350-1450* (Cambridge, 1987), p. 179.

[13] On Ferrara in general, still indispensable is A. Frizzi, *Memorie per la storia di Ferrara* (2nd ed., Ferrara, 1846-48).

The creation of the Este *signoria* in Ferrara, the first of its type in northern Italy, has given rise to several interpretations, which have variously focussed on the economic basis of the city, depressed under Venetian pressure to allow the victory of landed interests; on the weakness of the Ferrarese nobility, which lacked rural strongholds from which to resist the Este; on the vast landed power of the Este family and its use, through feudal grants, to recruit and reward supporters; and on the importance of regional Guelf leaders in protecting and promoting the first Este lord, Obizzo II.[14] Despite these advantages, Este power remained for some time not wholly legitimate or complete: it was not until the 1330s that they finally secured, at high financial cost, acceptance by the pope, overlord of Ferrara, in the form of a papal vicariate; and until the mid-century the Este were still sharing some political matters with the commune, as seen in the duplicate appointment of ambassadors.[15] Nevertheless, Este power in Ferrara was unchallengeable, partly through their immense wealth, partly as a result of outside support. Already in the thirteenth century the Este had attracted to Ferrara Guelf exiles and allies from other cities, and in the fourteenth century a cosmopolitan court emerged, with counsellors and officers drawn from all over northern and central Italy.[16] With the acquisition of further territories (Modena 1336, Reggio 1409, and places in the Romagna) and with the expansion of Este administration and the elaboration of a 'courtly space' (palaces, ceremonies and entertainment), a regime was created that was remarkably stable. No other *signoria*, established so early, lasted so long. Revolts and dynastic crises of course there were, but the Este hold on Ferrara was noticeably more robust than their hold on Modena or Reggio. The causes of this are presumably to be found in the family's continuous presence in or near Ferrara, in the relative weakness of the Ferrarese aristocracy (certainly compared to their Modenese or Reggian counterparts) and also perhaps in the political structure of the city itself. For the presence of a lord and his court could cause local difficulties: that it did not in Ferrara might be related to the way that the Este organised acceptance of their rule and deflected criticism of it.[17] Did the commune have a role here?

[14] A. Castagnetti, *Società e politica a Ferrara dall'età postcarolingia alla signoria estense (secoli X-XIII)* (Bologna, 1985), pp. 216-17; Dean, pp. 28-108; idem, 'Venetian economic hegemony: the case of Ferrara, 1200-1500', *Studi veneziani*, n.s., xii (1986); A.L. Trombetti Budriesi, 'Vassalli e feudi a Ferrara e nel Ferrarese dall'età precomunale alla signoria estense', *A[tti e] M[emorie della Deputazione] F[errarese di storia patria]*, ser. 3, xxviii (1980).

[15] E.g. A. Theiner, *Codex diplomaticus Dominii temporalis Sanctae Sedis* (Rome, 1861-62), ii, 135-38 (1342).

[16] Dean, *Land and Power*, pp. 77-91; Jones, p. 89.

[17] On deflection of criticism: R.G. Brown, 'The Politics of Magnificence in Ferrara, 1450-1505', Univ. Edinburgh D.Phil., 1982, pp. 61-74.

It could be argued that the Este largely suppressed the commune and transferred many of its functions to their own officials. Such an argument would focus on two areas. First is the fact that the elaborate communal apparatus described in the statutes of 1287 was clearly no longer in existence fifty years later. These statutes, though already bearing the imprint of Este power, still provided for a *maggior consiglio* of 200 and a minor council of forty, and for their detailed operating procedures (initiation, speeches, voting, attendance, record-keeping).[18] The statutes remained full of stipulations that certain actions by communal officials needed the prior consent of the *maggior consiglio*. The commune also had, on paper, a structure of ordinary offices in charge of law enforcement, finances, food supply, trade and movement; and there were all the usual restrictions on periods of office, repeated office-holding and so on.[19] Already by the 1320s – if it was not a fiction even by 1287 – this structure had been scaled down: although the ordinary officers did remain, the key council was now one of twelve, not forty, presided over by a *giudice (dei savi)* appointed by the marquis.[20] Significantly the rules and procedures operating in this council were never written down. The *maggior consiglio* was reduced to a fleeting existence, convened (if that is the right word) only to hear certain private business that by law had to be made public (such as bankruptcies). The second point is that some communal functions were indeed, during the fourteenth century, transferred to the Este, most clearly the collection of gabelles and military security. In the 1340s it was still the communal *massaro* who farmed out the gabelles and received their revenues, but by the 1360s control had passed to the Este *camera*.[21] It was also the marquis who appointed guards to the many river routes into and out of Ferrarese territory.[22] Over remaining communal functions it could be argued that the marquis had complete control: he technically appointed all communal officials, and it was always after discussion with him that the commune's remaining taxes (mainly the property tax or *colleta*) were levied.

This transfer of functions obviously reflects the growth of the Este administration in the second half of the fourteenth century: the emergence of the chancery and *camera* and the branching off of various financial and judicial functions. But there are three qualifications to be made. First, the process was slow, despite the fact that the *signore* had had the power to dispose of communal property since the constitution of the *signoria* in 1264.

---

[18] *Statuta Ferrariae anno MCCLXXXVII*, ed. W. Montorsi (Ferrara, 1955), Lib. II, 90 a-1. 1.

[19] Ibid., II, 181-203, 207, 209, 224-45, 289, 292.

[20] Frizzi, ii, 291-301; A[rchivio di] S[tato], F[errara], Liber provisionum, fos. 51v-61v.

[21] A[rchivio di] S[tato], M[odena], A[rchivio] S[egreto] E[stense], Notai camerali, B. Nigrisoli, *passim*; ASF, Lib. prov., fos. 30, 31, 56v, 57v, 60v.

[22] ASM, ASE, Cancelleria, Leggi e Decreti, regs. A 1 and A 2, *passim*.

It was not until 1474 that the communal council, which had traditionally met in ecclesiastical space (first the cathedral, then rooms above the cloister of the church of S. Romano), moved to new offices in the Este palace itself.[23] Secondly, the process of transfer was patchy: property confiscated from rebels was still being adjudicated to the commune in the 1390s, not to the *camera*; in conducting commercial relations with Venice, the Este insisted on observing the terms of the old communal pacts with Venice, notwithstanding much altered political and economic circumstances.[24] So the evidence of dismantling of communal institutions is not clear-cut, and has to be set against other evidence which points in a different direction, namely that of the commune having a more active role.

It is useful to start by considering some interesting changes in communal nomenclature in the middle of the fifteenth century: the council of *savi* then became in communal records a *senatus* and, at the beginning of every year, in the registers of their deliberations, a fresh page would be headed *S.P.Q.F.*, *Senatus Populusque Ferrariensis*.[25] Is this merely the adoption of voguish classical terminology, or is it a sign of institutional confidence, of the council having a role that some liked (mistakenly?) to think resembled that of senates in other places (Rome or Venice?) or at other times (ancient or modern?)? The latter view would be supported by developments in the previous half-century, during which the Este seem to have tried, at various stages, to find a positive role for the communal council.

Full documentation for much of the fourteenth century is lacking, most of it apparently destroyed during the Ferrarese tax revolt of 1385,[26] though there survives a register of selected deliberations for the period 1321-82. But it does seem as if the council of *savi* was disorganised and inactive by the late fourteenth century. This is suggested by the records themselves: the surviving registers of deliberations do not start until 1393, with the succession of Niccolò III, and for some years they remain rather chaotic and near-illegible, as if no one was expected to refer to them.[27] They then break off altogether from 1403 to 1418. But from 1418 there is abundant evidence of matters being put into order, of the reins of

---

[23]   Frizzi, ii, 304.

[24]   Biblioteca Estense, Modena, Documenti Campori, Appendice, 1251, fos. 35 (29 Jan. 1384), 52-55 (5 June 1392); ASM, Notai camerali, Z. Coadi, 1 Apr. 1393; cf. ASM, Leggi e Decreti, reg. B III, fo. 166 (1404) and reg. B IV, fo. 53 (1421); Dean, 'Venetian economic hegemony', p. 68.

[25]   A[rchivio] C[omunale,] F[errara], Libri delle Deliberazioni, reg. F, fo. 85v; reg. G, fo. 1; cf. 'S.P.Q.F.' in Florence: A. Brown, 'Florence, Renaissance and Early Modern State: Reappraisals', *Journal of Modern History*, lvi (1984), 298.

[26]   Frizzi, ii, 294; iii, 368-72; J.E. Law, 'Popular Unrest in Ferrara in 1385', in *The Renaissance in Ferrara and its European Horizons*, ed. J. Salmons and W. Moretti (Cardiff and Ravenna, 1984).

[27]   ACF, Libri, A, *passim*; C (1), fo. 28v.

communal administration being taken up again. A new tax assessment (*estimo*) was launched and two *savi* were delegated to review the accounts of the *collete* imposed since 1410. Measures were taken to pay off communal debts and groups were appointed to review the *massaro*'s accounts for the years 1412-17.[28] At the same time, the proposal was aired to reopen the university of Ferrara, closed to save money in 1404.[29] In 1420 all inhabitants of the *contado* with titles of citizenship were ordered to appear before the *giudice* and *savi*, a measure obviously aimed at attacking fiscal fraud in the aftermath of the *estimo* revision.[30] There is evidence of inquiries being made into tax declarations and into individuals' tax status. Greater fiscal pressure was obviously being applied, combined with a firm insistence on the different fiscal treatment of citizens and *contadini*, which generated some protest in 1422.[31] It is also from 1418 that we find more frequent use of supernumerary attendance at meetings of the *savi*: so-called *adiuncti*, persons specifically invited to attend a particular meeting, presumably because considered expert in some matter or personally involved or in order to give greater weight and representativeness to the proceedings.[32] In the following years meetings afforced in this way were held to discuss matters such as petitions for tax remission, the coinage, the funding of repairs to bridges and conduits, clerical tax exemptions, proposals regarding cloth imports and the wool trade, the university and the plague.[33]

A more significant series of changes were made in the years following 1432. At the end of that year, the marquis ordered the *giudice* to initiate a system for the regular replacement of *savi*. Existing arrangements hardly constituted a system at all, with the same group of men being left in charge for years at a time. Now it was envisaged to replace two of the twelve *savi* every two months, though the system actually implemented involved instead the election every year of ten new *savi*, with two being retained from the previous year.[34] In addition, the practice of having additional members was formalised: the *adiuncti* became a fixed group, changed annually. This was the system that then operated for the rest of the fifteenth century: new elections every year of ten *savi* and six *adiuncti*. It is important to note the principles on which this reform seems to have been based: regular turnover of members, more formal arrangements for

[28] Ibid., fos. 20v, 22v, 30, 36-37v, 38-39, 53, 54v.
[29] Ibid., fos. 24-25.
[30] Ibid., fo. 69v.
[31] Ibid., fos. 77-v, 79-v, 84, 101, 105v, 135v-36v, 155.
[32] Ibid., fos. 21v, 24-v, 25, 45, 65-66; cf. Frizzi, ii, 301; S. Bertelli, *Il potere oligarchico nello città-stato medievale* (Florence, 1978), p. 8; S. Polica, 'Le famiglie del ceto dirigente lucchese', in *I ceti dirigenti nella Toscana del Quattrocento* (Florence, 1987), pp. 374-84.
[33] ACF, Libri, A, fos. 61-62, 79, 82, 85-86, 95; C (1), fos. 21v, 24-25, 148, 156-v, 172, 176, 182; C (2), fos. 8-v; D, fo. 54v; F. fos. 54v-55v; G, fos. 1, 10v.
[34] Ibid., C (2), fo. 30v; D, fos. 27v, 45v, 57; F, fos. 19, 30, 34v etc.

supplementary or auxiliary advice, a limited element of continuity from one year to the next. Further reform and innovation followed. In 1433 an oath of secrecy was imposed on the *savi* and became a standard feature of their admission to office (secrecy would have been necessary only if the decisions to be taken were important ones).[35] Also in 1433 a new inventory of communal property was drawn up and an investigation launched into tax exemptions in the *contado* (followed in 1434 by a new *estimo*).[36] In 1436 a new procedure was set up for the annual appointment of officials to maintain communal property and rights, and the council's offices were refurbished.[37] In 1440 came an order from the marquis that the *savi* were to hold regular meetings, every Tuesday and Thursday (later relaxed to Thursday only), with a fine for non-attendance.[38] In these years too, the registers of council proceedings become much better organised and more clearly written.

Secrecy, annual elections, regular meetings, greater firmness in investigating and maintaining communal rights all indicate that the communal council was being deliberately promoted in these years. Coincidentally, almost the same process, of cataloguing rights, establishing officials to maintain them and creating greater order and clarity in the making and keeping of documents, was at work at the same time in the Este administration itself, such that it is hard to believe that there was not a single mind at work here, possibly that of Leonello d'Este, Niccolò III's classically-educated son, who was given authority in routine internal administration by his father in 1434.[39] The reforms certainly continued in Leonello's own reign (1441-50) and amounted to a general overhaul of communal structures, not just of the communal council. Already under Niccolò, the office of *podestà* had been revised and new standing orders had been issued for the *officium bulletarum et custodie*, which dealt with movement into and out of the city and with sanitation, prostitution and horse trading.[40] Then, after 1441, the food-supply office was reformed, an inventory was made of communal munitions, and a tighter system of stock control was instituted there.[41] There was tax reform in 1443, when the *datea*, a tax on crops paid to the Este, was reduced and the remaining receipts reassigned, one half to the commune, one half to the cathedral fabric.[42] The university was the subject of a major

[35] Ibid., C (2), fo. 36. For punishment of unauthorised disclosure: ibid., fo. 38v. Cf. similar provision in the new 1440 statutes of Rovigo: N. Di Lenna, *L'ordinamento della visconteria di Rovigo* (Lugo, 1918), pp. 28-29.

[36] ACF, Libri, C (2), fos. 9v, 35, 36-37; D, fos. 8v, 9v.

[37] Ibid., fos. 46v, 50; L.N. Cittadella, *Notizie relative a Ferrara* (Ferrara, 1864), p. 4.

[38] ACF, Libri, F, fos. 42-v; G, fo. 29v; Frizzi, ii, 304.

[39] ASM, Notai camerali, A. Villa, 22 May 1434.

[40] ACF, Libri, D, fo. 11; ASF, Archivio storico comunale, Serie finanziaria, sec. XV, b. 9/17; Cittadella, p. 289.

[41] ACF, Libri, F, fos. 68v, 69, 71, 77, 79v.

[42] Ibid., fo. 76v; Frizzi, ii, 308; A. Sitta, 'Saggio sulle istituzioni finanziarie del ducato

expansionary reform in 1442, and hospital provision in Ferrara was centralised in 1444 with the creation of the Ospedale di S. Anna: in both, the commune was intimately involved.[43] In 1446 the civil and criminal law statutes were revised and in the following year sumptuary legislation was eventually issued (after years of pressure from the *savi*).[44] There can be little doubt that it was this rapid succession of reforms and innovations that brought the commune a more positive self-image.

The commune, then, seems to have been important to the Este, but what did it do? There were seven main areas of responsibility.[45] First came maintaining and revising the tax assessments (*estimo*) and setting every year the level of direct tax (*colleta*) based on them.[46] This involved dealing with changes in individuals' circumstances, with petitions for remission and so on and debating and deciding on questions of liability and exemption (here there were the usual and constant problems regarding the tax status of citizens living in the *contado* and the tax burden of *subburgenses*).[47] The *estimo* was periodically revised.[48] The level of *colleta* depended on the charges envisaged in the coming year and covered salaries and expenses, and the costs of public works and of servicing the commune's debt. The second area of communal action regarded food-supply: controls on milling, supervision of the movement and trade of grain, the regulation of food prices (especially meat).[49]

This shaded into the third area, that of economic regulation. It was the commune that issued wage and price controls in 1350 following the Black Death[50] and that regulated secured money-lending.[51] The council was

---

estense', *AMF*, iii (1891), 164-65.

[43] ACF, Libri, G, fo. 26v; A. Franceschini, 'Il sapore del sale: ricerche sulla assistenza ospedaliera nel sec. XV in una città di punta: Ferrara', *AMF*, ser. 4, i (1981), 65-77; G. Pardi, *Lo studio di Ferrara nei secoli XV e XVI* (Ferrara, 1903).

[44] ACF, Libri, G, fos. 20-v, 24v-25. This followed proposals of 1420 and 1434: ibid., C (1), fo. 103; D, fos. 4, 5-v.

[45] Cf. Frizzi, ii, 304; Sitta, pp. 108-17.

[46] On the *estimo*: ibid., pp. 156-64; Frizzi, ii, 305-7.

[47] *Stat. Ferr.*, VI, 53; Biblioteca Comunale Ariostea, Ferrara, Capitoli per l'estimo (1400), Cl. I, 740, fos. 3v-4v, 5v, 6 (clauses 8-10, 14, 17).

[48] ACF, Libri, B, fo. 42 (1410); C (1), fos. 20v (1418), 36-39, 42 (1419), 196-200 (1428); D, fos. 9-v, 30v, 41-v (1434-35).

[49] ASF, Lib. prov., fos 29-v (1327), 35-v (1339), 44v (1346), 45-46v (1347), 54-v (1323). For meat prices and meat trade: ACF, Libri, A, fos. 33, 45, 87, 91; C (1), fos. 150, 181v; C (2), fos. 24-v, 31-v, 33, 38-39; D, fos. 31v-32, 33v, 62v. For bread prices: ibid., C (2), fo. 23; D, fos. 12v, 36, 39, 40, 51v, 77v; wood prices: D, fo. 55v; F, fos. 43v, 48; and milling controls: C (1), fo. 51; C (2), fos. 21v-22v, 25-26, 28-v, 29v, 30v, 33v; F, fos. 56v, 76.

[50] ASF, Lib. prov., fos. 46v-48v; cf. M. Becker, 'La esecuzione della legislazione contro le pratiche monopolistiche delle arti fiorentine alla metà del secolo quattordicesimo', *Archivio Storico Italiano*, cxvii (1959); W.M. Bowsky, 'The Impact of the Black Death upon Sienese Government and Society', *Speculum*, xxxix (1964), 21, 26, 30.

[51] ASF, Lib. prov., fos. 58v, 61-v; ACF, Libri, C (1), fos. 79, 102-v, 108, 145v-147 (insert), 155v, 160, 173v, 188, 193; C (2), fos. 4v, 10-v, 15v; F, fo. 86v; G, fo. 17.

also involved in guild matters, ordering regular guild offerings to the Church (1322), intervening in disputes between guilds (1399), revising guild statutes (1422), considering petitions to create new guilds and dealing with the wool guild (from the early 1430s this was claiming more and more time in council meetings as the wool industry in Ferrara expanded).[52] The official attitude to the guilds did not long remain that of 1287, when Obizzo d'Este had abolished them as illegal corporations: by contrast, in 1430 the proper management of the wool guild was identified as the most important problem facing the Ferrarese 'republic'.[53] There were also deliberations on the coinage: although the Este were slowly appropriating the Ferrarese coinage (renaming the coins *marchesini*; introducing portrait heads), it still remained a communal matter to some extent and the coins still carried the communal arms.[54]

The fourth area of the *savi*'s activity was public education. The commune hired an arithmetic teacher in 1418 and a grammar teacher in 1429. It was the commune that engaged Guarino da Verona in 1436 and that issued in 1443 an order against 'unlearned teachers opening schools'.[55] It was also the commune that funded the university (a number of large meetings were held in 1418 to discuss how to pay for reopening it).[56] The fifth area was public health: the commune was ultimately responsible for provisions taken against the plague in the 1430s, though in close consultation with the marquis and with his health officials.[57]

The sixth area was law and order. Despite the fact that the *podestà* was chosen by the *signore*, the commune set the level of his salary, formulated his duties, made provision to cover for him in his absence, and made him gifts on his departure from office.[58] In addition, the commune made amendments to the civil and criminal law (1320s/1330s), regulated procedure in the law courts (1363, 1403-4) and hired a police chief for the

[52] Frizzi, ii, 296-97; ASF, Lib. prov., fo. 57; ACF, Libri, A, fos. 4, 40; C (1), fos. 23v, 181v, 186v; C (2), fos. 5, 15v, 23, 29-v, 32v, 35v, 37v; D, fos. 1, 3, 6, 14, 32, 33, 69; E, fo. 18v; F, fos. 28v, 31-v, 32, 41, 50v; G, fos. 1v-2.

[53] *Stat. Ferr.*, VI,, 60; ACF, Libri, C (2), fo. 5: 'Per prefatum dominum Judicem propositum est quod sibi videtur fore aliqua membra in nostra republica que sunt grandis importantie et male gubernantur et primo ars lane . . .'

[54] V. Bellini, *Delle monete di Ferrara* (Ferrara, 1761), pp. 97-99, 108, 118, 123. For communal involvement: ASF, Lib. prov., fos. 35v, 37; ACF, Libri, A, fos. 9, 79, 80, 82, 95; C (1), fo. 22; C (2), fos. 8-v; D, fo. 50v.

[55] ACF, Libri, C (1), fo. 20v; C (2), fo. 2v; D, fos. 49v-50v; F, fo. 81v; Sitta, pp. 110-11; F. Borsetti, *Historia almi Ferrariae gymnasii* (2 vols., Ferrara, 1735), i, 28-29, 31, 47-49, 50.

[56] ACF, Libri, C (1), fos. 24-25; Pardi, pp. 31-34, 263-64.

[57] ACF, Libri, D, fos, 53-55, 56, 63; F, fos. 23v-25, 30v, 33v-34, 36; Cittadella, pp. 392, 399.

[58] ASF, Lib. prov., fos. 24-v (1351), 25 (1332), 54v-55 (1323), 58v, 59 (1326), 63v, 73v (1354), 78 (1379); ACF, Libri, D, fos. 9v, 11.

contado.[59] However, direct communal concern with law and order seems to have been more common in the fourteenth than in the fifteenth century: in the fourteenth century the *savi* even tried to deal with the disruptive effects of magnate power and family quarrels;[60] but in the fifteenth, such interventions, or the problems they aimed to solve, were lacking. The final area of communal responsibility lay in the general area of defence, in the maintenance of bridges, dykes and fortifications, in inspection, the organisation of repair work and the occasional hiring of troops.[61]

What does all this amount to? Was it just routine administration, providing the basic services of security and welfare on which the urban community depended and implementing decisions taken by the *signore*, but cloaking them in a communal facade? Or did the commune represent a channel both for the local community to express their views and to have some control over their lives, and also for the Este to involve in government members of the local community who would not be seen at court? Was the grasp of signorial power so weak that it had to leave some matters (or only unpopular ones?) to a semi-detached institution? Or was there some other reason for the Este to allow the communal council to survive? The evidence at this point is conflicting. On the one hand, it is clear that behind all the commune's activities stood the *signore*, instructing it, issuing orders, privileges and exemptions, and taking initiatives which the commune had to adapt to. Thus if the commune administered the *estimo*, the marquis ordered exemptions and set the level of *colleta*;[62] if the commune managed the food-supply, the marquis issued licences to export grain;[63] if the commune regulated money-lending, the marquis authorised Jews to operate in Ferrara;[64] if the commune had responsibility for maintaining fortifications, the marquis decided when they were to be repaired or rebuilt.[65] In each case, it was the lord who gave and dispensed, the commune which regulated and paid: a distribution of functions that reflected the importance of *giving* in the political structure.[66] And certainly it looks as if the *signore* did use the commune to take unpopular decisions. This might especially be the case in matters of economic regulation, but is

[59] ASF, Lib. prov., fos. 27, 53v-54, 57v, 58v, 62v, 71v, 73, 74, 75v etc; ACF, Libri, A, fo. 65; B, fos. 3-4, 8; C (1), fos. 20-v, 34, 66v, 173, 188, 192; D, fos. 57v, 64; G, fos. 20-v.

[60] ASF, Lib. prov., fos. 27 (1334), 53v-54 (1323), 57v (1322) etc.

[61] Bridges: ACF, Libri, A, fos. 6, 10, 18, 43, 83-86, 92-93; C (1), fos. 129, 148 etc; dykes: A, fos. 11-12, 31, 35, 38, 50; C (1), fos. 165v, 172, 179v, 182, 185 etc; walls and fortifications: A, fos. 52-55, 191v-92; C (1), fos. 187, 191v-92; C (2), fos. 38, 49; D, fos. 3v, 8, 57v.

[62] E.g. ASM, Leggi e Decreti, B IV, fos. 108, 113v.

[63] ASM, Leggi e Decreti, *passim*.

[64] E.g. ibid., B III, fos. 114-21, 292.

[65] ACF, Libri, C (1), fos 191v-92; C (2), fo. 21v; D, fo. 57v; E, fo. 30.

[66] T. Dean, 'Notes on the Court of Ferrara in the Later Middle Ages', *Renaissance Studies*, 3 (1989), 364.

well illustrated by the measures taken against the plague in 1438. This came at a delicate time for the marquis, who was about to host a Church Council, to be attended by the leading ecclesiastical and secular dignitaries of the Greek and Latin churches. With fears of plague growing, the marquis suggested that the commune find a place to which to send any people stricken by it. The commune decided on the monastery of S. Lazaro, but the marquis was unhappy with their choice, wondering whether it would be 'honest' to disturb the monks and fearing that they might complain to the pope. So he advised that a rumour should be started that the commune had decided to build a new hospital and that some display should be made to encourage belief in this, but that if any people actually contracted plague, they should be sent to S. Lazaro anyway.[67] The political value of a non-centralised government is here made plain, as in other areas of Este lordship.[68] It is also true that the commune made direct financial contributions to the Este and their court: granting tax immunities for *familiares* and estate-workers, maintaining horses for Este service, making wedding gifts and commissioning commemorative statues.[69]

On the other hand, there is evidence of the commune expressing views at variance with those of the marquis. This can be seen in occasional instances of opposition to the marquis's decisions, successful in each case.[70] It can also be seen in the transmission to the marquis in 1420 of a list of grievances concerning the gabelles, controls on Jewish money-lending and sumptuary legislation.[71] These instances, in which the commune is to be found having its own views, are supported by the whole practice of extra-conciliar consultation, which became permanent in these years: there would have been no need for this had the commune simply been implementing the marquis's orders. The marquis was also keen to remit private petitions to the *savi* for investigation or advice: petitions for citizenship, tax rebates and building licences. Guild matters were also passed on in this way.[72] That there was real discussion in the formation of the commune's view is indicated by the taking of votes[73] and the

[67] ACF, Libri, F, fo. 24; Franceschini, pp. 128-29.

[68] Dean, 'Venetian economic hegemony', pp. 68-69.

[69] ASF, Lib. prov., fo. 34v; ACF, Libri, A, fo. 68; C (1), fos. 19v, 176; C (2), fos. 16v, 17-18, 23; D, fos. 13v, 37, 39v, 49v, 66; F, fos. 45, 83.

[70] Over milling controls, the appointment of a *barisello*, and a proposed block sale of Este property: ibid., A, fo. 41; C (2), fo. 33v; D, fos. 57v, 64v.

[71] Ibid., C (1), fo. 102v. On the connection of sumptuary laws and anti-Jewish feeling: D.O. Hughes, 'Distinguishing Signs: Earrings, Jews and Franciscan Rhetoric in the Italian Renaissance City', *Past and Present*, cxii (1986).

[72] E.g. ACF, Libri, C (1), fos. 165, 176v, 178-79, 180-81; ASM, Leggi e Decreti, reg. B IV, fos. 79v, 122v, 152, 184v-85.

[73] ACF, Libri, C (1), fos. 21v, 24v, insert 145v-47; 173v-74; C (2), fos. 8, 26v-28; F, fos. 31-v.

registering of dissent.[74]

Who, finally, were the *savi*? Does their identity help us to determine the role of the communal council and its relation to the court? Was the commune run by an oligarchy of men close to the marquis? Did it become the preserve of an increasingly exclusive local elite?[75] Or did it afford opportunities for wider participation in matters of local importance? The first and clearest point regarding membership of the council is that the *savi* included very few nobles. Nobles *were* among the *savi* in the first half of the fourteenth century, but appear less frequently thereafter: this presumably reflects the slow transfer of functions from the commune to the Este. After 1350 there is only a scatter of members of noble families,[76] and the *savi* seem to come predominantly from the business community: they are mainly notaries, bankers, cloth merchants and artisans. As a result they were probably not very close to the court. Although some of the notaries and bankers did work occasionally for the Este, that does not make them part of the court milieu. Few of the *savi* were Este vassals, and it would be difficult to claim that they were politically experienced. They seem rather to be connected with neighbourhood associations (*contrade*). These *contrade* were the smallest social and administrative units in the city and were arranged into four quarters. Each *contrada* had its own *massaro* or *sindico* and each quarter had its own *savi* (distinct from the communal *savi*).[77] Little of this local structure is now visible to the historian,[78] but we know, from a list of the *massari* of one *contrada* (S. Romano) in this period, that a substantial proportion of *massari* (nearly one half) went on to become communal *savi*. Prominence in the neighbourhood seems to have made certain individuals more eligible as *savi*.[79]

The council's contact with the court came not so much through the *savi*, as through their president, the *giudice de' savi*, although this post was, during the fifteenth century, captured by members of the local nobility prominent at court. Whereas in the fourteenth century it was held by foreign lawyers attached to the court and from around 1400 by native bureaucrats and courtiers, from the mid fifteenth century it became the

[74] Ibid., A, fo. 75; C (1), fos. 156v, 161, 190.

[75] Ventura, pp. 17-18, 28-29, 58ff., 118ff.; R.P. Cooper, 'The Prosopography of the "Prima Repubblica"', in *I ceti dirigenti*, p. 247; M. Ascheri, 'Siena nel Rinascimento', ibid., pp. 425-26.

[76] E.g., for the period 1425-1435: Antonio and Geminiano Costabili, Esau and Vitaliano Trotti, Guglielmo Contrari, Ettore Sacrati, Piero Marocelli: ACF, Libri, C (1), fos. 173v ff., 178ff., 181ff.; D, fos. 27ff., 45v ff., 58ff.; F, fos. 19ff. Cf. the 1320s-30s: ASF, Lib. prov., fos. 23v-63v.

[77] Sitta, p. 114.

[78] Lists of the *savi* for the *quartieri* are given in: ACF, Libri, C (1), fos. 1-7v (1418-19), 119-23 (1421-23).

[79] British Museum, Add. Ms. 38024, 'Register of the Contrada of San Romano'.

preserve of Ferrarese noble families (the Costabili, Trotti and Ariosti).[80]

There were certainly oligarchical tendencies in the membership of the council, but these were not very strong and were strongest in fact in the period when the council seems least active, as if no one could be bothered to replace sitting members. The available evidence can be divided into three periods. In the first, 1321 to 1382, we have 94 name lists for meetings from 38 years. This is perhaps too small a sample for so long a period, but the lack of continuity of membership is noticeable, for 90 per cent of the 269 names sat on only four or fewer occasions. Even when a good number of meetings are recorded from one year, the turnover of *savi* was high.[81] In the second period, 1394 to 1432, a sequence of pools of no more than twenty individuals provided the *savi* for a number of years, and for long stretches of time the same small group of men remained in charge (thus 1394-99, 1420-24, 1426-29).[82] In the final period, from 1432, there was a widening of participation, though again with a small group of twenty forming a core and holding about half of the available seats in the period.[83] Throughout the period from 1321 to 1450 there is little evidence of domination by a small group of families as has been abundantly perceived elsewhere, usually in cities under republican rule. Despotism, it seems, could at least keep oligarchy at bay.

How should we interpret all this? One explanation would see the commune as no more than an artificial creation, a decoy organisation which took the harsh decisions that would otherwise imperil loyalty to the Este family. The Este were thus able to perform the familiar rulers' trick of distancing themselves from their own government, especially when the results of decisions were likely to create discontent. This allowed the Este to sacrifice unpopular communal officials as necessary, making a 'theatrical gift' of them to placate opposition.[84] Yet it was not only harsh decisions that the commune took: it was involved in a wide range of measures to improve common welfare, while the Este proved quite

---

[80] A combination of Frizzi, ii, 302; ASF, Lib. prov.; ACF, Libri; and ASM, Leggi e Decreti, allow the following list of *giudici* to be compiled: Tassino da Rovigo 1321-30; Gasparino Stanga da Cremona 1331-41; Albertino da San Pietro di Cremona 1341; Lapo Meliorati da Prato 1342-50; Dino da Montecatino 1350-51; Jacopo Salimbene 1353; Filippo da Marano 1354-63; Giovanni Toscani 1365-67; Gasparino Tacoli da Reggio 1371; Pietro Guaitamisteri da Modena 1373; Tommaso da Tortona 1379-82; Gerardo [Confalonieri] da Fratta 1393-96; Giovanni Spadari 1396-98; Bartolomeo Barbalunga 1399-1400; Niccolò Perondoli, 1403-?; Antonio Banchi 1415-?; Niccolò Ariosti 1418-21; Bartolomeo Barbalunga 1421-33; Aldrovandino Guidoni 1433-37; Niccolò Ariosti 1438; Giovanni Gualengo 1438-44; Agostino Villa 1445-52. Cf. the fantasy of A. Maresti, *Cronologia et istoria de' capi e giudici de' savii della città di Ferrara* (Ferrara, 1683).

[81] ASF, Lib. prov., *passim*.

[82] ACF, Libri, A and C (1) *passim*; C (2), fos. 1-4.

[83] Ibid., fos. 30v-54; D, E and F, *passim*.

[84] Law, *ubi supra*; Brown, *ubi supra*.

capable of taking unpopular decisions themselves.[85] The division of business between the commune and the Este palace-administration simply does not fall neatly enough to fit the view of the commune as a mere facade. It looks much more like a forum dealing with delegated business of a sort that needed local consultation. Obviously we should not delude ourselves into thinking that the commune represented an *alternative* form of government, nor that consultation was not free from influence by the powerful.[86] 'The convenient revival of republican institutions . . . made no difference to the source and facts of power' (Syme). But it remains the case that much business of local importance was shifted onto the shoulders of middling citizens who had no place at court. Was this 'self-government at the lord's command'?[87]

---

[85] E.g. in the matter of large-scale building works: F. Bocchi, 'La Terranuova da campagna a città', in *La corte e lo spazio: Ferrara estense*, ed. G. Papagno and A. Quondam (Rome, 1982), pp. 172, 174, 177-79. There was similar resentment to large building schemes by Niccolò III and Borso.

[86] When, for example, twenty-six citizens, representing 'bonitas et quasi totum totius' of the *contrada* of Boccacanale, met in 1406 to discuss a request to close and privatise a road so that Bandino Brancaleoni (on whom, see Dean, *Land and Power*, p. 138) could build on the site, can we doubt that a lead was given by those citizens who were also Este officials or counsellors (Uguccione Contrari, Basilio Baldini, Niccolò Perondoli)?: ASM, Leggi e Decreti, B III, fo. 226.

[87] Cf. A.B. White, *Self-Government at the King's Command* (Minneapolis, 1933).

List of Subscribers

Abulafia, Dr David
Artifoni, Dr Enrico
Bernasconi, John G.
Bowsky, Prof William M.
Bridgeman, Dr Jane
Britnell, Dr R.H.
Brown, Alison
Capie, Prof Forrest
Cardini, Dr Franco
Chambers, Dr D.S.
Chittolini, Dr Giorgio
Clough, Dr C.H.
Collingwood, Vera
Crawford, Michael H.
Davies, Prof J.K.
Dean, Dr Trevor
Denley, Dr Peter
Dickson, Dr Gary
Dobson, Prof R.B.
English, Edward D.
Epstein, Dr S.R.
Fryde, Prof Edmund
Gelichi, Dr Sauro
Gibbs, Robert
Ginatempo, Dr Maria
Grierson, Prof Philip
Haines, Keith
Harriss, Dr G.L.
Harvey, Miss Barbara F.
Hay, Prof Denys
Highfield, J.R.L.
Holmes, Prof George
Housley, Dr Norman
Hoy, P.C.
Jones, Dr Michael
Keen, Dr M.H.

Kent, Prof F.W.
Knapton, Dr Michael
Larner, Dr John
Law, Dr John Easton
Lewis, Dr Gillian
Leyser, Prof Karl
Loud, Dr G.A.
Luzzati, Prof Michele
Markus, Gilbert O.P.
Norman, Dr D.
Palliser, Prof D.M.
Partner, Dr Peter
Paton, Dr Bernadette
Petralia, Dr Giuseppe
Pinto, Dr Giuliano
Pirillo, Dr Paolo
Reynolds, Susan
Roncière, Dr Charles de la
Rosser, Dr Gervasse
Rubinstein, Prof Nicolai
Ruthenberg, Prof M.S.
Ryder, Prof Alan
Simons, Prof Pat
Spufford, Dr Peter
Stephens, Dr John
Stringer, Dr K.J.
Sutcliffe, Anne-Marie
Taylor, John
Varanini, Prof G.M.
Waley, Dr Daniel
Ward-Perkins, Brian
Weinstein, Prof Donald
Wickham, Dr Chris
Williams, Dr Ann
Wilson, Dr Stephen
Woodhouse, Prof J.R.